Dhadi Darbar

Dhadi Darbar

Religion, Violence, and the Performance of Sikh History

Michael Nijhawan

OXFORD
UNIVERSITY PRESS

OXFORD
UNIVERSITY PRESS

YMCA Library Building, Jai Singh Road, New Delhi 110 001

Oxford University Press is a department of the University of Oxford.
It furthers the University's objective of excellence in research,
scholarship, and education by publishing worldwide in

Oxford New York

Auckland Cape Town Dar es Salaam Hong Kong Karachi Kuala Lumpur
Madrid Melbourne Mexico City Nairobi New Delhi Shanghai Taipei Toronto

With offices in

Argentina Austria Brazil Chile Czech Republic France Greece Guatemala
Hungary Italy Japan Poland Portugal Singapore South Korea Switzerland
Thailand Turkey Ukraine Vietnam

Published in India
By Oxford University Press, New Delhi

First published 2006

ISBN-13: 978-0-19-567967-0
ISBN-10: 0-19-567967-9

Typeset in Naurang (Times New Roman) in 10/12
by Excellent Laser Typesetters, Pitampura, Delhi 110 034
Printed in India by De-Unique, New Delhi-110 018
Published by Oxford University Press
YMCA Library Building, Jai Singh Road, New Delhi 110 001

ਸੋਹਣ ਸਿੰਘ ਸੀਤਲ ਦੀ ਯਾਦ ਵਿਚ

The most difficult art is that of infinite melody, which launches itself and risks itself, wandering on the path that it itself invents and that never returns to itself, whose leap is sustained only by its restlessness, exposed, exploring unceasingly another fragment of the earth, flapping like the edge of a flag in the wind, going forward without profit or help, always at the stage of being born, cheerful, in turmoil, tormented, twisted, torturing, strange to hear, emanating from the body's roots like birds taking flight all around the leaves of a tree, burgeoning, divergent, an open exodus that those trouvères, finders who go nimbly from novelties to finds, suffer and chant.

—Michel Serres, *The Troubadour of Knowledge*, pp. 100–1

Contents

APPENDICES

Illustrations

MAP

Acknowledgements

At the outset I would like to acknowledge the people who have contributed to the completion of this book. I would like to first thank Veena Das, Roma Chatterjee, and Martin Fuchs who provided invaluable intellectual and moral support at different stages of my work. I owe inestimable gratitude to them. Vasudha Dalmia has been a great source of inspiration and intellectual support both during my stay at the University of California at Berkeley in 2001 and subsequent visits. I strongly benefited from her scholarly advice and friendship. My affiliation to the Department of South and Southeast Asia Studies at the University enabled me to write chapters of this book in a challenging and inspiring academic environment for which I am thankful. Several other people at Berkeley and throughout the United States have read parts of earlier drafts of the work and have commented on it in workshops and conference presentations. Among them I want to specifically thank Barbara D. Metcalf, Gurinder Singh Mann, Mita Banerjee, Katja Neves-Graca, Lawrence Cohen, Kelly Pemberton, Farina Mir, Gibb Schreffle, and the participants of the South Asian Modernities workshop at the Townsend Center for the Humanities, UC Berkeley. I thank Suzanne McMahon at the South Asia Library for helping me locate photographic material. Among the scholars with whom I collaborated during my fieldwork I want to especially thank Virinder Kalra and Tej Purewal for their scholarly advice and friendship. I also want to thank Surjit Singh Kalra for bringing me in touch with diaspora performers and introducing me to Birmingham's gurdwaras. At Heidelberg University, I am indebted to William Sax for his supervision of my work and for comments on an earlier draft of this book. Along the way, comments and suggestions by friends and colleagues have helped to rework earlier ideas and drafts of the book. Thanks go to Anna Schmid,

Christian Meyer, Khushwant Singh, Roshanank Shaery, Pratiksha Baxi, and Patrick Eisenlohr. The usual disclaimers apply and all errors remain entirely mine.

Ethnographic fieldwork remains partial and unfulfilled without friendship and mutual trust. I do not know how to thank all the people who have welcomed, hosted, and supported me in the Punjab and the diaspora setting. Among the dhadi performers who offered unconditional support and truthfulness, I would like to thank Inderjit Singh 'Ankhi', Ajaib Singh and Jagdev Singh Chandan, Shareef Idu, Mohammad Shareef Ragi, Kamal Singh Baddowal, Charan Singh Alamgir, Baldev Singh Billu, Gurbaksh Singh Albela, and Pawandeep Kaur with her sisters Sunit Kaur and Sangit Kaur. Many other artists and individuals, too numerous to mention here, helped me during my research. I am hopeful they will forgive me for not recording all their names. I had the good fortune to associate closely with Jagdev Singh Jassowal, chairman of the Professor Mohan Singh Trust and patron of Punjabi performative arts. I would like to thank him for his generosity, hospitality, and for all his help in contacting people on both sides of the border in the Punjab. I also thank Upkar Singh and family for providing textual material and for their hospitality; Wariam Singh Sandhu for sharing his deep insights into Punjabi literature, culture and society; and Atam Hamrahi for the entertaining literary discourses. Janmeja Singh Johl generously shared important video material on Sohan Singh Seetal. Sumitra guarded Seetal's books under her bed. In her role as Seetal's housemaid and in her great understanding of the everydayness of culture, she stands out. Sardar Panchi bestowed us with a special honour by reciting and sharing ghazals on the memory of exile and migration. I would like to express my deepest gratitude to him as well as to his wife Jaswant Kaur and daughter Surender Kaur Sima.

I would like to thank the following for their assistance and support during archival and fieldwork research: the staff at the Punjabi Bhawan Library in Ludhiana; the Sikh Missionary College at Anandpur Sahib; the staff of Parker Guest House at the Punjab Agricultural University in Ludhiana; broadcasting director H.S. Batalvi at All India Radio, Jalandhar; Adam Nayyar at Lok Virsa, Islamabad; Abdul Ghafur Darshan from Lok Virsa, Faisalabad and his family; Abdul Rashid at Jalandhar; Shubha Chaudhuri, director of the American Institute for Indian Studies, Gurgaon; Urvashi Butalia then at Kali for Women; Jatinder Kaur Walia and the management committee at the Sri Guru Singh Sahib gurdwara in Hounslow.

Fieldwork in India and Pakistan (1999, 2000, 2002) was made possible by fellowships that I received from the Cusanuswerk Bonn and the German Research Council (Collaborative Research Center 619 'The Dynamics of Ritual').

My research would not have been possible without the moral and emotional support that I received from close friends and family. In this respect I would like to my express my deepest appreciation and love to my parents and parents in-law, my sister Susanne and my brother-in-law Subin. Roshanak, Latha, Sushant, Fauzia, Khushwant, Taru, Christian, Mita, and Frank taught me what friendship is all about. Veena Nijhawan devoted many hours of strenuous work to fill gaps in my Punjabi transcripts and translations. Her contribution to the completion of this book remains not fully reciprocated by these words of appreciation. Shobna has been the source of strength during these years of fieldwork, travel, and hardship. There are no words for the friendship and love we share.

Introduction

A popular anecdote that I heard when I conducted my fieldwork in Punjab speaks of an encounter between a singer-composer and a leading Akali Dal politician. Both met in July 1955, in the course of the agitations that were launched by the Akali Dal (a political party that represents Sikh interests) to influence the State Reorganization Commission's (SRC) decision on the future boundaries of the state of Punjab. The stakes were high at that time for both sides involved. The Akali Dal politician was in a difficult negotiation with Congress, as both parties strived toward reaching a compromise according to which Sikhs were to be granted significant political weight and the right for religious self-determination within a Punjabi-speaking state of the Indian nation. The formation of a reorganized Punjabi state after the Partition in 1947 could only be achieved through fierce political negotiations, sustained by agitations upheld through Sikh popular support. The encounter between the politician and the singer-composer, or troubadour as I would like to call him, happened under what became known as the first phase of the Punjabi Suba Morcha. Thousands of Sikhs went voluntarily to jail in order to protest against the SRC recommendations to merge the sliced territory of East Punjab with the neighbouring former princely states, Himachal Pradesh and small sections of Uttar Pradesh (known as PEPSU plan). An implementation of this plan would have resulted in the Sikhs losing their majority base in a Punjabi-speaking state.

In such times, people in Punjab sought strong leaders who could persuade people to follow their example through their own sacrifice. The example set by the martyr bands (*shahīdī jatthās*) of the pre-Partition period, the Sikh response to Gandhi's Satyagraha marches still resonated in the postcolonial situation. The politician and the troubadour both knew it. For the troubadour, the stakes were high as well; he feared that his profession was not deemed necessary anymore, as many of his companions had crossed to the other side of the border. His own political engagement in the pre-Partition years that promised independence and self-rule had left him with a four-wheeled carrier and a broken family and he felt as though his voice had been stolen.

In this situation the encounter between the politician and troubadour was somewhat tragicomic. The politician spoke hesitantly, an experienced diplomat who knows how to veil political strategy in words of praise and appeals to shared virtues: 'You troubadour, why don't you join us and with your folk wisdom and refined voice serve to propagate our cause of fasting-to-death?' (The politician himself would later break his fasting-to-death rather ingloriously.) The troubadour in turn had inherited something of the wit that characterized his ancestors. He believed that in diplomacy there is neither enmity nor friendship (*nītī vic nā koī dā dushman, nā dost*). So he tried to be diplomatic too and answered: 'Master, fasting-to-death is none of my business. This is what you have to achieve. So you go ahead and even die for it. You will become a true *shahīd*. Afterwards, it will be my work to write a song about you.'

Narrated to me by contemporary performers, those who followed the footsteps of the travelling troubadour, the story is amusing and ironic at the same time. First, if I read it in the ethnographic and historiographic material gathered in this book, its irony has to do with the ambivalent position of the singer-bard, who is supposed to give voice to 'heroes' dead and alive, many of whom, in his or her eyes, do not deserve the recognition. Punjabi common sense has captured this relationship in proverbs and idioms that account for the subjection of cultural production to the calculated demands of patronage. If daily survival depends on service to the patron, one saying goes, the question of individual expression and voice simply does not arise: *roṭī kamāuṇā, roṭī khāṇā*—for many performers it is a question of earning a livelihood. Punjabi folk wisdom captures the relationship between the patrons and gift receivers in precise terms, categorizing the performers as the class of the *mangtā* (those who demand). Yet, common sense is also prone to error. In fact, it might be asked if the economy of survival necessarily stands in a causal relationship to the economy of linguistic and material exchange. In the above anecdote this is not the issue. The troubadour's wit lay not in fulfilling a traditional function in which his sharp speech would be socially sanctioned by a ritually framed exchange (such as in the case of the course of life cycle rituals). His wit acquired its cutting edge through his evocation of Sikh heroic discourse. This occurred at a historical juncture when the common cause was seen to be betrayed by political calculation; this dislodged the patron's claim and anticipated his crooked discourse. The parameters that shaped the troubadour's discourse, on the other hand, were set by allusions to religious language and nationalist concerns. And so, it seems to me, the direction in which the patron-client relationship would be traditionally tracked became ironically reversed.

The issue that is raised here has social and epistemological implications beyond the given content of this story. At first sight, this book traces the relationship between a performative tradition and the political and religious elite in Punjab. The story certainly has to do with the relationship between words crafted through a painful process of carving memory and landscapes in an oral tradition, with the printed words of the political tract, published and disseminated with great success by a small elite. However, I am not speaking about the difference between the oral and the written, nor about the differences between artisan work and educated language. I want to use the anecdote in a different way, for it carves out two opposed positions of knowledge production that I will further explore: one inhabits the position of political power, an expanding force of subjecting others to differently qualified interests and goals, maybe something that Punjabis mean when they say someone is driven by *loṛ* (need, necessity); the other takes the reverse stance of witted recognition, situated at the margins, striving for truths other than those claimed by politics. The paradox faced by the troubadour is that he recognizes the fictionality of this bipolar division while being captured in a web of relations in which his deepest emotional evaluations remain inexorably linked to the political eruptions of collective memory. He must be articulate in languages that are his own and yet not owned by him. He needs to disempower himself in order to be heard.

Paradoxically, as I shall argue, in the realm of Punjabi performative traditions it is, more often than not, religious idioms and language through which these dynamics are played out in creative ways. Cultural performers find emancipatory aspects in religious language where one would suspect them simply following ideological messages propounded by religious institutions. The point is that for the performers I am concerned with, access to religious discourses is culturally mediated through a variety of situated genres. As social and cultural institutions these genres not only inherit within their framework a pluralistic history, but also narrative modes and forms of aesthetic evaluation that can be engaged in constructive dialogue with the value system of religious belief. This dialogue is not without ruptures and ambiguities. In various places this book will return to the social history of this paradox.

Central to this book is the historiography and ethnography of the Punjabi *ḍhāḍī kalā* ('the art of minstrel singing') or *ḍhāḍī paramparā* ('dhadi tradition'), a tradition or genre of bardic performance that constitutes one of the extant forms of oral epic performance in South Asia. Dhadi performers appear as a group of three to four singers and musicians, who usually play the *sāraṅgī* (a string instrument) and a small drum called *ḍhaḍḍ*. The contents of dhadi song and narrative, as I shall analyse below, are mostly heroic tales of legendary and historical figures such as the Sikh martyrs that play a particular role in this analysis. I explore the different ways in which this genre became related to agendas of religious and political identity formation in twentieth-century Punjab. Analysing performative texts and ethnographic narratives at critical junctures in colonial and postcolonial Punjab, my interest is not so much in considering each and every historical argument on the potential causes of crisis or motivations for violent action. The main thread that runs through the text is less ambitious in historical breadth and more concerned with an anthropological understanding of the sociocultural processes that shape the way in which popular culture makes sense of these events and thus gives form to historical consciousness. This does not imply that I prefer an isolated study of cultural memory or consciousness that does not take account of historical genealogy. On the contrary, I claim this study of popular performative culture as an apposite part of a critical project of historical anthropology. As Chatterjee and Ghosh (2002: 19) point out, an 'appropriate analytic of the popular' has been needed to free the project of critical historiography from its 'cage of self-constructed scientific history.' Disputes around the destruction of the Babri mosque in Ayodhya and the upsurge of an aggressive anti-Muslim rhetoric with its heavy borrowing from popular as well as scientific representations have made this move all but necessary.

I argue in this book that it is particularly important to reconsider the role of vernacular traditions of (his)story telling through which alternative forms of historical imagination are cultivated. The importance of hagiographies, mythologies, and epic performances feature centrally in this regard. They must be approached in non-reductionist ways, not as the hallmark of a traditional past but as a constitutive element of

South Asian modernity. There is ample evidence for such a perspective. In the colonial period, reformist agendas reinvented traditional genres in which they could accommodate contemporary discourses. This had serious consequences for the way in which Hindu as well as Sikh reformists reconnected past and present. Anti-colonial protest movements vested their slogans in traditional poetic forms, and even in the postcolonial situation we find a continuing audience and patronage interest in mythology, epics, and theatrical performances of the past.

Walter Benjamin's argument that the secular forces of historical knowledge production have displaced what he considered the former integrity of the epic is often cited today. Undeniably, there is something to his melancholic insight that in modern times the storytelling tradition acquires its beauty in the recuperative gesture that acknowledges its indispensability at the point of its anticipated disappearance. With due respect, it must also be said that this viewpoint is part of a modern predicament that, as far as South Asia is concerned, seems to miss important cultural differences. To my knowledge, the storytelling tradition has not been ruptured in such fundamental ways as it is often believed. Storytellers flourish and even if modes of production and transmission have changed with the advent of new media technologies, in many parts of South Asia storytelling performances remain important sites of knowledge production and aesthetic experience. In this context, the storytelling genre is neither a remnant of an idealistic past nor a degenerated modern form; for the people concerned it is a cultivated practice that faces practical and epistemological challenges of different kinds.

The most important of these challenges has to do with recent situations of crisis and violence in which the evaluative framework provided by the storytelling genre is tested in its agentive capacities. In this book, I am concerned with the particular discursive and aesthetic modes through which identity politics and communal violence are translated and reworked in the social fabric of Punjabi performative practice. This is a significant issue because one is likely to think about the relationship between agendas of violence and folk culture as mutually exclusive domains. Yet, as the modern history of folklore indicates, both domains are often tied in a problematic framework of cultural politics. Cultural politics in Punjab are no exception to this. Thus, if today bards praise and eulogize the heroic deeds of martyrs and, in this way, project images of ideal moral conduct and heroism, then this has a strong potential to generate and sustain agendas of violence. The remembrance of trauma and violation that has become the theatre of Sikh collective memory, specifically after the events of 1984, in fact has threatened to reduce the bardic profession to an oral resource from which to draw images of otherness. If the collective psyche is mirrored in the folk narrative, it is just a small step to take images of torture and persecution, related to religious concepts of death and salvation, as lens through which to perceive the other ('the vicious Muslim' or 'the effeminate and treacherous Hindu'). To a significant extent, the politicization of folk discourses has determined the way dhadi performers become socially recognized, how their presentations are evaluated as providing deeply felt symbols of belonging and identification with larger causes, thus suggesting conceptual linkages to the dynamics of ethnonationalism as described in the European context.[1]

The importance of this combination of the political with folk discourses cannot and should not be ignored; it has shaped the very manner in which the performative form under consideration, the dhadi tradition, has been portrayed by the few historians and anthropologists who have mentioned it. Thus, in a paper written in the journal *Asian Music*, Joyce Pettigrew (1992) described dhadi bards as the popular voice of Sikh resistance. Based on interviews with diaspora performers and the scarce material on the tradition that she could gather from Sikh sources, Pettigrew captured the most relevant performative aspects of the tradition and gave an account of the Sikh performers' self-understanding as people's historians. In their commemorative function, Pettigrew notes, the performers 'regard their role as being one confined to the narration of events' which are presented 'in accordance with the information they receive from those around as to what the Sikhs are feeling' (ibid.: 90). Pettigrew made a strong point in demonstrating the linkages between the Khalistan movement and the cultural performers who praised the deeds of militants as heroic achievements in the spirit of Sikh martyrs of previous centuries. The relationship between dhadi performance and Sikh martyrdom is also captured in Lou Fenech's (2000) work in which he provides a broader historical perspective on the commemorative role of the Sikh dhadi performers. Drawing on hagiographical sources and various vernacular tracts of the nineteenth and early twentieth centuries, he argues that the Sikh reformists found this tradition particularly suited to disseminate their historical discourses throughout rural Punjab, precisely because the commemorative role the bards played there was firmly established within the ritual framework of shrine veneration where the issue of martyrdom had been cultivated for a long time.

Pettigrew as well as Fenech were not too concerned with the broader framework of dhadi performance that is historically accounted for, but restricted their argument to Sikh history; I underline the significance of Sikh representations in this book.[2] As I will argue, however, the framework of the dhadi genre is historically not confined to the performance of Sikh history—up to Partition, there was a large group of Muslim and low-caste performers with a broad repertoire of epic and folk narratives. They have been more or less erased from historical consciousness. In some respect, however, this absent other has had a lasting influence even in contexts, as I shall argue, in which the Sikh perspective is discursively predominant.

A more substantial critique must be voiced in terms of Pettigrew and Fenech's reckoning of the expressive and rhetorical function of bardic performance, which in my view does not go beyond the established framework of folkloristic analysis. Questions of the creativity involved in manipulating the inherited cultural repertoires, schemata, and stories are seldom, if ever, asked. To the extent that themes of sacrifice and suffering penetrate dhadi performative texts, this is seen as the result of an ideological imprint on the bardic genre. The normative accounts the performers give about their 'commemorative function' is taken for granted, and here lies a potential fallacy as this kind of acknowledgement misses the important distinction between forms of self-representation and an empirical study of performative practice.

The anecdote of the troubadour meeting the Sikh politician indicates the potential faultlines that exist in the relationship between politics, religion, and cultural performance. The bard's commitment to normative values, as I have argued, is an evaluative judgement, an implicit form of social criticism cloaked in the language of tradition, not simply a mirror of that tradition. As I want to demonstrate in this book, even in contexts in which performers become complicit with agendas of violence, the meanings that are generated and perceived in their performances are ambivalent and conceal a plurality that cannot be read at the purely ideological level. In that respect my approach is significantly different from previous approaches in Sikh and Punjab studies. What is presented here moves beyond the folkloristic approach toward a non-reductionist anthropological endeavour that considers (vernacular) language and artistic performance as dynamic and interpretive practices. In this way, I hope not only to portray a useful and more realistic account of a performative genre, but also to show in what different ways people who inhabit the space of Punjabi performative culture have made a difference in carving out possibilities of a future that is shared by Punjabis of different religious and social affiliations. To better situate my objectives, it is first necessary to delineate my departure from the folkloristic approach.

Locating the Dhadi Bard: Genre and Community

People in Punjab refer to dhadi as a tradition (*paramparā*) in the sense of a particular body of discursive and aesthetic knowledge that has been handed down over many generations. The consciousness of a particular heritage is expressed in various ways—in the guardianship of new patrons, including media institutions such as All India Radio, in the reverence of performers towards the elders (*buzurg*) from whom they receive instructions, and in the common claim that it is necessary to keep 'folk tradition' alive in modern society. The idea that folk tradition has to somehow 'survive' under conditions of modernity indicates the extent to which folkloristic discourses frame the contemporary perception of musical culture in Punjab.[3] I could deduce this during the course of my research work when, for instance, I spoke to contemporary patrons of Punjabi 'folk arts'. People told me they considered their work important, as the 'spirit' of *Punjabiyat* would reside in the folk domain. A broad range of vernacular magazines replicate this notion of cultural primordialism. The pervasiveness of these associations between notions of folk and Punjabi identity, however, are not sufficiently explained by reference to the prototype of early European nationalism. There are at least two conceptual points that must be mentioned here. The first has to do with the issue of translation, the second with the relationship between community and genre.

The term 'folklore' or 'folk tradition' has no direct equivalent in Punjabi and other Indian languages. It is usually translated as *lok vartā* (a name for a very particular narrative genre) or *lok sahit* (and *lok sangīt* or *lok gīt* in reference to musical forms), which indicates that the category of folk is reconfigured in India according to the old hagiographic genres of North Indian vernacular literature.[4] In this way, the category of folk is situated in a different evaluative framework; it traces a different spectrum between past and present and takes on different significations. It also competes with different forms of cultural identity as they are distinctively shaped by Indian models of social differentiation between regional groups, religious communities, tribes, castes, and classes. The notion of folk, writes Chatterji (2003: 567–8), acquires its meaning not only in contrast to civilizational perspectives, but also as an internalized scheme of self-assertion through which communities valorize their identity in relation and sometimes opposition to modern conceptions of identity. One of the crucial points therefore is how these forms of self-assertion are shaped by very specific concepts of religious community and regional culture in relation to particular performative genres, and to the individuals and groups that are known as the transmitters of these genres. More often than not, these are people at the social periphery.

Anthropological scholarship on South Asian performative tradition has addressed the issue of genre and community through a new methodological approach to what formerly constituted the field of folkloristics (Appadurai *et al.* 1991; Blackburn and Burkhalter-Flueckiger 1989; Blackburn and Ramanujan 1986; Champion 1996). Thus, in their seminal contribution to the study of oral epics in India, Blackburn and Burkhalter-Flueckiger emphasize the role of narrative traditions for the self-definition of communities (1989: 6). Traditions of storytelling, they argue, are crucial as they are 'especially sensitive to shifts in that group's history' (ibid.: 7) and have in their oral and written form 'that special ability to tell a community's own story' (ibid.: 11). General implications of this idea are not restricted to the study of oral epics but can be applied to other narrative and performative traditions in South Asia (Blackburn 1996; Chatterji 1998, 2000; Flueckiger 1996; Gold 1992; Leavitt 1997; Raheja and Gold 1994; Sax 1995; Kavita Singh 1996). The relationship between narrative repertoire and (performative) community as shared culture has been emphasized by Flueckiger (1996: 25), who argues that the local organization and interpretation of genres has to do with the various 'ways in which performance identifies and gives identity to various levels of community: the folklore region that shares a repertoire, the folklore community that shares rules of usage for that repertoire, and the folklore group whose members are the performers themselves.' Text and performative context are intrinsically bound to each other in articulating what we can describe as the 'social imaginary' of a community, including the imagined history and cosmology which usually co-structures contemporary cultural life and modes of individual and collective agency. Flueckiger demonstrates that the notion of community is a pluralized domain with different forms of communal self-understandings and intracommunal differentiations. Her emphasis on shared culture must be put in perspective, however, with notions of practical and discursive reflexivity that I consider constitutive of the relationship between individual and collective representations.

Think for instance about the work of Chatterji (1998, 2004) and Trawick (1986) who have both argued that the formation of personal voice within the performative framework of South Asian folk genres is based on fundamental ruptures between self and community rather than on shared notions of belonging. As Trawick demonstrates in her analysis of the Paraiyar crying songs, it is significant to identify the moments of personal expression because these are acknowledged—not only by the singers, but by the addressee as well—as potential sources for an emerging symbolic order that breaks with certain shared conventions and evaluations. To a certain degree, therefore, one has to be sceptical about defining a homogenous relationship between community and folk tradition (cf. Chatterji 2004). Community is not something naturally given, but is constantly created and reconfirmed even at the basic level of neighbourhoods or *jātīs* (local castes). Accordingly, this book will explore how dhadi as a performative genre offers narrative repertoires and aesthetic forms, through which individuals and groups find the means to create and define themselves at various levels of 'community'. Here I have in mind processes operating at the local level where, for instance, we find formerly low-caste actors claiming higher status. More important, it concerns the movement from the local to the translocal level of the religious community. For contemporary performers, the ability to acquire a voice in bardic performance partially depends on how they are able to shape their self-image in terms of their affiliation with the Sikh community. However, the way they acquire voice in that process is not reducible to this move.

The ethnographic data that is presented here offers an interpretation of the multifaceted, and sometimes ambiguous, linkages between the dhadi genre and Sikh community; community is translated here either as *panth* (the religious community that is linked by shared rituals and notions of spirituality and piety) or *qaum* (the religio-political community in the sense of a corporate or national identity). This book argues that the relationship between the dhadi tradition and the Sikh community is not free from tensions and ambiguities. The dhadi genre emerged as a culturally specific media and performative practice of rural Punjab. It has its own cultural attitudes and aesthetics which do not always fit into the agenda of political and religious actors.

Against the background of this discussion, I employ the term dhadi tradition, in non-folkloristic terms, as a genre of artistic possibility within a larger field of cultural practice. I have in mind linguistic genres, literary narratives, stylistic conventions, and tastes—in short, aesthetics—along with the value systems that make the dhadi tradition a particular body of knowledge and a way to remember and forget. It means that I am attentive to the potential collapses of the field of 'folk tradition', once it is framed by folklorist discourses, into the realm of identity politics. It also implies that performative practice has no clear-cut ideology to defend. This is what new ventures in the anthropology of performance have suggested in dismantling the antiquarian legacy and aestheticist approach that defined the subdiscipline of folkloristics in the first place.[5]

With these qualifications in mind, I explore the dhadi tradition as an important field of cultural production—a key site for studying processes of collective self-definition and historical imagination, a way of understanding the pastness of the present (Appadurai 1991). The significance attributed to this field of cultural production comes with the warning not to overemphasize its 'efficacy' and 'function', its representative role in symbolizing Sikh religion or Punjabi culture as a whole. Far from taking such a perspective, I follow a trajectory that works through the many historical layers within ethnography. What counts in the first place is the perspective offered through the practices and narratives embodied in a particular performative scene.

Troubadours in Times of Trouble

Two events with large-scale repercussions for contemporary Punjabi society have directed this work from its very inception: the consequences of Partition violence in 1947 and the 1984 crisis when militancy and counter-insurgency raged in Punjab. The territorial reordering of the region in 1947, along with the tremendous social upheavals and transitions caused by large-scale migration and violence, constitutes a legacy that resonates in various spheres of political, social, and everyday life.[6] This memory was overshadowed—some would say they relived the Partition experience—by the events around 1984, beginning with the Indian Army's infamous attack on the Akal Takht in Amritsar, followed by the assassination of Prime Minister Indira Gandhi in 1984 and the anti-Sikh riots in the same year. For more than a decade, Punjab was caught in violence and guerrilla warfare, leaving many observers dumbfounded.[7]

Both events have shaped Punjabi memories in unforeseen ways; they have resulted in a retelling of biography, in a new unfolding of time, streaming out of a dark shadow. Partition and 1984 necessitate a different telling of this troubadour story, a different pattern of melodies and narratives than suggested by political claims to uniformity and repetition, a different thinking about culture and experience that begins by turning away from the spectacular.[8] The spectacular character of violence in Punjab has been depicted in many books, articles, and popular films such as Ammtoje Mann's *Hawayein*. The representations and images that one comes across in a Bollywood film provides a rather distorted picture of violence and the mindless frenzy of rioters on the street, the motives behind their action remaining untreated. This kind of cinematographic imagery hardly helps in understanding the many faultlines created by such violence in its subtle and long-term dimension.

'Partition as an accomplished fact is something of a blurred achievement,' says Suresh Sharma in a recent conversation with Javeed Alam on this matter (1998: 100). And by this emphasis on 'blurred achievements', Sharma makes an important point, albeit one that has been made by other scholars before him. Events such as they occurred in 1947 or 1984 are often retold to follow an inherent logic, neatly woven along boundaries of religious or political affiliation—here are the true believers, there is the corrupt state power. Here is democracy to be safeguarded, there are the terrorists who threaten the social fabric. Two sides of the same coin. The idea of a 'blurred achievement', as I would like to understand it, suggests a different kind of telling, one that strives for truths that, in Veena Das' words (1995b: 23), have to be recovered from socially embedded narratives and from the perspective of the socially marginal.

An anecdote from my ethnographic fieldwork indicates what I have in mind about this different telling. This incident occurred during one of my daily visits to a well known dhadi musician. I was listening to the musician's instructions on how to press the fingers and how to handle the bow when, after a somewhat tiring experience, I asked him to demonstrate different musical styles that were played by other, non-Sikh performers, some of whom we had met at a recent public event in the vicinity. What would be the difference, I asked. Obviously surprised by this question (by then I should have learned the difference between, say 'Sufi' and 'Sikh' modes of performance), he said, 'oh... they... they play only *shānt rasa*, *dukh rasa*... they are just singers (*gauṇwāle hai uh*).' Rather than performing such songs, Sikhs would represent themselves as the singers of a particular genre, the *vār*, 'authentic' expression to rouse fervent passion (*jos̀*). All of a sudden, however, he began to play melodies that Sikh bards would not perform at public events. It happened suddenly and smoothly—so smoothly, in fact, that the musician seemed to lose control of the situation for some considerable moments. He stopped playing and put aside his instrument. That afternoon I found the troubadour seized by the effect of his own musical gesture. An ambivalent desire that constitutes the fragile boundaries of his life (as a religious performer) broke through. Memory elapsed in the ethnographic encounter in ways in which it was not anticipated. A single musical gesture opened a path to unspoken truths and partitioned lives, embodied in the performative voice. The chapters in this book are on the search for these slippages as they make it possible to problematize the relationship between culture and individual in non-reductionist ways.

The anecdote evokes a social arena which is defined by discourses that distinguish between dhadi performers of different religious affiliation. The fact that Sikh and Sufi performers would form parallel and mutually exclusive traditions is a valid description of actual performative practices, and at the same time a normative discourse that prevents us from recognizing the arbitrariness of that distinction when read into the past. I do not suggest that the tradition was characterized by a syncretism of various forms of spirituality. As I will demonstrate, there are enough indications to infer that performers (according to the regional focus with its dominating religious centres and patrons) had preferences in following Sufi saints or the Sikh path, and some of them venerated the pantheon of Hindu gods. Certainly, the Sikh tradition had a very unique role in adopting the dhadi genre. Notwithstanding these different orientations, however, the internal elasticity of bardic practices in Punjab is an undeniable fact. In the example given above, it speaks through the bard's confrontation with a negated part of the self. The larger question here is, why and how certain forms of bardic activity have been disavowed, and what this tells us about the changing forms of interaction between different religious traditions in Punjab. For instance, do we find the Partition replicated in the strict separation of Sikh and Sufi dhadi bards?

In various ways, the fieldwork anecdote serves as a good metaphor for the 'blurred achievements' of culture in the wake of violence. This book explores some of these scenes, seeking to understand how history is played out through the sensory modalities of performative practice, how modes of experiencing and narrating the world through the view of a particular culture are made accessible through the anthropological encounter. Anthropology, as I would like to understand it in this context, paves the way to a different understanding. It is without doubt partial and positioned and does not claim authority in the name of objective and eternal truth. And yet, it seems to me the best possible way of framing the cultural encounter in its particular epistemological dimension. Confined to the patient work of daily interaction and bestowed with moments of enunciation, the anthropologist strives for such scenes in which the finding of culture becomes a rare possibility. It is a finding that results from a gesture of holding back, as Serres (1991) would have it; a finding that draws an analogy to what Das (2000) has luminously described as the process through which people find themselves possessing a voice in culture. Without denying the structural inequalities that continue to shape the way anthropological narratives are generated and transmitted, the anthropologist and the bard as his or her interlocutor can be placed in a related epistemological position, that is, in the role of the one who finds, the troubadour.

Thematic Threads

As an anthropologist, I began to work with the dhadi performers without prior knowledge of their tradition. I had to slowly accommodate my interest in the social history of Partition to a more complex analysis of performative forms, while I found their aesthetic dimension difficult to grasp initially. Undergoing a longer process of acquaintance with the performers, their repertoires, stories, and personal concerns, the new focus turned out to be what I think is a genuine way in exploring culture in the aftermath of violence. The work with Punjab's troubadours also opened the historical archive and offered interesting pathways that I have willingly explored in the form of a historical anthropology. I believe that this book testifies to the way in which the anthropological encounter with the dhadi tradition made it possible to create linkages between past and present so that my efforts in historicizing events (a necessary undertaking for any concerned historical anthropologist) were interrupted, transformed, and shaped by the evaluations and interpretations of the persons I worked with. The structure of this book mirrors these dynamics. To the extent that it resorts to historical narrative, it acknowledges the emancipatory languages of historical reasoning. As these modes of reasoning are constrained in their applicability on the 'unassimilable' or 'untranslatable stuff' of history (Ramaswamy 1997: 3), alternative modes of interpretation are given strength, even if they come at the price of 'inconsistency'.

While the book is structured along a linear historical axis (precolonial, colonial, postcolonial), the thematic emphases in each chapter change according to the material I could access and the ethnographic paths my work has taken. In the first part of the book the reader is confronted with problems of how to assess the significance of the dhadi tradition within and beyond the Sikh tradition. What I offer is a partial perspective that depends on other (mostly western educated) historians' access to medieval texts in different (Braj, Punjabi, Persian) languages. On the one hand these texts are consistent in portraying the dhadi genre in specific performative dimensions. On the other hand we are confronted with differing interpretations on the social and religious embeddedness of the dhadi subject. The second part of the book uses dhadi vernacular tracts to probe into questions of historical agency and performers' intervention into the cultural modes of history, myth making, and the creative possibilities of voice production in different genres. My inquiry is framed by an interest in the relationship between popularized religious practices and elite agendas, which, as representatives of the subaltern studies school have argued, are historically intermingled and dependent upon each other. I consider this approach useful to historicize concepts of martyrdom and violence as they are addressed in the final part of the book. The final part is based on ethnographic material and revolves mainly around questions of violence, representation, and processes of community formation in the last two decades of the twentieth century. The Punjab crisis in the 1980s had a lasting impact on Punjabi social and cultural life and my discussions in the last two chapters are to be largely understood against this background.

Chapter 1 is a brief introduction to Punjab's cultural geography and the place of the dhadi tradition therein. Unlike the other chapters, I have made use of non-Sikh sources to account for a broadly defined historical perspective on the precolonial situation in which we find dhadi performers affiliated with the poet-saints and royal darbars. Chapter 2 examines the gendered dimension of Sikh religious aesthetics through Sikh hagiographical sources. I have situated this historical discussion in a framework that reflects my interlocutor's interpretive work that has also guided my path toward these historical sources. Tracing the linkages between the dhadi genre and Sikh religious aesthetics through this lens, I want to show how an earlier generic understanding of dhadi musical aesthetics got replaced through a modern discourse that distinguishes between secular and religious languages. I am thus able to demonstrate how historical consciousness of the dhadi tradition alternates between a form of self-identification and alterity.

Chapter 3 investigates vernacular dhadi texts of the early twentieth century. These texts show that dhadi performers were active participants in the emerging nationalist movement (in Punjab and the Sikh diaspora in North America). The chapter introduces a well known Sikh performer of the pre-Partition years. This case allows reconstructing in detail as to how the dhadi tradition became a 'suitable' form of religious self-representation. In theoretical scope, the chapter engages with subaltern history and the place of performative traditions therein. If subaltern theory has seen such traditions as critical, yet limited sites of identity formation, I develop a more optimistic approach in thinking about translatability and the development of emancipatory discourses within the parameters set by so-called 'subaltern' cultural formations.

Chapter 4 explores the relationship between martyrdom and territoriality. I argue that this relationship has become crucial to a wide range of phenomena in modern contexts of religious violence but, with notable exceptions, has remained largely unexplored from an anthropological perspective. The question here is how historical anthropology might capture the relationship between language, agency, and territory in a colonial scenario of urban and rural identity politics in Punjab. The chapter is structured around the 1935 Shahidganj incident in Lahore and draws comparisons to contemporary disputes over sacred sites in South Asia and beyond. I am particularly concerned with the dynamics between identity politics and the shared repertoire of performative languages that stretches across religious boundaries. The chapter traces a chain of discursive appropriations in which Sikh concepts of martyrdom are laced with Islamic discourses. This is interpreted as a ritualized struggle over sameness and difference in a universe of shared religious spaces, past and present. In this regard, the chapter is in critical dialogue with the Girardian framework of mimetic violence and sacrificial crisis.

Chapter 5 departs from my earlier analysis of dhadi discourses and explores other genres of literary expression through which dhadi performers have articulated their concerns. The reference here is to Sohan Singh Seetal's texts in which he narrated the experience of Partition violence in 1947. Partition not only led to significant changes in the social fabric of the dhadi performative community with many musical specialists migrating to what had become Pakistan, it also engendered in performers a new sense for the inherited forms of generic expression. What can and cannot be said about violence and suffering through particular performative genres? The chapter reads through a range of documentary, poetic, and prosaic genres which, I argue, mark the return of tropes and idioms that form a process of mourning Partition that is suppressed on the discursive level of dhadi narratives.

Chapter 6 resituates my previous argument on martyrdom and representation in drawing attention to the relationship between images, music, and pain. The context is set by the Sikh militant movement of the 1980s and its diasporic perception. In the course of the Punjab crisis many dhadi performers played a critical, if ambivalent, role. Rather than recapitulating the entire history of this conflict, the chapter analyses the relationship between martyr images (photographs of torture and video productions) and the imagistic language of dhadi musical recitation. Demonstrating the intrinsic relationship between these modes of representation, I argue that martyr images draw their emotional power by collapsing what Roland Barthes held to be the difference between denotative and connotative meanings in photography and art production.

Chapter 7 delineates the contemporary struggle of Punjab's dhadi performers. Although the genre has acquired an unambiguous format in accordance with the dominant paradigm of institutionalized Sikh religion, forms of dhadi self-representation are still cast in a language of difference in relation to religious institutions. If the previous chapters indicated a process of merging popular concerns with various nationalist and religious agendas, the present chapter emphasizes the re-emergence of a 'subaltern' form of dhadi agency within the normative framework of Sikh religious language. In theoretical perspective, the chapter engages with Judith Butler's work on performativity and voice. Following Butler's critical reading of Althusser's model of the commanding voice, I try to develop an alternative perspective on subjectivity and voice production in the dhadi performative scene.

The book, in short, offers an interdisciplinary approach to the study of Punjabi history and culture. The structure is not that of a classical anthropological monograph on a 'folk tradition'. What I offer is a critical reading of cultural texts and discourses through which, I believe, we gain a new perspective on the formative role of cultural performance in twentieth-century Punjab. Nevertheless, it should be evident throughout my text that the arguments developed are partial and written from a particular perspective, as it has been enabled and mediated through the anthropological encounter with contemporary Punjabi performers and the people I met during my fieldwork.

Signposts: Opening Boxes

My entrance to the field site began with the opening of steel boxes. Jagdev Singh Jassowal, my fieldwork interlocutor opens his boxes, extensions of his local memory, filled with countless notes torn out from newspaper reports, tape recordings, and old photographs in which I see him with politicians, musicians, religious persons. Jagdev Singh is sitting in front of us (at that time I was accompanied by my wife) on his wooden bed, wearing his pyjama, immersed in the many little ornaments through which he recollects his life. He does not talk much; he simply throws out document after document and points to it with his long fingers. It is a strange scene, one that he said was foretold in a letter from Australia that he received the week before we knocked at his door. For us it was completely unanticipated. Stranded in this city by mere accident on our way to Amritsar, the wrong address of a deceased musician in our pocket, we found ourselves drawn into a puzzle that, months later, we still tried to slowly disentangle.

Jagdev Singh's residence in Ludhiana, as it later turned out, has been the meeting point for many known and unknown artists, poets, and bards. A true Sardar, former politician and patron of a local folk mela, he has been known for his generosity in hosting artists and poets from all over the Punjab. While loved by many, he draws on himself the anger of others for his stoicism to organize cultural events in times of crisis. His house accommodates all these emotions and stories, offering guest rooms built around an open courtyard in which a neem tree provides protection from the intense sun. This little 'village in town' turned out to be one of the main sites from which the work presented in this book took its directions. I would sit there for hours, meeting people, discussing topics or taking decisions of whom to meet or where to go next. I would wonder about what would be the next thing emerging once the lid was opened.

Once a local poet, Sardar Panchi, who later became a dear friend, came by to recite one of his newly written poems. Recently he presented this poem to a large gathering at the Attari-Wagah border, which I was

FIGURE 1: Jagdev S. Jassowal, collecting books at Seetal Bhawan
Courtesy Michael Nijhawan

unable to attend. I had my tape recorder with me. Jagdev Singh sat next to Panchi, again occupied with finding some book or manuscript in one of his steel boxes. As the recitation progressed, he grew more uncomfortable. The poem was on the amity of Punjabis across the Indo-Pakistan border and had a very painful tinge to it. On that afternoon, the poet could not end his recitation. The frequency with which Jagdev Singh's steel box was opened and shut increased significantly, until it became such a distraction that the poet was simply unable to recite. Boxes are not just metaphors for stored memories, they also have a psychic life endowed with potentialities that come alive with the voice of the local poet. My first encounter with Punjab's troubadours was made possible through this opening and closing of boxes. They offered valuable traces of a forgotten history of dhadi bards and yet, in responding with their clapping one-dimensional sounds, showed the limitations of the historical archive. The performative scene opens and transgresses the potentialities of the historical record.

Jagdev Singh took us to the local crematory where two years before our arrival he lit the funeral fire for Sohan Singh Seetal, Punjabi novelist, writer of popular tracts on Sikh history, and dhadi bard. Jagdev Singh still grieved this loss as he recollected the scenes of the day of the funeral: how he carried his body, mourning the death of a real troubadour, the one whose voice they loved above everybody else's. Jagdev Singh pointed to the empty wall above the cremation site which had many holes and cracks in it. A lizard hides where he wanted to see a memorial for his forgotten hero. We then moved on to Seetal Bhavan, the bard's house and former publishing press that was then occupied by new tenants, who seemed to know little about who lived there before. Near the gate, in the small one-room building for the house servants we found Sumitra, Seetal's former housekeeper. It was a scene of reunion. Sumitra invited us in and soon afterwards opened a small box stored under her bed. She took out five copies of Seetal's publications, handing them to us. She had been waiting for someone to guard her treasure, she said. When we later found the remnants of Seetal's press in the neighbours' house, we knew why. Tons of unbound pages lay scattered across the floor; heat and dust had left their imprints on them. In the midst of this heap we located some old dhadi books and tape recordings, some of the last traces of the troubadour's voice. From there on the exploration began. Confronted with such a scene, the anthropologist learned that the spectre of cultural pessimism he thought had been exorcised in years of 'self-reflexive' thinking still haunted him. The only solution was to take another step and enter the contemporary performative scene, searching for some rare reincarnation.

FIGURE 2: Ethnographer and Jagdish Singh Chandan
Courtesy Michael Nijhawan

Notes

1. The issue here is the relationship between folk discourses and nationalism. Due to the popularization of Herder's concept of the folk and with the development of folkloristics in the nineteenth and early twentieth centuries, agendas that propagated the origin of the nation in the folk got a boost in the European context. Greek nationalist scholars attempted to locate the cultural continuity of the Greek nation in the vernacular genres of the peasants, thus contributing to the emergence of a new national culture in modern Greece (Herzfeld 1986). With the defeat of the Ottoman Empire in the First World War and the subsequent halt of religious discourse as the main source of moral reinforcement, Turkish intellectuals also took recourse to minstrel's songs as the source of a new national language. Ironically, it was the formerly most marginalized people, glossed as 'non-Islamic folk', who now achieved the status of culture heroes (Basgöz 1978: 128). Other discourses in which the origin and prehistory of the nation was conceptualized in terms of an ahistorical folk tradition emerged almost half a century later in China, Yugoslavia, and the erstwhile Soviet Union (Oinas 1978). According to Shiach (1989: 102), folk collectors in Britain were interested in tracing an original political voice in the people's folk narratives, in the hope that 'tunes, songs and other forms of folk culture could be revived as part of the living culture, thus mitigating the worst effects of industrial society'. Very early on, folklore scholars had complained about the incorporation of folk songs and genres in nationalist agendas, where they served to exclude parts of the population as 'others'. The most poignant example of course is National Socialist Germany, where folk songs and festivals were a major source to mobilize the youth and to instill an exclusive and anti-Semitic idea of the great German and Aryan nation (Dow and Lixfeld 1991; Meier 1992). See also Cocciara 1981.
2. Both authors refer to other genres such as the *lok gīt* or popular epics, but they confine their analysis to the context of Sikh patronage in which, they argue, these forms rarely find use.
3. Tradition, as has been argued by many, is not at all a neutral term, but one that has a specific (Western) historicity within discourses of modernity. For a long time, 'tradition' has been considered a remnant of the past and thus a counterpoint of modernity. Such discourses on 'tradition' have been comprehensively discussed in the 1980s. The idea of a fixed category against which modernity defines itself was criticized (Appadurai *et al.* 1991; Ben-Amos 1984; Shils 1981), the politics of the 'invention of tradition' (Hobsbawm and Ranger 1984) were studied and, in turn, criticized for the implicit assumption that there might be other cultural domains that would be less invented and thus in some way 'more real' (Kapferer 1988: 210).

4. Trilochan Pande made the point that until quite recently, 'Indian scholars have not accepted, and they still do not accept, the narrow use of the word *lok* in its strict sense of the European folk as the history of civilization and the social pattern of India have been much more different than those of the countries of the West' (Pande 1963: 25).
5. Whereas for a long time, classificatory and antiquarian interests defined the folklorists' agenda (Thompson 1977), scholars began to realize that the field of folkloristics offers tools beyond recording customs and stories. Individuals and groups had to be taken into account, and the meaning 'behind the story' had to be resituated in the actual social world of people; the issue had now become of asking in what different ways people were explicitly and implicitly placed as agents within narrative representations and other artistic forms (cf. Ramanujan 1999a, c). Furthermore, the interest in content had, if not to be replaced, then at least to be accomplished with a strong focus on performative contexts. Initiated by the linguistic turn in anthropology and due to the impact of the new performative approaches to the study of language and oral tradition (Finnegan 1977; Abu-Lughod 1986; Bauman and Briggs 1990; Briggs 1988), folklore studies underwent a paradigmatic shift that is probably best represented in the publication *Towards New Perspectives in Folklore* (Bauman and Paredes 1970). See also Briggs and Shuman (1993); Flueckiger (1996); Paredes (1993).
6. While people celebrated independence from colonial rule, in Punjab (and Bengal) people were traumatized by communal violence and displacement. Most of the Sikh and Hindu refugees who came from the western regions of Punjab lost family members in the turmoil of the events of 1947. Similarly, Muslim families who fled to Pakistan were subject to attacks and killings by violent mobs. An extensive body of literature has been produced to account for questions of displacement and the loss that Partition meant to individuals, families, and communities. Apart from the many historical treatises that focused on the processes and politics of the emergent event (Chandra 1989; Hasan 1993; Hodson 1985; Schechtman 1949), I want to mention here the anthropological and sociological contributions. I consider to be most important: Butalia (1998); Das (1995b), Menon and Bhasin (1998); and Pandey (1997).
7. Tens of thousands of people were left dead, many of them killed during militant attacks and riots. A large number of young male Sikhs, 'suspected terrorists', were killed in the course of police counter-insurgency (Human Rights Watch 1991, 1994). Many rural and urban neighbourhoods had become subject to violent disputes or had an atmosphere of uncertainty and terror. The 1984 anti-Sikh riots, in particular, resonated the fundamental trauma of the geographical and political Partition of the subcontinent in 1947 (Das 1990).
8. See Veena Das (1995).

PART ONE

Framing the Dhadi Past

MAP: Major Sikh Gurdwaras in Punjab
Copyright © mapsofindia.com

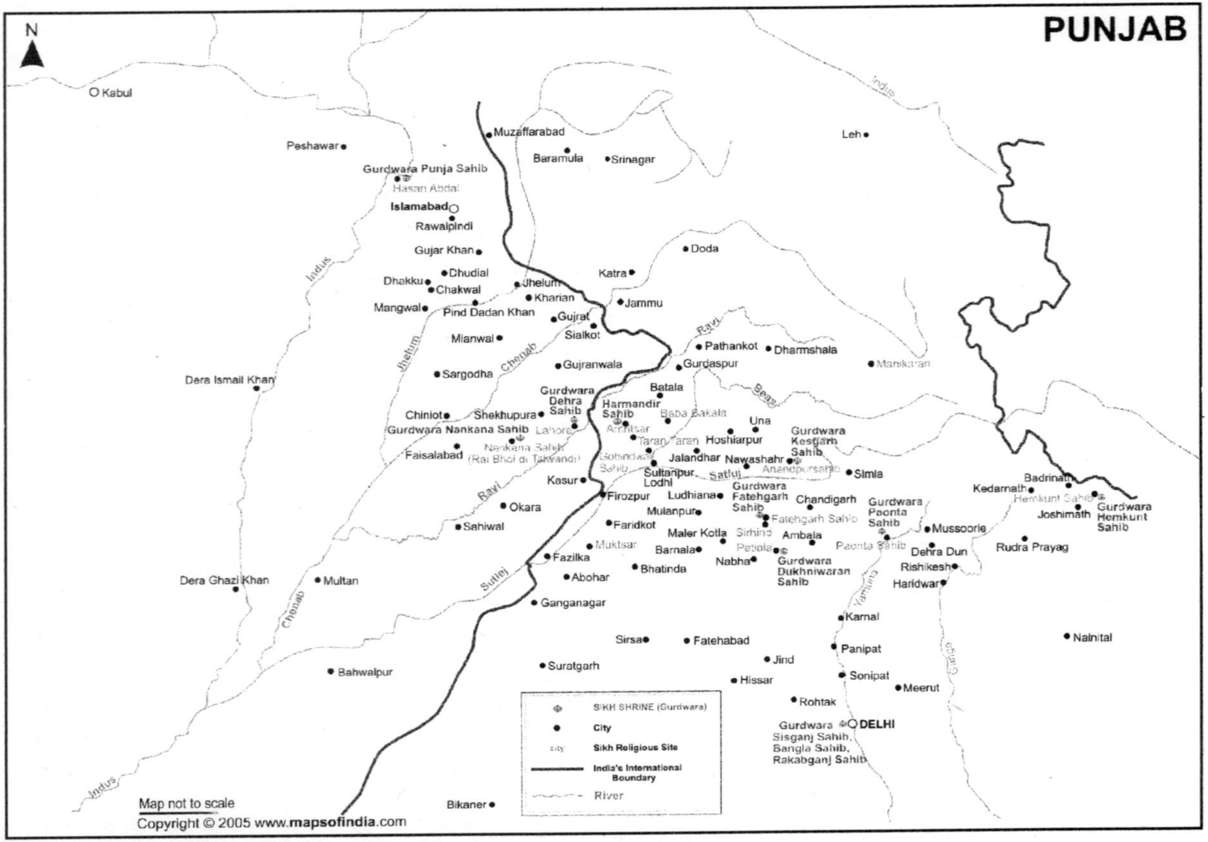

I

Cultural Geography and the Dhadi Past

The River

> Like the flow of the river, life's chariot keeps on moving. It knows no end. Its magnificence lies in movement. Its players are also its spectators. Indeed, greater pleasure lies in the performance rather than the reception of the play. But as an eternal law, the player has to change the place at the given time. Sometimes the spectator becomes the player and sometimes it is the other way round...No one is capable of grasping its complete structure. It can contain strange ceremonies, unforeseen incidents that are hard to visualize. Sometimes, things which seem unrealistic are within the reach of the possible (Seetal 1972: 220. Translated by Michael Nijhawan).

It all begins with the river. The cultural geography of Punjab has been shaped by the flow of rivers. It is the land of the wanderers, pastoral tribes, and peasants who have cultivated it. Over the centuries, they have created the cultural space of Punjab. The *pagus*, as Michel Serres reminds us, represents the traces left by agricultural work, the furrow on the earth, as well as the carved pages that make the stuff of vernacular history. Reading it requires the knowledge of the educated as much as the knowledge of the peasants, artisans, and troubadours.

Punjab is the land of rivers. Located next to the Himalayas in the north, the rich Gangetic plain in the southeast, the Rajasthan desert in the southwest, and the Indus in the west, Punjab (that is, land of *panj* 'five' *ab* 'water') derives its name from the five rivers Jhelum, Chenab, Ravi, Beas, and Sutlej, that flow through it. This designation, however, is a modern one. The ancient texts interpret Punjab as the land of seven rivers.[1] They begin with the Indus (or Sindhu) as the river and add the Kabul river as one of its main tributaries.

It is the river that has named the land. The criss-crossing of streams makes a patchwork of cultural subregions, the *doaba*s (do ab literally, land of two streams). Along with adaptations to the particular ecology, they are marked by variations in Punjabi dialect and cultural tradition. There is the Bist Jalandhar Doab between the Sutlej and Beas in the east bordering the Shivalik hills, the Bari Doab to the west where the big cities of Lahore and Multan are located, the Rachna Doab between the Ravi and Chenab, the Chaj Doab bordered by the Jhelum in the west, and finally the Sind Sagar Doab that borders the Indus and the Sulaiman mountain range. Here we reach Peshawar, the entry point to the Hindu Kush mountains and Kabul. In the Indian Punjab after 1947, the name 'Doaba' designates the Bist Jalandhar Doab, where people speak a particular Doabi dialect. Other regional identities that are based on cultural-linguistic boundary markers are in the names Malwa and Majha. The Majha area includes the districts of Amritsar and Gurdaspur. Malwa stretches from the districts of Ludhiana and Patiala to Faridkot and Ferozepur in the west. The importance of cultural geography is instrumental as there are many more names that designate smaller subregions, such as the *ilāqā* ('area' or a group of some adjacent villages) or *beṭ* (low alluvial lands), and *ḍhāhā* (abandoned bank of a river).[2] The last two terms indicate the importance attributed to rivers because of their rich mineral deposits that form the large alluvial plain of the agricultural heartland.

Punjab, sprinkled with the sweat of countless farmers, is also drenched in the blood of centuries of war and colonization.[3] It is the ground upon which innumerable bards have wandered, commemorating the histories of these battles, praising their patrons, cursing others, and singing of the pain of separation. The patterned surface of riverbanks and greens is also a metaphor for their cultural heritage: the patterned structure of collective memory, the vernacularization of Punjabi history. It is the psyche of the river that flows through the veins of Punjab's troubadours. For a beginning, let us think of it as a symphony of difference.

Punjab's troubadours look back on a long history that relates bardic musicians from Sindh to Rajasthan with the countless bards in the Himalayas, Sufi poetry with Sikh and Hindu devotional literature.[4] Their travel through North Indian history is shaped by invasions and migrations over the Kabul route. The early Sufi shrines in Sindh and the bards they attracted are integral to the picture.[5]

How does one locate the dhadi bard in this historical landscape? In a way, the name dhadi functions as a metaphor that is inclusive, embracing. In the medieval period (up to the fifteenth and sixteenth centuries) it signified a wider spectrum of bardic tradition, which is why we often find dhadi to be translated simply as 'bard' or 'minstrel'. With the emergence of the Mughal chronicles and Sikh hagiographic material, we find a clearer picture in terms of a specific genre of song recitation. Punjabis have heard the voice of dhadi in this distinctive format. It is a repository of specific narrative repertoires; enshrined in its sounds are idioms of Sikh devotional life, as well as popular forms that span across different spheres of saint veneration. In the chapters to come, the reader will mainly engage with the modern period and the relationship between Sikhism and the dhadi tradition. As this tradition existed during the times of Guru Nanak, its origins must be traced to non-Sikh contexts, some of which have continued to inform the broader spectrum of Punjabi performative culture up to the twentieth century.

The Troubadour of Poet-saints

Among South Asian scholars who have devoted their attention to the dhadi tradition, Charlotte Vaudeville (1962: 40–5) has probably offered the first detailed essay in her study of the Dhola-Maru epic in which dhadis are mentioned as the singers of this ballad. According to her reading, dhadi performers have been associated with the various poet-saints of North India and the sociotextual communities that were formed by them.[6] The term *ḍhāḍhī* occurs frequently in various poetic and Hindu devotional texts. Sur Das (1483–1563), the 'blind bard' and founder of the Vallabhacharya sect used the word dhadi in his lyrics as did Guru Nanak.[7] Even if they used the term dhadi in a metaphorical sense without clear indications of its precise sociocultural meanings, it is clear that the tradition was known to them and important enough to find a place in the sacred texts.

The North Indian Sant tradition contributed immensely to the creation and proliferation of a Punjabi vernacular language with its refined poetic genres. The *dohā* (a small couplet), for instance, is one of the poetical forms that have been used by many of the sants and gurus (Schomer and McLeod 1987). According to Vaudeville (1999: 273), the dohas not only mark 'the dawn of vernacular literature in northern India: they constitute the most ancient evidence of popular literature in old Rajasthani.' It seems that the doha is genealogically linked to the dhadi tradition. Francesca Orsini's (2004) recent discovery of the Qutubshatak text strongly underlines this observation, as the *doha* is narrated in the voice of a dhadhini—a female dhadi performer. Following Vaudeville and Orsini, it can be argued that the dhadi bard has a distinguished place in North Indian vernacular traditions despite the evidence of their low social position.[8]

Note that Vaudeville traces the bards' social origin to the Jat and Mina pastoral tribes, arguing that the dhadi bards have been the hereditary service castes for them. This is important insofar as it allows us to understand why the Sikh tradition (with the large constituency of Jats) later patronized dhadi bards. It is most likely that dhadi bards have emerged from these pastoral tribes.

In terms of performative format, Vaudeville found that dhadis were primarily vocalists, while they were also often reported as players of the *cikara* and *sarangi* and the drum instrument *ḍhaḍḍ* from which they have most likely taken their name.[9] The Qutubshatak text also mentions drum and other instruments. Most importantly, it mentions the dhadhini as a vocalist who plays a drum: '[84] What did the Dhadini sing? She lightly alaped a [hali] and lightly played the drum.' Other historical references in this matter, however, are rare and much of the argument about the performers' social origins rest upon historical speculation.[10]

If today the dhadi tradition in Punjab is at least popularly linked to Sufi vernacular poetry, this is due to the spread of Sufi mysticism through Amir Khusrau and Sheikh Farid. Otherwise we do not find strong evidence for a patronage system in the Sufi context. Khusrau and Farid, however, were two figures who strongly appealed to the bards; it is documented that many bards took on Muslim names in the fifteenth and sixteenth centuries. Even in the contemporary setting, many bardic performers I spoke with considered Sheikh Farid their spiritual guide, Pakpattan remaining one of the centres where bards would meet for the annual *'urs* celebrations. Pakpattan, which was earlier known as the ancient city of Ajudhan—centrally located on the east-west trade route—was an important place for the development of Sufi devotionalism in South Asia. Baba Farid was among the most important figures to reformulate Islamic doctrines. The Sufi Pirs not only reformulated Islamic doctrines and concepts in Punjabi vernacular idioms, their followers have also functioned as proprietors, landlords, and patrons, having established important institutional structures of ritual worship at the locations of Sufi shrines.[11] The Punjabi countryside is still dotted with innumerable *dargāhs* and the smaller, wayside shrines that people call *jaṭherās*. They indicate the enormous veneration for the Sufi saints outside the boundaries of the esoteric Sufi orders that has lasted to the dawn of the twenty-first century. Punjabis of different religious affiliations participate in the 'urs and '*samā* rituals that are organized and performed at these shrines.[12] The rich poetic and musical inheritance associated with the popular Sufi tradition in the Punjab constitutes the core of Punjabi folklore, music, and poetic expression, transmitted orally by dhadi bards.[13] Present at festive occasions, Punjab's dhadi bards render Sufi thought in the form of oral epics, the most popular of them being *Hīr Rānjhā*.[14]

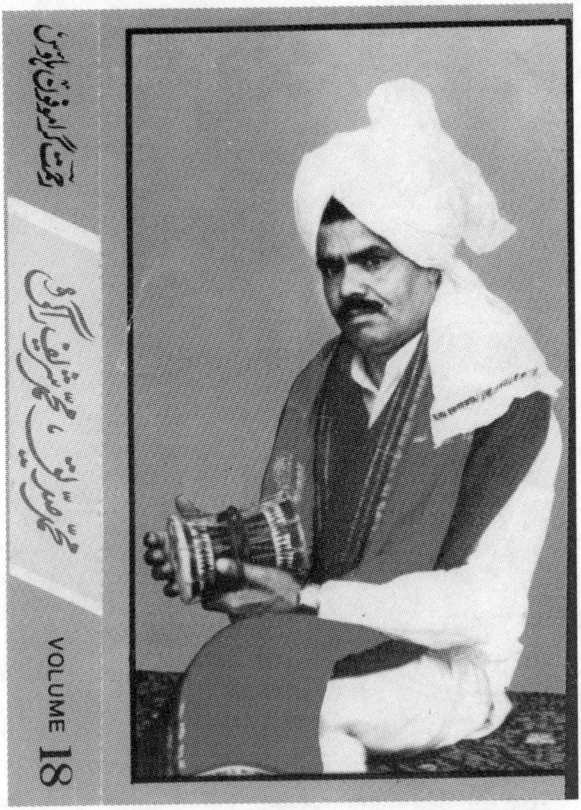

FIGURE 3: Cassette cover, Dhadi Mohammad Shareef Ragi, Rahmat Gramophones, Faisalabad
Courtesy Michael Nijhawan

FIGURE 4: Cassette cover, Dhadi Mohammad Shareef and Mohammad Shareef Ragi, ‘Lok Git’ (Folk Songs), Rahmat Gramophones, Faisalabad
Courtesy Michael Nijhawan

The Making of the Darbari Dhadi

The appreciation of the bardic profession is expressed in numerous miniature paintings of medieval times that depict one of the poet saints in the company of one or two male musicians. Most prominent in that regard is Guru Nanak's portrait in which he is seated under a tree in a novel posture beside Bala and Mardana, the latter playing the *rabab*. Often cited for its pluralistic message (Bala the Hindu and Mardana the Muslim), the painting also depicts an ideal of vernacularization, 'the speaking voice of popular culture', as Uberoi (1996: 79) calls it, with the green parrot in the tree symbolizing the vernacular tongue. Figure 5 indicates that the ruling class liked to be portrayed in a similar fashion; Izzat Khan, the then governor of Sindh, sits next to a sarangi player amidst a larger assembly of musicians. Bor (1987: 54) deliberates whether it is the first depiction of an Indian sarangi player, presumably a portrait of Allah Dad Dhadi mentioned by the chronicler Nawab Saif Khan Faquirullah. What this portrayal shows is that popular religious traditions alone did not cultivate poetic recitations and inspiring songs of the dhadi genre. Early on, this form was a recognized genre patronized by the royal court, the *darbār*. We can therefore speak of the emergence of the darbari dhadi: the bard who is employed by the (royal) patron whose praise he or she sings.

Travelling from under the shade of the tree to the inner domain of the darbar, the image of the dhadi bard gets enshrined in the memory of royal power. Indications that dhadi performers became part of the vibrant Mughal court culture can be found in chronicles such as the *Ain-i-Akbārī*.[15] Daniel Neuman says that the name dhadi was used for a class of local musicians who were ranked below other musicians of Persian origin, such as the *atai* or *huzūrī* and *gunijan* or *darbārī* (Neuman 1980: 86–7).[16] The troubadour's entrance to the court started at the bottom, the roots of his tree were in the poor countryside.

It is not clear today what role the dhadi bard played in the court. Wade's analysis of Mughal paintings only reveals that dhadi instrumentation—specifically the string instrument, the sarangi—entered the Mughal court at a later stage.[17] More important were the drums that are depicted frequently in the highly conventionalized Mughal miniature paintings. The drum players had a particular role in projecting state authority. In the context of the small kingdoms (as for instance in the Central Himalayas), the drum not only constituted a symbol of royal power, in India it was also commonly regarded as a part of the king's

FIGURE 5: Prince and friends in the company of a sarangi player among other musicians

amlā, the extended 'royal family' that included groups of different *jātī*s according to their specific ritual and kinship relations with the emperor (Joshi 1995: 113).[18] This might have also been the reason for Guru Hargobind's patronage of the musicians, even though, as I have pointed out, the bards were known to the Sikh gurus before the time of Guru Hargobind. In his aspirations to royal power, he welcomed the dhadi musicians in his court.[19] If today the Sikh dhadi performers speak of their gatherings as dhadi darbar, they relive the historical tradition of the aura of courtly power and elegance, paying homage to Guru Hargobind whom they consider the original patron.

Virah Gīt or Bīr Rasa?

From the historical material that has been handed down and explored so far, it can also be learned that the dhadi tradition has undergone transitions in terms of performative style and aesthetic format. While it would be appropriate to think of dhadi musicians as masters of different tunes, narrative registers, and musical genres, the changing patronage context has eventually led to gradual changes in the broader public perception of dhadi music. Such transitions can be documented for the modern period—as I will demonstrate later on—but it might be wise to assume that similar changes took place in the framework of historical developments discussed here. Most notably, it seems to me, is a shift from the *virah gīt* (songs of love and separation) to the martial aesthetics of *bīr rasa* that have been favoured under the patronage of royal power. We do not need to construct a false dichotomy here. But there are indications for gender-related differences associated with the performance of each of these genres.

The image of the dhadi singer as it is linked to martial aesthetics comes down to us through a Persian chronicle that can be traced to the seventeenth century. Joep Bor reports:

> According to Faquirullah (1665/66), *dhadhis* were the oldest community of musicians, and originally Rajputs. They sang *karkha*, which was 'composed in four to eight lines to sing the praises of the war-lords, the brave soldiers, and to narrate the affairs of battles and war'. He also informs us that the Punjabi *dhadhi*s played the *dhadh* (a small-sized *dhol* to which they owed their name), and sang heroic ballads, called *bar*. They were sung by at least two persons; the ustad, who was the leader of the group, tunefully recited the opening lines while the *shagirds* (disciples) followed, sometimes repeating the lines, sometimes returning to the opening section (Bor 1987: 62, original italics).

The presumed Rajput origin of the tradition is noteworthy as it deepens the question of why and under what circumstances the Sikh tradition welcomed dhadi performers in its realm when, at the same time, the relationship with the Rajputs was characterized by widespread antagonism. The chronicler might have misjudged this connection, but we might also have an indication here of a phenomenon of cultural appropriation.

In any case, the contemporary format of Sikh dhadi resonates strongly with Faquirullah's seventeenth century portrayal. The generic links to vernacular poetry and characteristics of the performative community suggest a continuity of the bardic genre in the way many contemporary Punjabis think about it. There are strong reasons to underline this historical continuity in aesthetic format (heroic genres such as the vār) and discursive orientation (martial ballads). The memory of persecution and war, specifically among the Sikh population, is vivid for all sections of society. Contemporary dhadi performers recall this history day after day at various public occasions in Punjab and amidst the Sikh diaspora. The genre has certainly retained the language of martyrdom and violence that has come from this history.

FIGURE 6: Dhadi Jattha Gurcharan Singh Gohlewar
Courtesy Upkar Singh, Amritsar

In contrast to this image, there is a female side to dhadi performance that leads to a somewhat different interpretation. Charlotte Vaudeville speaks of female dhadi singers, Francesca Orsini examines a text in which a dhadhini is the pivotal focus, and Bonny Wade argues that female dhadi performers were present at the Mughal court.[20] In the light of the predominant image of dhadi as a male genre, what are we to make of this female inheritance? As I shall further argue in Chapter 2, there have been interpretive moves to associate the female voice and performance of dhadi song with the aesthetics of bīr rasa. But in a historical perspective, this seems to be a more recent development. There is strong evidence that the sarangi and aesthetic images that are associated with courtesan culture had a stronger impact on public consciousness than other associations. Originally a folk instrument, the sarangi received royal patronage when it became associated with the culture of courtesans (*tawāyyaf*). The dominant sound-image of the sarangi, argues Qureshi (1997: 14), has been associated with the courtesan song. The instrument's body with its ornamental designs and names, testifies to this courtly tradition in which women's voice played a special role.

The sarangi, writes Qureshi (2000: 820), is 'highly adorned with motifs of refinement that directly articulate the milieu of Indo-Muslim feudal culture. Two architectural shapes dominate the head of the instruments. A delicately fluted arch and tower-shaped niche together frame what are really two pegboxes for three and a single string respectively, like elegant windows that invite the viewer's eye into a courtly interior...[referred to as] *mehrāb* (prayer niche) and *minār* (minaret).' Today, the sound/image of the sarangi is also perceived as the female voice of lament and longing. This is not unique to the classical tradition; it influenced the broad spectrum of performative culture, including the dhadi tradition. The culture industry makes frequent use of this feature, so that we hear the sarangi's disembodied voice in popular film and media reportage. Dhadi performers who specialize in singing popular ballads and oral epics portray the voice of the heroine with the tormenting sound of the stringed instrument.

It makes sense, therefore, to conceptualize the format of dhadi performance as we know it today as a complex crossing of different aesthetic styles and preferences that show historical continuities as well as ruptures in performative practice. This is not to suggest that 'folk' and 'classical' traditions had not developed different aesthetic styles and meanings, not to speak of the different forms of musical apprenticeship. But there has certainly been considerable overlap, mutual influence, historically shifting preferences as well as changes in musical and narrative repertoire. In some regards, it seems that the rhythmic pattern of the dhadd has become associated with the military exercise of royal power. In other contexts we hear vibrating the chords of lament and longing in the historical voice of the sarangi. In that way, the dhadi tradition incorporates, at least partially, a Punjabi history of acculturation in a historically specific, generic form.

Notes

1. See Grewal (2004) for this point.
2. See Bhatti (2002).
3. The first major development of industrialization was in the creation of an extensive irrigation canal system, the so-called Canal Colonies, under British colonial rule. Areas that were formerly unsuited for agricultural production because of their dry, sandy or semi-arid land, suddenly became centres of agricultural production like Lahore, Ferozepur, Lyallpur, Jhang, and Multan. A second major boost to agricultural production in the Punjab—both in regions that are now the Indian and Pakistan Punjab—came with the 'Green Revolution' in the 1960s, when new seeds and fertilizers were introduced and the techniques of agricultural production were further modernized and intensified.
4. See for instance Chandola (1977).
5. See Pannke (2002).
6. The term 'Sant' has become customary to designate these poet-saints—troubadours with wisdom—and founders of vibrant traditions of anti Brahmanical Hinduism. There is a vast field of scholarship on these religious traditions and I am only scratching the surface in these introductory pages.

   > While the Sants use Vaishnava names for God, they do not worship the incarnations of Vishnu or accept the Vaishnava scriptures, and are not affiliated to any of the orthodox bhakti schools or sampradays. They are also indifferent to the authority of the Vedas, reject the priestly prerogatives of Brahmans and oppose the outer forms of devotion associated with saguna bhakti. Finally, while the orthodox Vaishnava tradition has affirmed at the level of doctrine that salvation is open to all regardless of social status, ritual barriers between high and low castes have not really been challenged at the level of practice, and leadership has remained almost exclusively in the hands of Brahmans. The Sants, by contrast, have been uncompromising in their opposition to caste hierarchy and exclusiveness, and the great majority of the leading figures in the tradition have been from lower castes (Schomer and McLeod 1987: 7–8).

7. Vaudeville (1999: 293) writes: 'Sur Dās mentions the dhādhīs in several padas in the Sur-sāgar. The poet addresses the Yādava, Nandgopa, Krishna's adoptive father, saying, "I am the Dhādhī of your house"—and,

in exchange, Nandgopa claims not riches, but the bhakti of Krishna. This confirms the association of the Dhādīs with the Jāts, who are Yādavas, descendants of Krishna himself: the glory of Nandagopa, Krishna's adoptive father, reflects on all his descendants.' There has been some speculation as to whether the poet-saint Sur Das was himself a dhadi, or whether it was just due to poetical convention and a self-conscious turn to a figure of a socially low caste that the name surfaces in this body of literature, a point made by John Stratton Hawley (1984). The fact that Guru Nanak has also used that epithet seems to underline Hawley's argument (Shackle 1993: 276; Harbans Singh 1992: 563–4).

8. There are several points where dhadis are mentioned in the oral epic *Dholā-Māru*.
9. In considering the sections in the Dhola-Maru where dhadis are depicted as singers of the *ulag*, Vaudeville (1962: 42) argues that they have been specialists in vocalizing this particular motif of the pain of separation: 'Les Dhadis sont en quelque sorte des "spécialistes" de ce type de chansons sur le theme de l'absence de l'epoux et du "Virah" de l'épouse.' This remark is intriguing as dhadi vocalists today continue to have this theme as the core of their repertoire.
10. Vaudeville (1999: 294) mentions a second source which accounts for the participation of dhadis in bhakti worship:

    > A specialist, S.M. Kothari, notes that the dancers' costumes are Rajasthani, and that while dancing they agitate little cymbals called *cham-cham* (an equivalent of *manjārā*). The main theme of their songs (now in Braj) concerns the genealogy of Nanda-Rai, Krishna's putative father, whose prosperity and glory they abundantly describe. This testimony is interesting in so far as it underlines the association of the dhadis with the pastoral tribe of the ancient Yadavas or Jadons of Rajasthan, and in particular with the Jats and Bhattis of yore.

11. See Eaton (1978, 1996).
12. Harjot Oberoi argues that until the nineteenth century, the Sufi shrine and its related rituals and festivals constituted the core around which all major popular performances, rituals, and traditions were concentrated and through which they were perpetuated (Oberoi 1997: 139–203).
13. Vaudeville assumes that dhadi performers converted to Islam during the time of prince Amir Khusrau (another famous Sufi figure of the Chisti order) in order to claim a more respectable social status (1999: 293). Whether there is sufficient support for this conversion narrative or not is unclear. However, according to the Mughal and Sikh documents, these performers took Muslim names and the veneration of Sufi saints was obviously the major focus of pious conduct in medieval Punjab.
14. See Grewal (1984) and Matringe (1996, 1998) for this point.
15. One of the earliest references to dhadi have been traced to Persian chronicles. Daniel Neuman refers to these sources, naming dhadis (dharis) the oldest musical community known in India. There has never been a

single category translated as 'musician' in the Indian context but rather a multitude of different names referring to distinct traditions and musical styles. The same is true in the case of dhadi, but unfortunately we can trace only few details in Persian chronicles. In the major chronicles dhadi musicians are recorded as 'singers', not as the players of particular instruments. Neuman refers here to Abul Fazl's *Ain-ī-Akbārī* (the chronicle of Akbar's court), the *Kitāb-ī-Nauras* (written by the ruler Ibrahim Adil Shah), and Mohammad Karam Islam's *Mādanul Mausīqī* that was written in nineteenth century Lucknow (Neuman 1980: 86–7). Bor cites Faquirullah (1665/66) and a Venetian travel account from around the same time in which the origin of dhadi musicians is traced to Rajput groups.

16. The epithet *huzurī* is still used in the Sikh context for the kirtan *rāgi*s at the Harmandir Sahib. It is sometimes applied to dhadi singers when they perform at one of the five representative *takht*s. The distinction between indigenous and Persian genres reflects the development of musical traditions in the realm of Mughal patronage. It seems that Indian artists were entering the court at the bottom of the hierarchy, but were subsequently capable of replacing the previously dominant Persian musicians.
17. In Akbar's court the sarangi was still virtually absent, whereas by the time of Shah Jahan, the popular folk instrument had found its way in. While dhadi performers are mentioned as singers in the *Ain-ī-Akbārī*, Faquirullah informs us that they play the dhadd (Bor 1987: 63), and in the *Mādanul Mausīqī* they are referred to as sarangi players (ibid.: 100).
18. Considering that Mughal court culture was a synthesis of Persian and Indian cultural traditions and aesthetic forms (Wade 1998: 27), we are safe to assume that dhadis became part of the Mughal court 'family'. Acquiring Mughal patronage the dhadi genre became crucial to the public symbolization of state power. Akbar is believed to have effectively used Indian cultural traditions in order to symbolically demonstrate and disseminate political-religious authority.
19. See Chapter 2 for a full discussion of the Sikh sources.
20. Female dhadi performers were not ranked as honoured court musicians. Nevertheless the miniature paintings depict them as players of the dhadd and as singers. Wade hypothesizes that they formed a *jātī* (local caste) in Rajasthan, whereas at present they are known as scavengers who provide services such as garbage disposal and caretaking (Karlekar 1995). At Akbar's court, women played a pivotal role in the establishment of cultural ties with the Rajputs. Akbar married local Rajput women in order to establish friendly relationships with the Rajput kingdoms. It is often noted that Akbar allowed the Rajput princesses in his harem to keep to their Hindu traditions which included the regular invitation of musical and dance performers at the royal darbar. Thus, North Indian dance, music, and literature became part of the Mughal court. The ruler's marriage practice was probably another reason for the dhadi genre to have entered the court.

2

Sikh Religious Aesthetics and the Gendered Dhadi Voice[1]

One of the distinctive features of Sikh religious practice is the variation between meditative-mystical and heroic-passionate aesthetics, which in their mutual relationship lend themselves differently to processes of political and social resignification. In this chapter, I wish to explore something of the background of this relationship as it is represented in the discourses and practices associated with the dhadi genre. The dominant image of the dhadi genre is that of a male tradition that cultivates heroic moods expressed in the notion of bīr rasa. What needs to be addressed in this chapter is an evaluation of the gendered dhadi voice, both in relation to and distinction from the aesthetics of bīr rasa.

It is a well recognized fact that dhadi singers were patronized by Sikh gurus and communities from the sixteenth century onward to give voice to the gurus' lives and later to commemorate their deeds as well as those of Sikh martyrs from the eighteenth century onward. Scholars by and large agree that this tradition became linked with the institution of the Akal Takht, thus representing Sikh political and military power. Due to this association, the dhadi genre has retained a language and aesthetics of martyrdom and suffering. These are also given testimony in the genre's modern, twentieth-century form, which has helped to make it a recognized agent of collective Sikh self-definition and political mobilization. However, the portrayal of the dhadi genre as a homogeneous form of religious self-expression throughout the centuries leads to the impression that modes of Sikh self-representation were always essentially the same. Folk genres are accordingly understood as manifestations of these representations.

This chapter argues that, on the contrary, the relationship between Sikhism and the dhadi genre is complicated even at a level where tradition presumes a high degree of conformity: the relationship between religious and folk aesthetics. My argument necessitates, first of all, a discussion of Sikh religious aesthetics in their practical dimension. It requires a reading of historical material through an anthropological notion of aesthetics that moves beyond what could be called 'ethnoaesthetics', that is, the mere recognition of cultural relativism in aesthetic experience. Differences in the way cultures construct aesthetic values and imbue those with notions of agency and power of course vary significantly.[2] This is certainly the case with liturgical forms in the Sikh religion which, in the believer's eyes, are permeated with sacred truths and transformative power. I will discuss Sikh notions of religious aesthetics in detail while working toward a broader understanding of (religious) aesthetics as value judgements or evaluative schemes. My anthropological approach to aesthetics, in short, refers to the formal and spiritual qualities of artistic production in the way in which they are mobilized within the broader field of social and cultural relations.

To provide the reader with a first outline of the argument pursued here, I briefly depart from my chronological ordering of this book and begin with an observation on contemporary practices of dhadi singing. The example provided here amounts to the 'martial aesthetics' that are commonly ascribed to dhadi singing. The case is directly related to the recent association of the dhadi genre with the rise of militancy and Sikh ethnonationalism in the 1980s that I will further discuss in subsequent chapters.[3] By the time I started ethnographic research, the militant movement in Punjab had ebbed, yet the memory that linked the passionate voice of dhadi singers with the violence and sufferings of the 1980s still had a sensory immediacy.[4] This book, through ethnographic analysis, delineates how this sensory immediacy may help read an entire range of social relations. The first issue that I would like to note here is the mediation of the relationship between voice and violence through a discourse on the efficacy of the female voice. The recognition of the female voice as such was not entirely new. For a long time, the voice of the string-instrument sarangi—without question the central idiom of dhadi performance—has been associated with the female voice of longing and lament.[5] In the recent context of political violence, however, a different principle of the invigorating female voice was given expression. The aesthetic evaluation of the female voice had practical consequences in that it allowed women performers to enter the previously male dominated tradition.[6] Women performers first appeared on the scene immediately before the Indian army launched its attack on the Akal Takht in Amritsar. A group of women performers known as the *nābhewāle bibiāṃ* started to perform heroic songs in the vicinity of the temple complex. The contemporary performers with whom I worked emphasized that the women's high pitched voices were deemed appropriate to arouse fervent passion (*jośʹ*), the expression of extreme agony, and the spirit of resistance.

FIGURE 7: *Music Times* magazine cover showing female Dhadi performers
Courtesy Michael Nijhawan

Let us turn to some of the women's voices. In 1999, I had a series of conversations with female singers and musicians, recent converts to Sikhism, whose motivation to perform the dhadi genre has to be understood against the background of this entanglement of performative voice with political violence. At one point I asked Pawandeep Kaur, leader of a dhadi group and one of my fieldwork interlocutors, why she was attracted to perform the heroic songs of Sikh martyrs, although all evidence suggested that more than a decade after the turmoil, it could be still potentially harmful to anyone bearing the name dhadi. Counter-insurgency measures of the state were occasionally directed against those taking an active role in commemorative functions. Her answer was:

> We do this to gain a state of inner peace [*assī apne man dī śāntī vāste karde hāṃ*]. It is good for us and there will be no '*tension*'. We will not incite tension. We shall neither incite tension nor shall somebody bother us. Brother, nothing wrong will happen to us. Brother, should we suffer pain, we will face it with honour, with our parent's honour, with the honour of our brothers and sisters we shall continue—that's all [*bhaī, jitthe unhā nūṃ ṭez pahūṃce, assī unhā dī leke izzat, mā-pī'u dī izzat, bhaiṇ-bhare dī izzat le ke turan, bas*].

FIGURE 8: Pawandeep Kaur and sisters forming a Dhadi Jattha
Courtesy Michael Nijhawan

Borrowing the English term 'tension' that has perpetuated public discourse during the last two decades or so, Pawandeep Kaur discarded my idea that her dhadi performance would be an expression of militancy or would spur the use of violence. Tension is something that has to be avoided by all means. Tension is what she knew for too long. It had prevailed in her life and had been a political condition under which her performative profession had become subject to general suspicion. Instead, the performance of dhadi would lead to the ease of tension.

Beyond the immediate context of violence, the rendering of aesthetic experience becomes related to the self-understanding of the performers as responsible public and pious actors. What is needed, said Pawandeep Kaur in our conversation, is the obligation (*firz*) and responsibility (*jummewāri*) of performing before an audience, and as another performer has re-emphasized it, 'what is presented on the stage must contribute to the Sikh community's well-being [*succajji sehat*] and progress [*sucārū sehat*]. This is different from any bad conduct that is without soul, without recognition [*sirāh*], without meaning (*be sir-pair* lit. without "head and feet").' In the contemporary context in which Sikh dhadi performers begin to reorganize their social network by dissociating themselves from corrupt patrons and a recent history of militancy and suffering, it comes as no surprise that they emphasize issues of reputation, social responsibility, and piety in clear distinction from 'bad politics'. Thus, on the one hand, Pawandeep Kaur's rendering of the dhadi genre as a religious way of life resonates the agenda of an entire performative community.[7] On the other hand, she tells us something about the internal processes of how female actors gain reputation in a male dominated performative community.

The point I want to make in quoting from the field encounter is that Kaur's evaluation of performative aesthetics appears to have further implications that I could not have anticipated in following an 'expressivist' theory in my question. The process by which she links self, performative genre, and religious tradition cannot be entirely explained in terms of discursive constructions, although it is through language that these issues are made accessible and intelligible. Pawandeep Kaur's statement is set against the background of a non-discursive idiom: the mood of stillness and ease of tension. With this emphasis she seems to collapse a distinction between what is commonly regarded as folk aesthetics and Sikh religious aesthetics.

In Sikhism, the process of forming the self in terms of religious piety is linked to the practical efforts of reciting, singing, and listening to the hymns of the Adi Granth in the form of the meditative kirtan ritual. Kirtan is considered as absolutely central, as it elucidates the devotee's constant active engagement with and enactment of the sacred text. As attested by Pawandeep Kaur and several other performers I worked with, the meditative idiom and mood of Sikh kirtan is employed here to reinterpret the passionate-interpretive form and performative aesthetics of the dhadi genre in the aftermath of political violence in Punjab. As I shall further explore, such reinterpretations of performative practice and aesthetics have significant ramifications for our understanding of religious practices in the Sikh tradition and beyond. It is therefore necessary to look at performative genres such as the dhadi genre not as homogenous forms, but as dynamic practices through which to understand a complex web of relations.

Religious Aesthetics, Ritual, and Music

For a long time, anthropological scholarship has dealt with aesthetic issues in the domain of ethnomusicology, often working with a broad definition of music as a cultural practice of arranging sonic pitches. The study of musical traditions in such different cultural settings like Papua New Guinea (Feld 1982) or North India (Qureshi 1995) have all led to a common understanding of how music, as a self-referential system of tonal organization, becomes intrinsically linked to extramusical processes (semantic, ideational, emotional, social, and political). Anthropologists and scholars in religious studies have also been interested in understanding the various musical and poetical forms in both liturgy-centred and performance-centred rituals. Music has been considered essential to practices of religious experience and self-definition.[8] Some scholars argue that music is especially suited to engender a sense of wholeness and transcendence. This seems particularly to be the case if the effects of musical sounds are construed in a way in which they are invested with (supernatural) power. Other, more cognitively oriented scholars have pointed out that the sequence and pattern of a musical performance have an immediate impact on the senses and in this way serve to structure ritual time and set it apart from ordinary time. This can, for instance, be witnessed in the Sufi qawwali ritual.[9] Here, as in many other musical traditions performed at Indian religious shrines, music intensifies the emotional attachment to particular places and thus helps to form moral communities in particular localities.

The frequent employment of poetical and musical genres throughout South Asia indicates that people are attracted to religious traditions not just because of the doctrines of a particular faith, but also because religious tradition is transmitted in a variety of performative repertoires and aesthetic forms through which the self can be shaped spiritually and ethically. There is sufficient evidence to suggest that what had for a long time been deemed as a merely entertaining or supplementing form of 'expressive' culture has, in fact, been instrumental to the various ways in which subjectivity and agency are constituted in religious practices.

Revaluations of performativity and musicality have certainly contributed to a reconsideration of dominant scholarly frameworks on religious tradition. This can be seen in A.K. Ramanujan's work on Indian folklore and literature, in which he has pointed out that Western approaches to Indian cultural and religious traditions had a tendency to omit the complex structure of performative practices. For far too long, argues Ramanujan (1999c), were such approaches preoccupied with a 'context-free' hermeneutic analysis that would not lend itself to the 'context-sensitive' forms of cultural practice and narrative tradition. Regarding the plural framework of Indian narrative traditions that are often part and parcel of religious rituals, he emphasized that right until the nineteenth century we find clear instructions in Indian texts that 'tell the reader, reciter or listener all the good that will result from his act of reading, reciting or listening' (ibid.: 42–2).

Recently, historians of religion have re-emphasized this line of thought. The deistic model of religiosity in particular, based on a clear distinction between arts as the domain of (secular) aesthetics and the essence of religion to be accessed by natural reason, has become subject to extensive criticism. As Donna Wulff has argued, 'Western students of religion continue to focus largely on the discursive symbols of theology and philosophy rather than on the presentational symbols of music, drama, and the visual arts' (1986: 673). In a similar vein, Kermani has pointed out that, 'the relatively clear separation between art and religion in the Western mind... is rather the exception, and one is tempted to turn the discussion of the aesthetic dimension of the Qur'an into the question of why this dimension is largely lost in the Western image of religion' (1996: 221). Wulff and Kermani defy the idea that religion is primarily accessible through its rational doctrines. At the same time, there is no attempt being made to return to European romanticist notions of a presumably universal religious (mystical) core in the diversity of religion which, as lucidly shown by

Jantzen (1989, 1990), had been current to post-Enlightenment thinking from Schleiermacher to William James. The important point these scholars make is that, even though aesthetics has turned out to be a specifically western construct that brought about a differentiation between secular and religious modes of experience, a different theory of aesthetics allows locating it within a broader field of social and religious configurations.

I agree with much that has been argued in the works just cited. However, I would also like to pursue a somewhat different line of thought. I will do so by shifting the emphasis from the narrow debate over religious hermeneutics and aesthetics, which is still framed in expressivist notions, to a broader investigation of religious and performative aesthetics as a sphere of practical engagement. I argue that, in assuming such a broader perspective, we can reach a position in which we are more likely to understand the historical transitions taking place within religious and performative traditions themselves. As my introductory example illustrates, it is not sufficient to confront hermeneutical and performative concepts in their applicability to non-Western forms of religion. Anthropologically speaking, the issue has to do with the culturally situated practices and discourses in which the relationship between religion and aesthetics is recognized and re-evaluated by social actors. To take this issue seriously, we should not lose sight of the fact that practitioners can and often do make clear distinctions between the ineffable mystical experience of the divine and aesthetic experience. The important fact is that we find an ongoing debate on the necessity and legitimacy of such distinctions, which are frequently drawn within the same registers of art, poetry, and music, as for instance between sacred and secular poetry in Islam (Kermani 1996, 2000).

In this regard, there is a common feature in my argument with Gade's (2002) work on the tradition of Qur'anic recitation in Indonesia, which concerns the idea of critical self-measurements against commonly held ideals of religious musicality. Gade proposes conceptualizing religious musicality as the key site for understanding how social actors internalize religious structure, enactments of religious musicality thus offering 'particularly accessible, audible points of reference for apprehending changes in religious self and system, as well as the interactions of these domains' (ibid.: 330). Gade has focused on how the self is measured against the background of non-discursive ideals of voice, talent, and 'taste', which I think accounts for the possible ways in which a performative tradition can become a site of alterity. Think, for instance, about Pawandeep Kaur's reassessment of the meditative mood of kirtan in the passionate dhadi voice; it helps to shape a new sense of self, attained through musical and religious training. This is appraised in terms of gaining self-respect and honour in distinction from a personal past of vulnerability and poverty.

My interest in this chapter, however, is not with the social psychology of this process, but rather with the gendered relationship between religious aesthetics and their historical and social conditions of possibility. I argue that the assessment of the dhadi genre in terms of religious aesthetics can be reiterated as a struggle with different aesthetic evaluations. These different evaluations are set in relation with different memories of the dhadi tradition. On the one hand, the term dhadi is incorporated in the Sikh scriptures as a concept of mystical communication with the divine. Sikh hagiography, in contrast, provides a different notion of how dhadi and religious aesthetics are related by signifying dhadi as a recognizable performative tradition in terms of Sikh patronage. This, in turn, places the relationship between performative voice and sacred sound on a completely different level. Conventional accounts of the dhadi genre tend to overlook these differences by assigning the tradition an unchanging substance over time.[10] I argue instead that it is precisely by looking at the transitions between these two different orientations—the mystical and the heroic-passionate voice—that we come to an understanding of the dhadi genre as a practice of aesthetic evaluation.

Dhadi in the Early Sikh Tradition: The Spiritual Dimension

Ardāsi suṇī dātāri prabhi ḍhāḍhī ka'ū mahil bulāwai
Prabh dekhdi'ā dukh bhukh ga'ī ḍhāḍhī ka'ū mangṇū citi na āvai

[*Srī Adī Granth Sāhib, Rāg Marū, Mahlā 5, Pauṛī, Pannā 1097*]

[God, the Great giver, hears the prayer, and summons the minstrel to the mansion of his presence
Gazing upon God, the minstrel is rid of pain and hunger; he does not think to ask for anything else][11]

The 'spiritual' meaning of the term *ḍhāḍhī* can be best appraised by relating it to Sikh cosmological concepts and the social vision of the early Sikh tradition. Let me remind the reader of the most basic principles shared by Sikh believers: whether Sikhism is considered a monotheistic religion or revelatory teachings open to adherents of other faiths in the Sikh gurus' teachings god (*Vahegurū, Ādi Purakh*) is regarded as the omnipresent creator of the universe. This is already expressed in the compositions of Guru Nanak (1469–1539), whom Sikhs regard as the founding father of their religion, and all the following historical gurus reaffirm it. God is regarded as immanent and transcendent at the same time. He revealed himself to mankind in the form and teachings of the historical Sikh gurus.[12] Their hymns are compiled in a sacred book called the 'Ādi Granth (later it acquired the status of the guru, thus: Guru Granth Sahib), to which the Sikh religion assigns the highest authority. In fact, it is regarded as the manifestation of the divine and is accordingly treated as the central element around which Sikh liturgical rituals are organized. The Adi Granth is considered unchangeable in its form and character and Sikhs find in it the basics of their faith. According to the hymns of the Adi Granth, the world came into existence by divine order (*hukam*). The hymns describe a religious path that follows 'neither Hindu nor Muslim' practice and custom. The gurus insist on the rejection of all ritualistic or ascetic practices as a means of salvation. The emphasis is on truthful and graceful living that follows an ethical code (*rahit*), which entails an active engagement with society and humanity. The worldly orientation of the householder is regarded as a prerequisite rather than a hindrance to salvation in Sikhism.

In some of the hymns in the Adi Granth, to which I shall now turn, the gurus refer to themselves as dhadis. Even though they use it in a rather metaphorical sense, it is clear that they are knowledgeable about this particular form of bardic expression. The first reference to dhadi appears as the last stanza of the tenth composition, Rāg Mājh, in a poem (vār) composed by Guru Nanak. We find here, that the guru as dhadi stands in mystical communication with the divine.

Ha'u 'Dhāḍhī vekāru kārai lā'iā
Rātī dihai kai var dhurhu phurmā'iā
'Dhāḍhī sacai mahali khasami bulā'iā
Sacī siphati mālāh kapṛā pā'iā
Sacā amrit nāmu bhojanu ā'iā
Gurmatī khādhā raji tini sukhu pā'iā
'Dhāḍhī kare pasā'u sabadu vajā'iā
Nānak sacu sālāhi pūrā pā'iā

(Srī Adi Granth Sāhib, *Rāg Mājh, Mahalā 1, Pauṛī, Pannā 150–1*)

[I was a minstrel, out of work, when the Lord took me into His service.

FIGURE 9: Darbar Sahib, Amritsar
Courtesy Michael Nijhawan

To sing His Praises day and night, He gave me His Order, right from the start.
My Lord and Master has summoned me, His minstrel, to the True Mansion of His Presence.
He has dressed me in the robes of His True Praise and Glory.
The Ambrosial Nectar of the True Name has become my food.

Those who follow the Guru's Teachings, who eat this food and are satisfied, find peace.
His minstrel spreads His Glory, singing and vibrating the Word of His Shabad.
O Nanak, praising the True Lord, I have obtained His Perfection.]

In these words, Guru Nanak expresses his belief that he was bestowed with divine insight and that he had been chosen by god to sing his sacred hymns. The name dhadi has a truly spiritual meaning in this context. Used as an epithet in Nanak's hymns, it is at the same time an expression of the devotional prayer and graceful calling of god's name.

It is important to note that the verses of the Adi Granth are hymns; they are sung and memorialized by devotees in *rāgas*. In fact, the spiritual meaning of these hymns can hardly be thought to exist separately from the musical-poetical forms; the latter would constitute an aesthetic supplement to the 'actual' meaning of the narrative content. The emphasis on music and poetic form is expressed in the structure of the Adi Granth as a whole. The book is divided into 31 subsections, each of which is attributed to a particular rāga, beginning with *Srī Rāga*. This indicates that the historical gurus were trained in classical North Indian Hindustani music and it indicates complex musical structures. They consciously chose complex musical structures to transmit the divine messages.[13] The sonic form was regarded as sacred and listening to sacred sound as transcendental. In contemporary Sikh liturgy, these hymns are recited in the kirtan or *śabad-kirtan*—the central devotional practice in Sikhism. It is a form of meditation that consists of singing and listening to the hymns of the Adi Granth in a congregational setting. Similar to the Islamic tradition (as for instance indicated in the debate on correct listening in the Sufi *samā*'), there are certain prescriptions and codes of conduct as to how the hymns are to be recited and heard. Furthermore, the Katha tradition provides extensive commentary as to how the different shabads are to be related to real-life concerns of every day living and moral conduct in the social sphere.[14]

Ideally, the mind has to be purified from the desires and interests of everyday life. Pious Sikhs will only recite and listen to the poetic hymns of the Adi Granth in a devotional posture and with proper attire.

This attitude is symbolized in practices such as cleaning hands and feet before entering the precinct of the gurdwara and in keeping the head covered before the sacred scripture, which is also considered to be the residence of the guru. Such prescriptions mark a clear boundary between the pleasure from listening to secular poetry (or music) and the religious aesthetics evoked through listening to the hymns of the Adi Granth. Unlike in the Islamic tradition where the doctrine excludes any form of instrumental music during prayer, Sikh kirtan has always been performed by the accompaniment of string and percussion instruments.[15] Some historical examples of instruments used for the kirtan include the *taus*, *sarindā*, and *jorī-pakhāwaj*. In modern times, the harmonium and the *tablā* have occupied their place.[16]

The importance attributed to sound also accords with the religious practices and teachings characteristic of the North Indian saint-poets. Some of these compositions were even authorized by the Sikh gurus and later included into the final canon of the Guru Granth Sahib. In one of these verses, Kabir, the famous saint-poet, says:

By union of the ardent seeker and the enlightened Teacher
Comes about success in unison and devotion to God
People consider my poems as songs,
Know these are meditations on the Divine.
Holy as the liberating sermon in Kashi at the time of death
Whoever chants or listens to the Name Divine with devoted heart
Saith Kabir, without doubt shall attain the Supreme.[17]

The inclusion of Kabir and other saint-poets' hymns indicates that the religious aesthetics of the early Sikh tradition shared important facets with the Sant tradition of medieval Punjab. This does not agree with a current view, according to which Nanak's religion was simply another form of *nirguṇa bhaktī*, which for many Sikhs entails a crucial misunderstanding of the uniqueness and self-constitutive character of the Sikh religion.[18] For the purpose of the argument outlined here, it is sufficient to say that the historic Sikh gurus lived in a wider cultural and religious framework for which the use of vernacular musical-poetical forms as a medium of religious aesthetics was innate.

To the extent that the Sikh gurus have withdrawn from seeing the divine in iconic representations (the Hindu notion of *darśan*), they have revitalized the sacred meaning of sound. Musical congregations have been a predominant way of worship since the formation of the first sangat. The belief that one could reach a new threshold of religio-aesthetic experience by performing a pure lyric in the kirtan has been a focus of Sikh ritual practice till today.[19] We can link this emphasis on aesthetic praxis and reception of divine sound to a shared notion of Indian aesthetics as indicated in the concept of *rasa* which I will elaborate below. There is a clear emphasis on experiencing the divine messages through their mood, taste, or tone of voice. Particularly in reference to Guru Ram Das (office of the Guru: 1574–81), commentators have put emphasis on the fact that for the early Sikh community (as it is true for the contemporary Sikh panth) the focus of devotional activities was not on the text's abstract meaning (though the written word was important) but on the liturgical-musical praxis of evocating the divine Name (Mansukhani 1984). The divine Name can be reflected upon in all its aspects (*nām simaran*) and it seems the compilers of the Sikh holy book have systematized this insight in a musical architecture that provided the text with its final form as *bāṇī*, which at the same time expresses the idea of text as an aesthetic object, a site of constant practical engagement (Bhogal 2001: 88).

It is in this framework of sacred sound and religious aesthetics that we can locate the 'mystical' meaning of the term dhadi in the Sikh tradition in its generic dimension. For Guru Nanak as well as for his successors, the liberation of mankind lay in inward meditation in the service of the 'True Lord'; dhadi is the minstrel divine engaged in this devotional practice.

Ḍhāḍhī tis no ākhi'ai ji khasmai dhare pi'āru
Dari khaṛā sevā gur sabadī vīcāru
Ḍhāḍhī daru gharu pā'isī sacu rakhai ur dhāri
Ḍhāḍhī kā mahalu agalā hari kai nā'i pi'āri
Ḍhāḍhī kī sevā cākarī hari japi hari nimatāri

(Srī Adi Granth Sāhib, *Gūjarī kī Var, Mahalā 3, Paurī, Pannā 516*)

[He alone is called a minstrel, who enshrines love for his Lord and Master.
Standing at the Lord's Door, he serves the Lord,
and reflects upon the Word of the Guru's Shabad.
The minstrel attains the Lord's Gate and Mansion,
and he keeps the True Lord clasped to his heart.
The status of the minstrel is exalted;
he loves the Name of the Lord.
The service of the minstrel is to meditate on the Lord;
he is emancipated by the Lord.]

It needs to be remembered that Sikh religious doctrine is not embedded in an entire belief system of mysticism or asceticism. As already mentioned, the practice of meditation and congregational singing is complemented by an equally strong commitment to the specific conduct of a social and pious life. Unlike *nāth* (*yogī*) or certain ascetic Sufi traditions, which stress inward meditation and the rejection of outward forms, the Sikh religion places an emphasis on the accomplishment of religious truth by associating oneself with the saintly community (*sadh-sangat*) of devotees. Everyday conduct and social service are therefore absolutely essential. Sikh belief and practice also reject any idea of mysticism according to which disciples would require a spiritual guide in the form of another human agent without whom the objectives of prayer and meditation could not be achieved.

The central focus in Sikh religion is the mystical meaning of scripture in its intellectual and aesthetic experience, evoked by means of meditating on, singing of, and listening to the sacred hymns. The emphasis on the intimate experience of god is mystical to the extent that inner communication with the divine is based on the concept of a 'path of love', which is not private and individualistic but similar to what Jantzen has found in her study of two paradigmatic cases of the Christian mystical tradition, 'quintessentially communal, public, and indeed political in its interconnections with integrity and justice' (1989: 71).

These political underpinnings of religious aesthetics and concepts of Sikh mysticism in fact have direct importance for my discussion of the dhadi genre. The name dhadi was employed in the sacred hymns not merely by poetic convention but presumably also by deliberate choice, in order to express the social vision of Sikhism in the way it was revealed to the gurus: the ordinariness and equality of all human beings in relation to the supreme lord. The Sikh gurus could not have missed the fact that the name dhadi was associated with a group of bards who were at the lower end of the social hierarchy. Although we must be careful not to project the negative social image of musicians of later periods upon the situation in sixteenth and seventeenth-century Punjab, it is very likely that bards were associated with service castes, and thus were regarded low and dependant on the patronage of powerful rulers, chiefs, and families. The increasing number of hymns in which the term dhadi appears is traceable in Guru Ram Das' compositions. As a matter of fact, this corresponds with the period in which historians trace the large-scale conversion of low caste groups to the emerging Sikh community.

The original Sikh community in Kartarpur that gathered around Nanak was already egalitarian in appearance, based on a rejection of caste and gender inequalities that were explicitly overcome in the form of sharing of food or by means of congregational worship. This orientation toward social equality and everyday life was further developed during the times of Nanak's successors Guru Angad, Guru Amar Das, and Guru Ram Das. Guru Amar Das (office of the guru: 1552–74) for instance, established the *manjīs*, positions held by appointed Sikhs who were given the task of education and handling of community affairs (Mann 2001: 13). During this early period of the institutionalization of Sikh religion, the community grew and central institutions such as the community kitchen (*laṅgar*), code of conduct (*rahit maryādā*), and a revenue system (*Das vand*) for the benefit of the underprivileged and the maintenance for the gurdwara were established. Followers streamed from all spheres; however, because of the rejection of caste inequalities, there existed a special appeal for low caste groups, which are said to have venerated the Sikh gurus in great numbers. At different junctures in the development of Sikhism, one finds allusions to the depressed situation of its followers. Social criticism runs throughout the scriptures and is one of the cornerstones of the Sikh religion, which is why the use of the name dhadi could be possibly seen as fitting into the socio-political dimension of religious thought as outlined in the Adi Granth.

Miri-Piri as Interpretive Grid: Recasting Dhadi as a Social and Performative Category

There is not much doubt that the Sikh gurus had bards (dhadis, *bhaṭṭs*, and other musicians) among their followers. Sikh iconography, for instance, depicts Guru Nanak with two disciples, one of whom is Mardana, the player of the one-stringed instrument, the *rabāb*.[20] Thus, by using the epithet dhadi, the Sikh gurus employed a distinct social category as an idiom of self-reference. While this fact seems uncontested, the question of what actual social role the bards held is somewhat ambiguous.

Earlier, I have indicated the metaphorical use of the name dhadi. In the literature I refer to in this section, we find numerous references to dhadi performers as heroic singers. In Bor's (1987) citation of Persian chroniclers (see chapter 1), there are generic associations with narrative-musical forms such as the vār, which in turn is one of the most frequent poetical meters used in the Adi Granth. As a matter of fact, the reference to dhadi in the Sikh scriptures occurs in the form of *pauṛīs*. This is the term used for short compositions that are either a subsection of a vār or take the form of a single short vār. The genre of the vār is usually translated as epic poetry. The 22 vārs and abundant pauṛīs included in the Adi Granth vary in their musical structure but some of them are attributed to bards who were specialists in heroic genres.[21] Guru Arjan specified nine vārs, with particular information on rhythm and style.[22] Significantly, these vārs are associated today with the dhadi genre.

For the Sikh tradition, the occurrence of a heroic vār in the Adi Granth reflects what is often described as a transition from a 'pietistic' to a 'heroic' period in Sikh history. In its application in modern historical analysis, the distinction between these two 'phases' sometimes involves the idea of a dualistic devotional concept in Sikhism. Yet, it has to be clearly stated that for a majority of Sikh believers, piety is not opposed to the concept of the heroic. A dualistic notion that distinguishes 'pietism' from 'heroism' or real life concerns is alien to Indic thoughts and certainly the result of a western inheritance of scholarly representations. What most people would agree with, however, is that due to historical circumstances, 'martial spirit' and militant resistance as ultimate forms of self-defence became an important facet of the Sikh self-representations. With this new political emphasis, I shall argue, we also find a new form of religious aesthetics introduced into Sikhism. The notion of dhadi serves as an ideal point of access to reflect on the social and political significance attributed to this transition.

The turning point in this matter is Guru Arjan's death in 1606, which is remembered as the first martyrdom in Sikh history. This event was followed by decisive changes in the Sikh tradition, introduced by Guru Arjan's son and successor, Guru Hargobind (1595–1644). The latter founded the institution of the Akal Takht (the eternal throne), hence the representation of Sikh political authority. It was erected opposite the sacred place of worship, the Harmandir Sahib in Amritsar. Guru Hargobind established a strong military force, wore the paraphernalia of royal power (he was called the *saccā pātśah*, the 'true king'), and established a royal darbār from which he issued his orders, or *hukumnāme* (Chhabra 1960: 196). This apparent mimesis of prevalent symbolic and political forms of royal authority led to a situation in which Sikhs were perceived as a potential threat to the legitimacy of the Mughal state.

In a nineteenth-century hagiographic genre, the *Gurbilās Pātshāhī* 6, it is mentioned that Guru Hargobind patronized dhadi bards; two of them are clearly named—Abdullah and Nattha or Nathmal Dhadi (ibid.: 200). Nathmal Dhadi is also held to be the author of an important hagiographical document written in Persian called *Amarnamah* which appeared around the time of the demise of Guru Gobind Singh in 1708 (Gurtej Singh 2000). This seems to be the first incident in Sikh hagiography with explicit reference to dhadi bards as a distinct social category. The text is not only significant in terms of its historical data and the insight it provides on the last days of the tenth guru, as a performative text composed by a dhadi bard it also includes within its formal structure metacommentaries on Sikh patronage of dhadi performers.[23] Some of the couplets that have been put together and translated by Gurtej Singh. They include explicit reference to the dhadis:

When the Sikhs hold celebrations, it is proper for them to listen to vars by Dhadis (135).
One mode of worshipping God is also listening to poems of heroic deeds from the Dhadis or traditional singers side by side with the exposition of the Guru's word (129).
Wasn't it the practice of Guru Nanak who always retained Mardana by his side? (138).
Inspired by Guru Nanak's example, the Tenth Guru always retained Nathmal Dhadi with him (139).
Dhadis must always accompany the Singhs who must not eat without the Dhadis [being around] (137).
Let Mardana's descendants [or those who follow his practice] first sing the Guru's shabads and thereafter let the Dhadis take the stage (130).
The singing minstrels are as dear to the Guru as the Singhs are.
This account of travels, Amarnamah, will be loved much by singers (63).
They were asked to often recite the Amarnamah to the Singhs (64).
A Dhadi surely is an asset to adorn any gathering [of the cultured] and Amarnamah enhances the worth of a Dhadi (146).
When the Singhs attain to power (sic!) and glory, they will ensure prosperity for singers (65).

The patronage of musicians fits into a larger historical picture in which the bards composed eulogies and panegyrics and in which they were instrumental to a process of recording and transmitting history. This role was not restricted to Sikh patronage. The transmission of Mughal religious and political authority, for instance, drew heavily from cultural performances and rituals in which dhadi and other musicians participated. It is most likely that Guru Hargobind and Guru Gobind Singh followed this pattern by calling dhadi musicians into the darbār. According to the Sikh hagiographies, this occurred for the first time when Guru Hargobind established his military force.[24]

Thus, Sikh hagiography links the patronage of dhadi bards with the militarization of the community. The majority of contemporary Sikh dhadi performers names Guru Hargobind as the founding patron of their community. Guru Hargobind not only introduced military exercises, he also created the Sikh ideal of the saint-soldier (*sant-sipāhī*) that can be traced to these historical circumstances. According to this narrative, dhadi performers were introduced to provide panegyrics on Sikh worldly power. Their contribution was to sing martial ballads to inspire the military followers of the religious leader. This transition in the organization of the Sikh community is conceptualized in the principle of *mīrī-pīrī*: the balance held between spiritual and temporal power.[25] As a consequence of the execution of his father, Guru Hargobind wore two swords that symbolized the dual structure of worldly and spiritual power. The dhadi genre, linked to the ceremonial order of the Akal Takht, hence became part of the miri concept and was therefore considered an agent of religious-political power. Until the present day, dhadi performers are associated with the Akal Takht and perform in the same vicinity. In other places, they are explicitly introduced as the heroic element to be distinguished from the congregational kirtan. In this way the narration of historical deeds and the eulogies of heroic deaths on battlefields has become the distinctive edge of dhadi performance in the Sikh tradition.

Rasa and Sikh Religious Aesthetics

I have referred to the nine *vār*s in the Adi Granth that according to my interlocutors, are directly associated with the performance of dhadi tunes. The narrative content of these hymns indicates a shift in emphasis on heroic aesthetics, which does not mean—to repeat a point raised before—that this change in emphasis would result in a dichotomy between pietism and the heroic in the Sikh tradition. The *maujdī kī vār* for example tells of two rivals at Akbar's darbar who die on the battlefield. The mood of these vārs is bīr rasa, the musical form that according to the Indian rasa theory corresponds to and evokes the heroic 'taste' or 'mood'. It is important to note that these hymns constitute *gurbāṇī* (authenticated language of the Sikh gurus) and are thus given voice in the Sikh kirtan. Accordingly, the mood of bīr rasa is conceptualized as a part of the mystical orientation of calling God's name, sometimes referred to as '*nām rasa*'. The first transition in the concept of dhadi aesthetics therefore has to do with a shift within the framework of Sikh sacred language. It is not a question of one form of dhadi being linked to sacred language and the other to secular discourse.[26]

Before further discussing the historical transitions of the dhadi genre and its re-evaluation in contemporary religious discourse, let me briefly turn to the notion of rasa, which is a popular concept of aesthetic receptivity in Punjab and which has also shaped the way Pawandeep Kaur and her sisters have evaluated their experience in practising bardic performance. I do not want to engage here in a theological or philosophical debate on whether the concept of rasa accounts for the mystical experience in liturgical ritual or not. What I have observed is that listeners and performers do employ the technical language of rasa in order to draw distinctions between both genres of public performance such as dhadi, and ritual liturgy. In the context of dhadi performance these assessments are important because they are linked to forms of aesthetic appraisal as well as notions of efficacy in creating particular, collectively shared moods. The mastery of various performative genres and the refinements of voice are seen as prerequisites to generating and experiencing these moods.

The early Sanskrit treatises on dramaturgy and aesthetic experience, in which the notion of the rasa is delineated, have linked technical mastery and religious experience rather than placing each of them on different planes (Wulff 1986: 674).[27] Thus, the evocation of aesthetic pleasure is not considered an end in itself. On the contrary, aesthetic experience is posited as a generalized emotive situation created by means of dramatic, poetic, or musical performance, which ideally is oriented toward a process of revelation. The experience of rasa is not a 'natural' state of feelings and sentiments 'expressed' on the stage, but a culturally stipulated concept for which, in the case of classical drama, several requirements of actors and listeners are posited (Gnoli 1956: 63–4).[28] Sanskrit dramatic theory explicitly describes the various techniques to be used by actors on the stage to produce seven to nine different types of rasa, such as *śānta* (the pure state of mind, what is thought to be the Buddha's state of mind) or *vīra* (the heroic state). But listeners too have to be familiarized with the various representational forms and underlying emotive states of mind that are thought to resonate in the process of dramaturgy.

With regard to the religious and cultural traditions in South Asia, *rasa* is differently assessed as a concept through which to understand the communicative and experiential processes in liturgical ritual and performative contexts. Such differentiations also apply within the same religious tradition. Thus, contemporary dhadi performance differs significantly from the framing of musical performance and reception in terms of sacred liturgy in the way discussed earlier. The emphasis continues to be placed on the heroic mood (bīr rasa), but equally important are notions of *dukh rasa* or *shant rasa*. *Rasa* as a modality of performative aesthetics, in any case, becomes related to rhetorical forms of voice production in oration and song, which serve purposes other than those expressed in Sikh kirtan.

The rhetoric of martyrdom and bloodshed predominates in contemporary dhadi performances, some of which will be further discussed in the following chapters. The efficacy of dhadi performance is conceptualized in terms of body heat (the blood is brought to a boil—*khūn vic joś paidā hai*) or the eruption of inner forces (*man andar ubāl āuṇā*). The body image of the Sikh dhadi bard is apparently different from the meditative posture of the kirtan singer and listener; the performers stand upright and hardly move their bodies during the performance, while maintaining a majestic and noble pose with the eyes fixed in one direction. In addition to the sonic forms, dhadi performances are assessed in terms of facial expression, gesture, and body movement. The dynamics of the body consists of the raised hand and the alteration of the singers' voices. Thus, although the bards do not use very complex facial expressions and meaningful gestures, they are certainly engaged in a manner in which the movement of the hand, the modulation of the voice, the play of gestures, and the symbolic meanings displayed by the body in terms of dress and posture constitute recognizable performative aesthetics that depend on their visibility rather than their audibility.

For the Sikh disciple, rasa as linked to the notion of ineffable mystical experience in Sikh kirtan is therefore not equivalent to the aesthetic concepts and representative contents of contemporary dhadi performance. In terms of a yardstick to assess standards of technical mastery and ritual or performative competence, however, the orientation towards rasa as a discernible object alludes to a shared framework of aesthetic evaluation in performative practice. This is the paradox that underlies statements that link evaluative judgements of both orientations. It is because of this shared framework that actors are able to revitalize linkages between the musical-aesthetic domains of dhadi and kirtan even though, today, dhadi is linked with the katha and exegetic tradition, rather than congregational singing. The next section shows that these linkages are also facilitated through ideas of voice and agency.

Dhadi as Heroic Spirit: Refashioning the Puranic Tradition

Sikh performers today face further interpretive problems as dhadi aesthetics are often associated with particular categories of social and religious difference.[29] Most of the references that are historically available in Sikh hagiography trace dhadi musicians with Muslim names. If we turn to colonial representations, we find that dhadi performers were glossed in derogatory terms as *mirāsī*.[30] Although this category originally represented a group of genealogists cum musicians, its social usage was expanded to designate a witty and vulgar character. Whereas for the Sikh gurus social class and religious background of the Muslim musicians was not problematic, it seems that in the contemporary context, the Sikh tradition faces some difficulties in bridging the two dissonant memories of the dhadi genre. On the one hand, it is remembered as an intrinsic part of the Sikh devotional tradition, and yet on the other hand, we have a suppressed memory of 'folk singers' who were patronized and had their origin in different cultural or even religious traditions. One might assume that these two perspectives are not mutually exclusive and indeed I have no intention to question the social legitimacy of this claim. But the puzzle remains as to how we ought to understand the transition from a devotional employment of the name dhadi as an intrinsic part of Sikh sacred literature to a performative genre based on secular representational modes—a transition that entails a shift from aesthetic to social categories as well as a shift from what is considered sacred language to vernacular representational modes. Further interpretive efforts are necessary to frame the genre as cultural practice and as an agent of Sikh collective mobilization in a historical perspective. In the following section, I propose that this transition be assessed in terms of an integration of different religio-aesthetic concepts, as can be inferred from the discourses and practices that have centred on another revered text in the Sikh tradition; the Dasam Granth.

Like almost every other religion, Sikhism comprises different traditions and schools of thought. One such example are the Namdharis (lit. 'bearer of the name') who emerged as part of a social movement in the nineteenth century and have been known to favour the *Chandi di Vār* and other text from the Dasam Granth. Another tradition is, the *Nihāng* Sikhs. I shall now briefly turn to show how the discourse on dhadi is linked to a particular inheritance of heroic aesthetics in Sikhism. Nihāṅg Sikhs were originally known as *Akālī Nihāng*, a heavily armed order within the Sikh panth, which traced specific relations to Guru Gobind Singh. In what follows, I concentrate on my conversation with Prem Singh, a contemporary Nihāṅg Sikh who was teaching the gurbāṇī classes at the Sikh Missionary College in Anandpur Sahib when we met. Prem Singh's account of the origin of the dhadi genre is interesting for at least two reasons. First, he knows the Sikh scriptures by memory and is particularly committed to seeing dhadi as an intrinsic part of the Sikh martial tradition as linked to the tenth guru; and second, we get an idea of how epic literature that is included in the Dasam Granth is assigned an authoritative voice.

The Dasam Granth (literally, the tenth book) is a bardic compilation of hagiographic and epic texts attributed to the lifetime of Guru Gobind Singh. Besides compositions such as the *Akāl Ustād*, *Jāp*, *Zafarnamā* which are regarded as authentic (that is, believed to be Gobind Singh's own or authorized words), the great majority of verses are martial epics and folk renderings of ancient puranic (Hindu) texts such as the *Devī-Mahātmayā* in the *Markandeya Purāṇā*. Titled *Chaṇḍī Caritra* or *Krishnāvtar*, we find the cosmic battles of the Hindu goddess Durgā depicted in epic narratives. According to the Sikh reformist tradition, the tenth guru presumably named the Dasam Granth a book of diversion, to be clearly separated from the status of the Adi Granth. This point seems convincing insofar as there is an absence of spiritual reverence or pious attitude towards the goddess Durga in the Dasam Granth. Yet, as Nikki-Guninder Kaur Singh (1993: 123) argued, we find significant evidence that as a *mythological figure*, the Hindu goddess is a crucial element in Guru Gobind Singh's religio-aesthetic world. Indeed, we can assume that she is reincorporated into Sikhism as a kind of archetypal figure, representing the aesthetic imagery and mood of the heroic, which at the time of Gobind Singh's endeavour to fight a holy war (*dharam yuddh*) against the Mughal rulers must have directly appealed to his followers. It is also likely that the poetic power of the Durga myths was relevant for the Khalsa brotherhood's military struggles in the eighteenth century.

Among the possible reasons for evoking the mythic power of Durga as a female principle in Sikhism, Singh cites the untamed female energy and sacrificial ethos attributed to Durga as creator and destroyer, the full independence of her character, and her purifying anger. Not only is the evocation of these heroic features expressed in abundant epic narratives, but the erotic flavour, the heroic mood (the martial, or *raudra*) constitutes 'the dominant rasa of poetry honouring Durga' (ibid.: 124). This brings us back to our interest in religious aesthetics, and indeed it seems to me, the reverence accorded to the Dasam Granth within the Khalsa tradition is due to the fact that it offers a key to the understanding of the particular heroic aesthetic values and ideals held by the last of the historic gurus. This holds true for the contemporary reverence paid to the Dasam Granth within segments of the Khalsa tradition. As the next section shall demonstrate, the meaning of the dhadi genre becomes associated with these heroic aesthetics.

For Prem Singh, the Dasam Granth had by no means lost its appeal at the end of the twentieth century. When my colleague Khushwant and I first met Prem Singh at his home in Anandpur Sahib, the latter was quick in pointing to heroic poems he had written, and which for him were related to poetry in the Dasam Granth. Responding to our questions on the origins of the dhadi genre in the Sikh tradition, he did not begin his account with Guru Nanak but instead with a reference to one of the poetic verses in the Dasam Granth in which the mythological origin of dhadi is conceptualized as the singer of the *kharkā* vār. Sikh dhadi bards are often remembered as the singers of this sonic form. The word *kharak* is onomatopoeic in denoting a breaking, cracking, explosive or rattling sound. The word is often used as a metaphor for an inner state of agony and pain. In this fashion it shares an important facet of poetry in the Dasam Granth, particularly in the *Bisnupaḍas*, where onomatopoeic forms are frequent in the depiction of battle scenes.[31]

The epic to which Prem Singh refers must be read as a creation myth: the origin of dhadi is accounted for, as well as other social categories such as the bhaṭṭs, or the *sayyid*s and *sheikh*s. The scene is taken from the Chaṇḍī *Caritra* (405) and describes a cosmic battle between Mahakāl (the creator and destroyer of the universe, eternal time) and the two demons Suāswirāy and Diṛhgadār. The Caritra consists mostly of the battles between the goddess (Chandi or Durgā) and various demons. Each of these battles represents the cosmic clashes between the forces of good and evil. It is in this particular story that the goddess, bearing the name Dulhadevī, expresses her wish to marry Mahākāl. She is called on by the latter to besiege the two demons as proof of her devotion. While she is fighting, the goddess' skills impress Mahakāl. He joins her and kills Suāswirāy. The battle with Diṛhgadār demands more effort. Sweat from Mahākāl's forehead drops on the earth.[32] From these drops Bhaṭṭacaryā was created, the founder of the bhaṭṭs. According to Prem Singh's account, from the latter's sweat 'Dhāḍsen, the first dhadhi singer, came into being. After 'Dhāḍsen was born, he sang a heroic song during this battle which aroused the warriors' spirits—the above-mentioned *khaṛka var*. It is mentioned as a decisive factor in winning the battle against the forces of evil. His son was Bhumsen who finally intervened in the battle to kill the demon.

Prem Singh insisted that Guru Gobind Singh did 'not confuse this Mahākāl with the Hindu Gods', but instilled an idea that he is superior to Kārtikeya (in Hindu tradition, the son of Shiva and Pārvatī). In his opinion, the myth itself cannot be regarded as the authentic voice of the Guru (*maulik bānī*), but as a new and exhilarating interpretation of the Puranas (*purāṇā ullkhdā kitā hoi'ā granthā dā*) by Guru Gobind Singh—a powerful mythic narrative of war. In this regard Prem Singh articulated a current interpretation according to which Guru Gobind Singh included mythological accounts of cosmic battles in the Dasam Granth in order to stir the passions of his followers to resist the Mughal army. According to this line of interpretation, the renderings of the puranic sources are not to be interpreted as a religious discourse that would entail the veneration of the Hindu gods.

Prem Singh's account of the origins of dhadi, therefore, has to be interpreted on two different planes of analysis. On the one hand, it articulates the dominating interpretive frameworks according to which Sikh literature is to be divided into authentic religious and interpretive-historical sources. In its position within Hindu religious cosmology, dhadi is the other; it belongs to the puranic tradition and is not considered as part of the Sikh belief system. By means of clearly distinguishing between authentic sacred literature of the Sikhs and these renderings of puranic epics, the Sikh tradition is able to account for the Puranas as historical sources even if they are not acknowledged in their entire cosmological dimension. This observation can be summarized by Hans' statement that the Dasam Granth is not a work of Sikhism *per se* but a 'Sikh textbook on received tradition' (1984: 62).

On the other hand, dhadi is reincorporated as a part of a particular aesthetic tradition into Sikhism. This is done in a manner in which the voice of dhadi is imbued with an agentive quality: the particular sounds and aural rhythms attributed to the primordial dhadi bard are decisive for the victory of the goddess over the demons. We can see this in the link between the inspirational quality of voice and the religio-aesthetic disposition it evokes—again based on a reinterpretation of the emotional concept of the rasas. Guninder Kaur has described very well the various poetic devices used in the Dasam Granth to create the heroic mood (here *raudra rasa* instead of bīr rasa). I will quote from her book at some length in order to show how the concept of the dhadi voice has to be read in terms of the particular aural aesthetics of the Dasam Granth:

One is repetition of sounds. It seems as if Gurū Gobind Singh had woven *raudra* rasa into the warp and woof of the language itself, into the very texture of the words! His frequent use of alliteration, assonance, and consonance lends a stimulating rhythm and music to the narrative. The constant repetition of sounds like *bha*, *gha*, *jha*, *ḍha*, and *ṛa* reproduces the heavy sounds of combat. In '*durgā sabhe saṅghāre rākhaś khaṛag lai*,' ... for instance the use of *bha*, *gha*, and *ṛa* makes the verse throb with excitement. Here, the sounds themselves suggest that the goddess is felling the giant-like demons. In another verse, '*bhakā bhuṅk bherī ḍhah ḍūh ḍaṅkam... ḍhakā ḍhukk ḍhalam*,' the martial rhythm is ringingly audible. The readers become saturated with the frenzy of battle and are carried away with it, feeling it flow turbulently in their own blood and nerves. In another line, '*taṇi taṇi tīr calāe durgā dhanukh lai*' the sound alone—a combination of the alliteration of *t* and the consonance of *lai*—reproduces the speed of action in actual fighting. *Durgā* is pictured here shooting arrows (*tīr calāe*) with all her might (*taṇi taṇi*). These devices are very appropriate to the description of battle-scenes. Another favorite device is the use of onomatopoeia. Gurū Gobind Singh subtly chooses words whose sound suggests their meaning. He reinforces *raudra* rasa by the aural effect of his diction. The different names used for *Durgā* like *Caṇḍī*, *Bhavānī*, and *Durgshāh* have a heroic ring. Furthermore, polysyllabic words or compound epithets—aurally very resonant—enrich the poetry.... In such instances a multiplicity of characteristics are brought together, heightening both sound and sense (Kaur 1993: 138).

This emphasis on the aural aesthetics of the poetry in the Dasam Granth provided an explanatory framework for Prem Singh's evocation of the dhadi voice as the arbiter of the heroic spirit. Prem Singh was aware of the fact, that the gurus (beginning with Guru Hargobind) patronized the dhadi poet-bards and that this corresponded to the historical transition of the Sikh community. The re-emphasis on the heroic dimension of dhadi on the side of the mīrī concept in Prem Singh's account thus involved a transition in religio-aesthetic meanings as well as a transition in agentive-psychological disposition. Born from the sweat of the fighting Mahakāl, the dhadi as the primordial singer of the *kharkā var* is the authentic voice of the cosmic battle. In our conversation, Prem Singh confirmed the view that dhadi performers were patronized 'to bring the blood in the Sikh bodies into rage' (*vārāṃ gā ke sikhāṃ andar josh ate jitt de sankalap nūṃ hor pekār karde rahe*). As the one to bring about a particular aesthetic quality, the dhadi has become reified as an agent in Sikh history.

Gendered Relations

In this chapter I have tried to find an explanation for the gendered relationship between the dhadi genre and Sikh religious aesthetics. Although contemporary Sikh performers frame the dhadi genre in religious terms of pious conduct, dominant discourses continue to allocate a notion of otherness to it, to the extent that it is seen as part of a mythological tradition outside the spiritual world of the Sikh religion. The transition from the evaluation of dhadi as part of Sikh sacred language to its recasting in terms of patronage and bardic performance has been partially the result of the historical developments that took place during earlier periods of Sikh history. But, I have argued that these developments should not be interpreted as fixed results of historical process. The turn to contemporary practices of dhadi performance leads us to a different picture. There are distinctive interpretative moves through which both perspectives on the performative tradition are bridged in contemporary perspective. I have identified these as the suspension of social references to the name dhadi by simultaneously revitalizing ontological meanings such as the sacredness of sounds and the heroic aesthetics inherited in performative genres.

The persistence of the dhadi genre as a form through which to articulate a pious Sikh self has been due to the influence of core traditions within the Sikh fold, which have assigned agency to the religio-aesthetic forms associated with dhadi representational practice. The martial tradition in Sikhism, in particular, has emphasized the heroic meaning of dhadi being linked to particular figures of the martial epic tradition, which finds its primary text in a broader field of puranic literature and localized practices of the veneration of martyred spirits. The framing of dhadi aesthetics in terms of a martial image and heroic tunes is of paramount importance for the interpretation of the agency of dhadi bards in the context of crisis and violence, as I will further explore in the second part of the book.

Thus, almost decades after the Khalistan movement ebbed, Sikh performers provide alternatives to deal with the dissonant memory in the dhadi genre. I have referred to Pawandeep Kaur's rendering of dhadi in terms of a dialectics between folk notions on female energy and spiritual notion of emotional lease. Another performer, Inderjit Singh, expressed somewhat similar ideas in one of our conversations:

> Dhadi is like a golden vessel (*ikk sone dā bhāndā*). While the vessel is made of gold, it remains upon you what you put into it. You might put juice, Coke or Seven-up in it. That is your choice. The dhadi tradition is this vessel, this pot. What some people make to resonate (*sunānā*) in it is completely their business.... In one direction, people delved in the sweet taste of the folk song (*lok gīt*), in the other direction, it was Guru Nanak who provided the unique *amrit* in singing the devotional songs.

Here, we find the idea that dhadi is a cultural form to be filled with religious or secular content. Similar to Prem Singh's interpretation, Inderjit Singh recognizes that the Sikh gurus were reflexively drawing on a shared repertoire of oral culture. But unlike in Prem Singh's discourse, the allusion to Guru Nanak places an emphasis on the phenomenology of sonic form as a vehicle through which mystical elixir (*amrit*) can become manifest. I would therefore argue that the assignment of religious meaning to a performative genre is due to shifting discursive constructions and historical interpretations, as I have demonstrated in this chapter. But more than that, such resignifications are the result of how people experience and practice religious musicality and aesthetics. As the most intriguing fact I have noticed in this context a move toward a revitalization of the spiritual dimension in Sikh dhadi aesthetics.

Notes

1. This chapter is a revised version of my article 'From Divine Bliss to Ardent Passion: Exploring Sikh Religious Aesthetics Through the Dhadi Genre' that appeared in the *History of Religion* (2003), 42(4): 359–85. I am indebted to Gurinder Singh Mann for providing extensive comments that have helped reshape the text.
2. Even though I am interested in the relationship between aesthetics and agency, as should become obvious throughout the chapters, I am not as pessimistic as Alfred Gell (1998) who argues that the anthropology of art has to be decisively non-aestheticist. For a critique of this position see Campbell (2001) and Layton (2003).

3. For the term 'ethnonationalism' see Gurharpal Singh (2000).
4. For a discussion of diasporic dhadi songs that represent the ideology of the Khalistan movement see also Pettigrew (1992).
5. See previous chapter for a discussion.
6. The emergence of female dhadi performers occurred under historical circumstances when their male colleagues with their 'orthodox' outer appearance were directly confronted with censorship by the state. In performing this genre one had to deal with these hazards of public speech. However, I would not consider the emergence of female performers as the direct consequence of such restrictions. Rather, as I have pointed out, the reassessment of the heroic voice provides the parameters by which the actual appearance of female singers is acknowledged.
7. See my discussion in Chapter 7.
8. For the North Indian context see in particular Leavitt (1997) and Qureshi (1995).
9. Qureshi (1995: 141).
10. My argument on how differently the Sikh tradition authorizes the dhadi genre does not entail a value judgement on either Sikhism or dhadi in terms of a coherent tradition in historical perspective. As will become sufficiently evident in the course of my discussion, we deal here with a category of social praxis and interaction (distinctions and interpretative efforts made by various actors) that has further complicated this issue.
11. Unless otherwise indicated the following translation are those by Khalsa (1995).
12. For a discussion of the Sikh belief system see Grewal (1998), Ray (1970), Daljeet Singh and Kharak Singh (1997) and Uberoi (1996). The canonization of the Adi Granth is expansively discussed in Mann (2001).
13. According to Sher Singh Sher (1996) these ragas are based on classical Indian music and indicate different temporal and emotive markers. Sher Singh also points out the Sikh Guru's preference of string instruments. Thus, the *sarinda* (predecessor of the sarangi) is attributed to Guru Arjan (ibid.: 323).
14. For this point, see Mann (2001).
15. The Sufi *qawwalī* is certainly an exception, yet as a form of ritual practice is also clearly distinguished from Muslim prayer and never falls into prayer times.
16. I am grateful to Bhai Baldeep Singh for sharing his insights into the history of instrumentality and religious musicality in the Sikh tradition.
17. Srī Ādi Granth Sāhib, Rāg Gauri, *Ashtpadi*. This translation is taken from Talib (1984: 335). For a discussion of Kabir's religion, see Vaudeville (1964).
18. Kabir, Nanak, and Dadu are often named as the influential sants (or poet-saints) in medieval North India. See for instance Schomer and McLeod (1987). Hew Mc Leod has proposed that the early Sikh tradition had been

merely another version of the sant movement. This idea has had a significant impact on how Western academia conceptualized Sikhism and has in turn been criticized by a variety of Sikh scholars. While many of the arguments against McLeod were polemical in character, J.S. Grewal (1998a) among others has pointed out that McLeod has failed to acknowledge crucial differences between Nanak and other sants—differences that in the case of Nanak's thought, were decisive in explaining the self-constitutive force of the Sikh tradition. Existing cleavages in Sikh scholarship notwithstanding, most historians would certainly agree that there was a shared common ground in the teachings of Kabir, Dadu, and Nanak. However, this similarity is restricted in important ways as only those hymns of Kabir or Sheikh Farid were included in the Adi Granth that fully resonated with Sikh doctrinal belief; those departing from the dominant view were left out.

19. According to Bhai Baldeep Singh (2001: 155),

> *shabad* kritan requires a perceptual awareness of the tradition of kritan maryada as it developed right from the times of the Gurus. This would mean a clear understanding not only of the raga forms but also of the classical folk forms used in kritan...[as] indicated in the Sri Guru Granth Sahib. With changing times these fundamental forms have been polluted and tampered with. For e.g. there are 22 *vaars* (odes) in the Guru Granth Sahib but it is a pity that only *asa-di-vaar* is recited today. The singing of these compositions was phenomenal as was the style of accompaniment on the percussive instruments. There were different rhythmic patterns played with each *vaar*. The enormous challenge that we face today is to recover and restore the original forms of these compositions as authenticated by the great bards of the *Gurdarbar* [all italics and transcriptions in original].

20. This group of Muslim performers still exists in Punjab (particularly in Lahore) and they trace their origin to the same Mardana who is said to have accompanied Nanak on his legendary travels. While the rabāb was an instrument used in Sikh kirtan singing, the same cannot be said of those instruments (sarangi and dhadd) that are characteristic for the dhadi genre in contemporary Punjab. Thus, although we find in the early Sikh tradition a combination of stringed and percussion instruments (sarindā and joṛī-pakhāwaj) which might have conceptually facilitated later uses of the folk instruments, instrumentation alone is not sufficient to account for the meaning of dhadi in the Sikh tradition.

21. According to the research on this topic presented in the *Sikh Encyclopedia*, the vār achieved a new status with Guru Arjan:

> The Gurus from the time of Guru Arjan onward had *Bhaṭṭs* and bards in attendance on them. After *Sattā* and *Balvaṇḍ*, whose *vār* was given scriptural status by Guru Arjan, we come across bards Abdullah and Natth Mall who sang *vārs* in the time of Guru Hargobind. They are believed to have written 72 *vārs*, though only a few fragments of these are still extant. Guru Gobind Singh had living with him a large

number of poets and bards, prominent among them *Mīr Mushkī* and *Mīr Chhabīlā* who recited *vārs* at the afternoon *dīvāns* (Harbans Singh 1998: 407).

22. These include: *Vār Malak Murīd tathā Cahndraharā Sohīā*, *Rāi Kamāldī Maujdī kī Vār*, *Tuṇḍe Asrāje kī Vār*, *Sikandar Birāhim kī Vār*, *Lallā Bahilīmā kī Vār*, *Vār Jodhe Virāī Purbānī Kī*, *Vār Rāī Mahime Hasne Kī*, *Rāne Kailās ate Māldeo kī Vār*, and *Muse kī Vār*. For a discussion of the var in Punjab literary history see Ganda Singh (1990).
23. Gurtej Singh (2000: 7–8) mentions also the role of dhadi panegyrics in the context of the death ritual as it has been prescribed by the tenth guru in distinction from Hindu funeral practices. Historically we must assume that dhadi performers were part of these death rituals and had a significant role to play in grieving death. Pettigrew's assessment of the dhadi tradition as a purely commemorative form that is distinguished from contexts of mourning is therefore, mistaken at least historically. In the present, dhadi performers also take part in shahidi niwas rituals which constitute spaces in which unnatural and heroic deaths are mourned, even if grief is articulated in aesthetic rather than discursive modes.
24. A further possible interpretation could be that, in order to build up military strength, Guru Hargobind exploited the 'martial nature' of the tribal *Jaṭs* who brought with them the heroic tunes of the dhadi tradition. This is a valuable idea insofar as *Jaṭs* are known to have venerated martyr-saints and to have inherited a heroic tradition. Yet, we have to be very careful not to essentialize heroism and violence at the level of tribal identity. See for instance Nonica Datta (1999). See also Das and Bajwa (1994). For a study of the political system of Jats see Pettigrew (1978).
25. For a discussion of the mīrī-pīrī system see Bachittar Singh (1996: 216–47).
26. While in the Islamic tradition we find strong emphasis placed on the *tajwīd*, the inherited tradition that prescribes minute details as to how the Qur'an is to be recited, a similar institution is missing in the case of Sikh religion. For a discussion of aesthetics in the Islamic tradition see Kermani (2000).
27. The theory of Indian aesthetics was presumably first developed in a treatise on Sanskrit drama (*Nāṭyashāstra*) attributed to the sage Bharata and further explored by the Kashmiri Shivaite philosopher Abhinavagupta (tenth to eleventh century). For a translation, see Gnoli (1956).
28. In the translation of Abhinavagupta, aesthetic receptiveness is equivalent to 'a mirror-like power of intuition (pratibhara)' that resides in the heart.
29. See Chapter 1.
30. I take up this issue in the following chapter.
31. The Dasam Granth offers a vast repository of poetic metres that still have not been sufficiently analysed and recognized as valuable sources by linguists and historians of the Punjab. Generally speaking both syllables (varnik) and syllabic instants (matrik) were used metres that are specifically related with the dhadi genre, such as the *baiṃt*. On the

relationship between metres and narrative meaning, the *Sikh Encyclopedia* says:

> In the Dasam Granth the battle scenes have been described through the metres Kabitt, Savaiyya, Padhistaka and Bisnupada. Savaiyya hitherto had been generally used for sensuous love poetry, but Guru Gobind Singh used it with consummate artistry for heroic poetry. To capture the sounds as well as the swift movements on the battlefield, he has used small metres like Padhistaka. Metres are changed frequently with a view to describing different types of combat. In this process the similes and metaphors are sometimes relegated to the background but where similes and metaphors dominate, the metres remain mostly unchanged (Harbans Singh 1998: 518).

32. The idea that these figures are born from the sweat of the fighting goddess clearly resonates the idea of *āsura*s in Hindu mythology. The *āsura*s are 'demons' that are born out of blood-semen (*rakt-bīj*). Thus, what we find here is a matter of great ingenuity. As A.K. Ramanujan has pointed out, many Indian oral epics and related narrative traditions can be understood as folk renderings of the ancient Puranas in which the epic heroes, gods, goddesses, and demons are reincorporated as 'bodies that sweat, stink, defecate, and menstruate' (Ramanujan 1993: 103). It seems that such an emphasis on bodily matters is placed here as well.

PART TWO

From the Colonial to the Postcolonial

FIGURE 10: Dhadi musicians in Canada, c. 1905–8.
Courtesy University of British Columbia Library, Special Collections and University Archives, photo neg. BC 489/1

This is the photograph of a group of four Punjabi men in Canada in the early twentieth century. Three of them appear to be Khalsa Sikhs—they wear bourgeois outfits and tightly knit turbans. The fourth person in the picture looks noticeably different with his loosely tied turban and the hourglass shaped membraphone in his left hand. In front of the second person from the left another Punjabi instrument is exhibited, the folk sarangi. Without much doubt, the portrait of this group indexes the format of dhadi song-recitation and is probably one of the first black and white pictures of dhadi performers that was ever shot. When I first saw this photograph in a Berkeley exhibition on Punjabi migration to North America,[1] I was quite surprised by the way the historical archive afforded me an alternative portrayal that seemed so at odds with popular representations of folklore genres and performative culture of that period, specifically if we think about ethnographic descriptions of folk entertainment and popular culture in colonial North India.

Consider for a moment the way in which folk performers were classified in the Glossary of the Tribes and Castes of the Punjab and the North-West Frontier Province (H.A. Rose 1970 [1892]). In this late nineteenth century ethnographic record that was published one or two decades earlier than the time the photograph was taken, we find dhadi bards, among other popular performers, described as low-strata folk-singers. Dhadi performers were categorized as an element of mirāsī social organization 'or disorganization as it might be called' (ibid. 109). The name mirāsi that is etymologically linked to the Arabic mirās ('inheritance') designated a group of village genealogists who played a vital role during the celebration of life-cycle rituals and other festive occasions. The Glossary lists different Mirāsi groups in the various Punjabi districts and lists dhadi performers as a subdivision of these groups, even though intermarriage rules and social rank differ from case to case. In Punjab, they are remembered as 'jokers' and good entertainers. In their search for the origins of the mirāsi and the related groups of performers, the compilers of the Glossary noticed their adherence to regionally varying forms of religious authority, including tales of an Arabian origin of the mirāsi. Yet the overall attempt was to label the bards 'indigenous to India', the most common reference being Rajput and Jat lineages. Whereas cultural authenticity was thus relocated to the remote past, the way this performative community was recognized in the colonial present was mostly grasped within the logic of civilizational discourse. Within this discourse the mirasi-dhadi was depicted as a service caste, sometimes of elevated status (for selected individuals with renowned artistic qualities) but generally at the very bottom of the social hiearchy. Furthermore, in the Glossary, the reader is given reassurance that tales about these groups (such as the use of effigies to ridicule powerful landlords) were recorded only to show 'how daring popular invention can be' (ibid.: 106). That satire and witty speech bear some significance to the social fabric of Punjabi rural life did not seem reasonable only if dated back historically, not so much for the present situation. What we find in their account, therefore, is an image of cultural degradation that defers any form of agency and historical subjectivity from the realm of mirāsis and related groups of performative such as the dhadis.

The story that can be perceived from the photograph, however, is different. It is a story that does not lend itself so easily to antiquarian constructions of folk tradition and low-caste identity. First, it tells us of a long journey and an unwelcome landing in the Americas. It is a story that places the dhadi tradition at a critical site of colonial modernity. Even though further information about the performers is missing, there can be little doubt that they were émigrés who made their way via

Singapore and Japan to Canada. Most likely they were among the c. 5000 predominantly Punjabi Sikh immigrants, who made their way to Canada between 1905 and 1908, just before the 'Continuous Journey' Act prevented further labour migration from the subcontinent. Not only was their coming to the Americas characterized by physical hardship, initially they were also subject to racism and hostilities that culminated in an anti-immigration violence in 1907 in Canada and California (Puri 1983).

Against this background of early twentieth century immigration to North America, how does one read this photograph? At the time the picture was taken professional photography flourished and much of its work on non-western traditions catered to primitivist and orientalist notions of the exotic. Photography was undeniably an important technique of colonial representation through which the western world consolidated its power in reassuring itself about the need to civilize the native Indian.[2] Is the photograph part of this endeavour so that the performers' aspiration of a life in the Americas becomes entangled in the conventional styles of colonial photography, their positioning in the salon something that conferred the sense of a caricature to the Western viewer? Or are there other possibilities of interpreting it?

Imagine for a moment that these four Punjabis have deliberately chosen to be framed in this way: a group of bardic singers in a Western salon with its aura of publicity and citizenry. From the perspective of early diaspora formation in North America, this thought is not too speculative. Notions of the public sphere were in fact instrumental to the political developments in colonial India, and the situation in the late nineteenth century Punjab was certainly no exception to this. Due to changing infrastructures of communication, social visions and political critique were expressed in a growing body of vernacular literature that circulated between Punjab and the diaspora. This form of knowledge transmission was by no means restricted to the literary consciousness of an emerging elite public sphere in Punjab (Talbot 1996: 26). On the contrary, vernacular literature was meant to widen discursive spaces to rural public arenas, and was thus necessarily dependent on performative spaces in which orators, bards, and other performers were key figures. Punjabi performative genres were assessed as important discursive resources of self-assertion and self-definition, cutting across class and caste boundaries.

Jane Singh (1990) has argued that Punjabi poetry and song were at the very core of the discursive and aesthetic repertoire that sustained the political movement in the North American diaspora setting at that time. If dhadi performers had a role to play in the larger political struggle that emerged in the Punjabi diaspora, then what lingered in the cultural repertoire of popular performative tradition were idiomatic and imagistic forms that affected the way political messages could be voiced, internalized, and transformed into different modes of action. Not only did literature articulate common experience and thus help to establish new emotional ties among the members of a 'scattered community', it acquired a political voice in the public sphere of the print media such as in the publications of the Gadar revolutionaries (ibid.: 114). The photograph, I would therefore argue, also shows a performative format that was a constitutive element of an emerging anti-colonial movement that tied elite discourses to what is usually called 'subaltern' participation in the public sphere.

If it makes sense to read the photograph against the grain of colonial representation, what is to be done with the internal framing, that is, with the differences that are marked by the composition of the four performers? Is it by mere accident that the person holding the drum is clean-shaven, wearing a loosely tied turban and thus does not appear to be a religious performer in the first place. Is it at all necessary to raise this question and think about a difference that for the performers themselves might not have been an issue at all? Their coming together in a single performative format indicates, after all, a certain openness of the dhadi tradition to accommodate different religious and social identifications within the same framework of performative culture. This resonates with the historical evidence that I presented earlier according to which dhadi performers, as hereditary musicians, demonstrated a high degree of flexibility in their association with various forms of political and religious patronage. Unmistakably, the early twentieth-century portrait of the group testifies to this kind of cultural flexibility.

But why, in the anthropologist's eyes, does the player of the drum stand out here? Having in mind the broad range of anthropological scholarship on performative traditions in North India which identifies drum players as low-caste subjects or Dalits, I cannot help but raise this question. Since contemporary performers in the Indian Punjab appear almost entirely to be Khalsa Sikhs, it seems to me no coincidence that, about a century earlier, Sikh religious symbols displayed in bodily attire and expression began to shape the framework of dhadi self-representation. Thus, if the photograph epitomizes a key issue of (diaspora) community formation, does it also entail a discourse on marginalization that is directed inwards and that can be anticipated in the displacement of the low caste or *mirāsī* bard, imagined in the drum player of the photograph?

Notes

1. I first saw this photograph in the Berkeley exhibition 'Echoes of Freedom. South Asian Pioneers in California, 1899–1965' (curator: Suzanne McMohan). The picture is not included in the catalogue (McMohan 2001) but was displayed as a huge, formatted photograph.
2. The name dhadi is mentioned twice: as a brief entry in the second volume of the *Glossary* and as a subcategory of mīrasī in the third. Two generic aspects of the dhadi genre are mentioned in the *Glossary*: 'The Dhádhi is one who plays the dhádh and sings the deeds of heroes dead and gone. Little else about him is known with certainty.'
3. For this point see Nayyar (2000: 764).
4. Ibbetson (1994 [1883]) and Rose (1970 [1892]) specified roles in gift exchange, patronage, and aspects of intermarriage. These are obviously some of the concepts upon which the understanding of caste society as a hierarchical social system rested. The particular emphasis is placed on the ritually defined relationships between different social categories 'within the whole of society'.
5. According to Neuman, the name dhadi was replaced by the term mīrasī by the mid-nineteenth century. Referring to a book written by Mohammad Karam Islam in 1856–7 in which no mīrasī is mentioned, Neuman demonstrates that a decade later one could observe, 'that as with all sectors of political and social life in India, rapid changes were taking place [and] within a short period of time, Mirasis begin to take the place of Dharis [dhadis], or at least the terminology changes' (1980: 130).
6. See for instance the eight volume work, *The People of India: A Series of Photographic Illustrations, with Descriptive Letterpress, of the Races and Tribes of Hindustan*', that was produced in 1891 by the Political and Secret Department of the India Office in London.

3

A New Dhadi Subject in Colonial Punjab

The question of agency and subaltern identity continues to haunt the project of writing minority histories today. There are at least two features that have made the relationship between both notions a difficult one to think about. One is the old but still relevant question of whether subaltern participation in the great historical struggles has to be seen as a generative political and social force or not. The second feature revolves around the question of what particular form subaltern agency assumes, considering that attributions of cause and effect are often incommensurable with a historicist worldview, or can only be grasped in terms of 'subaltern consciousness'. Let me briefly address both these issues.

In a widely recognized contribution to the historiography of the Indian nationalist movement, Partha Chatterjee (1993) held cultural traditions as significant discursive sources through which the Indian nationalist project carved out alternative models of Indian sociality and historical imagination. In his book, Chatterjee made the important point that, in distinction from European history, Indian reformists and nationalists considered popular religion and related forms of cultural expression as vital sources to define the inner, cultural as well as spiritual space of the nation. If in this context language was recognized as 'a zone over which the nation first had to declare its sovereignty and then had to transform it in order to make it adequate for the modern world' (ibid.: 7), it pertained not only to the learned languages that constituted the publicizing activities of the reformist and nationalist elites. Chatterjee also held that popular performative spaces of religious and political participation were in significant ways tied to the formation of community and nation.

Emphasizing the self-constituting process of subaltern identity formation, Chatterjee, however stepped back from his provocative thesis, suggesting that the 'mark of subalternity' would still be characterized by an inability on the part of the subaltern classes to translate dominant political discourses (such as the dominant dharma projected through religious orthodoxy) into alternative projects that could challenge the encompassing claims underlying the powerful modes of (nationalist) representation (ibid.: 181).

Through this sustaining of a constrained form of subaltern agency, Chatterjee sets a specific task and responsibility for a critical project of South Asian historiography, which is the excavation of the 'fragmented oppositions' produced through the historically situated dynamics of dominance and subordination. His perspective on subaltern agency provides us with a useful but partial framework for historical analysis. As Fuchs (1999) has pointed out, Chatterjee advanced a dialectical model of subalternity that is different from the 'autonomy' model proposed by Guha (1988) and others. By focusing on the relationship between elite and non-elite discourses rather than confining each of them to a closed cultural and social universe beyond which their actions have either no meaning or might appear awkward and unintelligible to the historical gaze, Chatterjee is certainly on the right track. Yet, as Fuchs argues, his shift to the dialectical approach poses a vexed issue as well (1999: 126). This is because Chatterjee posits subaltern agency as a mode of negating dominant discourses.[1] In that way, non-elite representations constantly fail to challenge the claims to power propounded through elite ideologies. Instead of explaining how social actors negotiate and interpret their world as meaningful and potentially open, says Fuchs (ibid.: 139), actors at the social periphery pose a problem for academic classification: the predominant question is *what* experiences and *whose* identities could be included under the rubric of 'the subaltern'. They are either confined to a closed identity without possibly transcending the limits of their own lifeworld, or remain subordinate within hegemonic discourses. In both renderings, marginalized groups always emerge as social categories that are constrained in their agency.

This analytic framework also informs the historiography of Punjab.[2] In his influential book on the Singh Sabha reform movement, Oberoi (1997) argued that the Sikh reformist agenda was successful in targeting iconoclastic and other religious practices associated with subaltern groups or what he referred to as popular or folk religion. Oberoi demarcates reformist religion and subaltern practices of sociability as utterly distinct modalities of public reasoning. Whereas the reformist elites engaged in the public sphere, the realms of popular religion and cultural syncretism were populated by professional bards and ritual specialists. He construes them as players in an 'enchanted universe' in which the motivation to participate in religious practices was not defined in terms of Hindu, Muslim, or Sikh affiliation but rather through shared beliefs in supernatural powers. While Oberoi has a valid point in emphasizing the role of popular religion, I think he makes a mistake in portraying folk performers and ritual specialists as icons for a rather static rural culture that could be traced back in time.[3] In his rendering, bardic culture is either characterized as a factor preventing social transformation and religious reform or, as in the case of the dhadi singers, as a form of expression that could be shaped according to the Sikh elite's own need of transmitting reformist discourses.

In what follows, I propose a somewhat different interpretation. I have cited Chatterjee and Oberoi because they touch upon an important point in referring to the cultural experts of public performance and mediation such as bards, orators, preachers, and artists. If Oberoi proposes the existence of two homogenous and temporally disjoint blocs of reformist elites and subaltern folks, Chatterjee in turn would argue that it is rather their inter-relationship that matters. In that regard, Chatterjee, is on the right track in identifying the expressive and representational modes of a performative tradition as a site of critical engagement in colonial modernity. Yet, what is missed is a full recognition of the self-constitutive character of particular social movements and a record of the specificities of how particular peasants, low castes, and other marginalized groups acquire agency in this process. Little historical evidence has been provided thus far to shed light on this aspect in the context of Punjabi history and society.

At this point, the second problem with the relationship between agency and subalternity has to be addressed. Among the crucial dilemmas for a project of writing minority histories, argues Dipesh Chakrabarty (2000), is the historian's search for historical agency and reflexivity on the part of the subalterns, when in fact those actors themselves seem to deny such agency or defer it to complex or non-human agents. In fact, one might ask, when supernatural agents and gods are evoked as the makers of history, what will be the role of the historian in accounting for historical agency and the idea of a speaking subject that underlines it? In response to Ranajit Guha's seminal paper on the 'Prose of Counter-Insurgency' (1988), Chakrabarty asks: 'What does it mean, then, when we both take the subaltern's view seriously—the subaltern ascribe agency for their rebellion to some god—and want to confer on the subaltern agency or subjecthood in their own history, a status the subaltern's statement denies?' (ibid.: 103) This is indeed a critical question, even if we should not assume an essentialist notion of the other's religious world view. Anthropologists like Keane (1997b) or Miyazaki (2000) have asked similar questions and demonstrated how agency is problematized, even in contexts where the adaptation of Western notions of a speaking subject (such as in Christian liturgical speech) seems to be uncontested.

Punjabi history offers various trajectories through which similar questions can be asked. The most prominent examples, in terms of the material I am concerned with, is the agency of the mythohistorical figure of the martyr that I shall explore in subsequent chapters. My trajectory in this chapter engages with both these conceptual problems. It consists of two argumentative moves that, by sidestepping an all-embracing discussion of the larger historical circumstances, will consider the specificity of interpretive practices and participatory models as they are shaped through the dhadi genre. In the first part of the chapter, I attempt to read a performer's autobiography as a mode of recollecting a past that breaks with the subaltern-dominance framework. I believe that the autobiographical material represents a mode of recognizing the proactive force of performative tradition in its irreducibility to ideological appropriation. In the second part I discuss two vernacular texts on the Sikh martyr Baba Deep Singh. I could trace these texts among the many dhadi tracts that I collected in the course of conducting ethnographic fieldwork between the years 1998 and 2000. I suggest reading two particular episodes that I could allocate to historically subsequent modes of genre expression. The transitions in terms of performative language and style deserve our attention, not because of some valid philological and cultural interest, but precisely because it is in these transitions that we can make out interventions into song, words, and key symbols of religious and political mobilization. I am particularly interested in knowing how the new forms of representational language emerging in the early twentieth century Punjab generated a sense of participation and engagement in national politics.

My writing will by and large abstain from reproducing the rhetoric of the 'subaltern fragment'. I emphasize this point even though much of my writing is informed by a project of critical South Asian historiography and anthropology.[4] My attempt to recognize the constitutive role of Punjabi performative traditions in this context might seem slightly overstated and distort the broader picture in which we see socio-economic and political forces working against the proliferation of oral culture. Yet, as scholars before me have argued, this picture is partial at best. The vast repository of performative culture does offer trajectories for understanding the relations of power and agency in an emerging public sphere in colonial modernity (see also Freitag 1989). It is, in fact, crucial to ask in what ways emancipatory spaces were fashioned through the various aesthetic and linguistic forms assigned to the traditional practices of performative tradition. Powerful discourses did certainly impact on performative languages, yet the ways in which this happened and with what results is not at all evident. Drawing attention to some of the Punjabi material, I hope to demonstrate that popular participation is not sufficiently understood in terms of the organizational and ideological adjustments to the discourses shaped by colonial and religious elites.

Subaltern Voice and Religious Virtue: Forming a Pious Dhadi Performer

At a time in which the first Punjabi settlers experienced hardship and turmoil in North America and elsewhere, the situation in Punjab was also far from peaceful. It was a time of social and political mobilization in which, it seems, many rural Punjabis took up the opportunity to voice their message through public song and drama performances, some of which were banned under British censorship law. It was around thar time that a 'son of Punjab' was born who was later recognized as one of the leading public performers of the dhadi genre—Sohan Singh Seetal. Seetal was born in 1909 in Khadivind (*Qāzīvinḍ*), a small hamlet located a few miles north of the town of Qasur at the Ferozepur-Lahore route. He did not grow up in a family of hereditary musicians. He started to perform dhadi because he grasped the political twist in poetic discourse and political oratory in his youth, at a time when the Akali movement mobilized the rural masses.[5] Launched by the Chief Khalsa Diwan as a non-violent struggle to take the Sikh shrines from the administrative purview of the colonial state, the Akali movement rallied around religious symbols and social reformist idioms. The objectives of the Akalis became a matter of major concern for the British who, fearing far wider repercussions for the legitimacy of indirect rule, responded violently. Led by self-proclaimed 'martyrs of the faith' (*shahīdī jatthe*), many of those who marched were willing to die and in this 'accomplishment' were venerated as heroes of the anti-colonial struggle in rural Punjab. According to his autobiography *Vekhī Māni Duniā*, Seetal was still in primary school when Akali activists used to come to there school and perform in the mornings (Seetal 1983: 72). In his writing, he devotes significant space to describing occasions of public performance, thus unraveling what he considered the creative intervention of singers and orators. As we shall see, apart from anti-colonial slogans, religious orientation is an important point of reference in his account of dhadi public participation around that time. What interests me particularly in this first reading of his autobiography is how this performer situates the formation of a pious self within a long journey through the broad framework of Punjabi popular religious and performative practices.[6]

Seetal was brought up in an environment in which the Sikh gurus were highly revered. His father's lineage traced the name Singh over many generations to the early eighteenth century. Seetal's father was a peasant belonging to the *viṛak got* from Gujranwala, whereas his mother's lineage was named *pannu* from *Jauṛa*. Both are Jat lineages, constituting the predominant ethnic group in rural Punjab. Seetal mentions that his grandfather and father were rather poor farmers; they owned a few acres of land and shared their house with neighbours. Life in the village is described as strenuous and difficult. Water scarcity or

FIGURE 11: Gyani Sohan Singh Seetal, Ludhiana *Courtesy* Jagdev Singh Jassowal

other shortcomings would frequently result in quarrels with over land and other ownership rights. Seetal compares his personal character with that of his maternal grandfather (*nānājī*). A very crucial aspect in his personal development was the dissatisfaction with his paternal line, which he expresses frequently. While his relationship with his father was close, most paternal relatives were a constant source of trouble; some of them consumed opium and did not work while others, such as his uncle Waddhawa Singh, even threatened him. Punjabi society is known for a patriarchic value system and kinship organization based on the *biraderi* rather than other caste differentiations. Against this background Seetal's emphasis on his closeness to the maternal side, and his frequent references to the good relations he had with women in the household are not merely incidental.

The relationship with his female cognates is also where he situates the role of religious conduct. Seetal frequently uses anecdotes to introduce and characterize particularities of his childhood and personal development. Such is the case in anecdotes referring to religious orientation. Seetal reports that he was very particular about purity. For instance, he always insisted on drinking from a clean (*succhā*) glass, and for this his two sisters would constantly tease him. Eventually, he agreed to drink water offered to him only if one of his relatives immersed the glass in a vessel in front of his eyes (to prove that it had not been touched). There is a perceptible narrative line in that matter. In a collection of autobiographical anecdotes (Seetal 1989) he observes a similar incident, when he would only take his meal after the Japiyi prayer was recited on a day when the villagers, including the Sikh families, celebrated the Hindu Devi puja. He also remembers his efforts to complete the path of the *Jāpujī* prayer at the age of six years. Seetal (ibid.: 48) assumes that his inner disposition slowly began to take shape in this early encounter with religious scripture (*man de andar hī andar kuch socnā śurū kar ditā sī*). In short, such anecdotes on mundane incidents depict him as a determined and pious person. His account of personal conduct gives expression to his *dhārmik* orientation. Everyday notions of purity (*ishnān*) and prayer appear to be central. Seetal points out that religious practice was held in high esteem in his family, although these attitudes were not to be taken for granted in the framework of the family at large.

The emphasis placed on religious conduct is further expressed in accounts that deal with his education. As a child he experienced great pleasure while listening to the Punjabi folk epics through which he got acquainted with discourses on saintly figures and mystical thought.[7] Subsequently, different religious teachers educated him. A travelling *Udāsī sant*, Hari Ram, is mentioned to have instructed him in *gurmukhi*.[8] This provided the basis for his interest in the Sikh scriptures. Later, a teacher named Murli Ram instructed him in Urdu. Murli Ram is mentioned as the one to set him 'on the right track'. When Seetal entered primary school, he skipped several classes because of his talent and then joined governmental school in Qasur. Within the colonial institution, Seetal studied English, Sanskrit, Hindi, Persian, and Arabic and became interested in history. His main interest, however, remained Urdu, the *ghazal* poetry in particular. One of his Urdu teachers at government school was Fakir Hussein, whom Seetal honours in almost panegyric terms. His favourite was the Urdu poet Ghalib from whom he cites various ghazals. For his later dhadi profession, this education in Urdu literature was of considerable importance. It formed the basis of his distinct oratory style and would eventually elicit the applause of the literate society when he performed on the stage.

Seetal's educational background is remarkable for a variety of reasons. First, as a poor farmer's son, he was not particularly 'suited' to follow this path. Agricultural labour and family obligations awaited him. Second, he pays reverence to various learned men, some of whom most certainly belonged to traditions that were not regarded as authoritative in modern reformist discourse. He traversed different sites of apprenticeship, such as in the student-teacher (*ustād-shagird*) relationship with the *Udāsī sant*. These different orientations notwithstanding, he projects a self that is clearly framed by pious and moral conduct, in line with traditional Khalsa values. Note that this happens in a historical period in which, according to Harjot Oberoi (1997: 343–4), the 'new episteme' of Khalsa Sikhism was firmly established and operative at the level of everyday religious practice. It seems that, for Seetal, the hegemony of Khalsa identity was no obstacle to shape his religious self through engagement in a pluralistic cultural and religious framework. He not only fully acknowledges existing popular traditions, from which he gained a great deal of linguistic and performative training, but also considers these as appropriate forms through which his moral virtues were shaped. And this extends right into the mīrasī framework that Oberoi has identified as the main target of the Sikh reformist agenda.

For the argument pursued in this chapter, these connections between a dharmik form of life and inherited modes of apprenticeship in the mīrasī framework are crucial to consider. We find evidence for this connection in sections of the narrative that deal with Seetal's early days as a dhadi performer. Seetal mentions the role of the mīrasī as family genealogists and ritual specialists. Much of Seetal's own recollection of his family genealogy is based on bardic memory.[9] Seetal was in fact trained for six months as a dhadi singer by Baba Chirag Din, a mīrasī bard who resided in the village. He refers to the beginnings of his dhadi career in an anecdote that portrays the poetic voice of another low-caste singer, a *rabābī* who was part of a theatre troupe of *Rāmgaṛhiās* who came to visit Khadivind.[10] Attracted by the singer's voice, Seetal would listen to the performance of the Sikh prayer *asa dī vār*. The young folk (*gabharū*) of the village who attended the performance were completely enamoured by the performers. As implied in the anecdote, they decided to start their own drama group (*naṭak maṇḍalī*) and approached Seetal in this matter. Seetal, who by that time was known to be among the few educated peasants in the vicinity, first rejected the quest. 'Since childhood I follow the religious (*dhārmik*) path. I told my compatriots: "I appreciate that you approached me in this matter but you know that I never go to listen to these itinerant singers (*bāhar de gauṇ wāliāṃ*), therefore I cannot join you in the drama group"'.[11] Yet, after a long discussion he agreed with his companions to form a dhadi jattha. As an important factor in his decision he mentions a local performer of reputation—Kishan Singh Orara—whom he regarded as a pious Sikh and religious dhadi.

The anecdote disguises the fact that this rejection of the ludic framework of drama performance (the *rāsdhārī* genre in particular) was mediated by post-Partition developments. By the time his autobiography was published, he looked back at a life during which he contributed to the establishment of a specific image of the Sikh dhadi. In the 1920s, the question of whether Sikh participation in cultural performances was appropriate or not was certainly an issue of religious piety. The texts discussed in the next section provide a clear indication for this. Yet, the way this is portrayed in his recollection probably lays too much emphasis on how this was practically achieved by means of conscious choices. In his autobiography, he mentions that even after Partition in 1947 dhadi groups performed at occasions such as weddings. According to the author, his negation of the ludic framework of the dhadi performance became manifest in the course of such a wedding. A person in the audience addressed Seetal and wanted him to perform a folk song (*ik hīr di kali sunā diho, 'lai tūr calliyā rāñjhāṃ cūcak dīye jaīye*').[12] Hailed by the ludic voice, Seetal felt offended (*eh sun ke mere dil te barī chot lagī sī*). His answer is cited as: 'Brothers! I'm really grateful to you. You taught me a lesson. You do not consider me to be a religious dhadi (*gurū ghar dā dhādī*) but rather a singer (*gauṇ wālā*). I swear today that I will never again perform kirtan in front of a marriage party and that I will also refrain from visiting wedding occasions'.[13] Seetal frames dhadi performance in religious terms and refers to his practice as kirtan, which is exclusively used for the recitation of gurbānī from the Adi Granth.

Seetal's aversion to what he called the folk singer's genre throws up several issues that seek clarification. We have learned that, like his teacher, many dhadi performers (specifically the sarangi players) were in fact mīrasī or bardic singers from the lower strata of Punjabi society. There is no way Seetal would have denied this. Obviously, the discursive effect of this affiliation on his understanding of dhadi practice has been something of great concern. The existing tension in his reappraisal of the dhadi subject therefore reflects the discursive power of colonial antiquarianism and reformist discourse that were, in their relatedness, instrumental in shaping the social image of Punjabi performative traditions.

I have just delineated the derogatory effect of colonial discourse due to which the dhadi performer was being subsumed under the general category of low bardic (folk) culture. As is particularly evident in the wedding anecdote, this image is associated with a sensual-subversive memory, playing upon problematic notions of male-female encounter and 'loose morals'. Sikh performers in that period tried to dissociate dhadi practice from this particular image by renaming it in religious terminology. Seetal therefore uses the word kirtan, the name used for the recitation of sacred Sikh literature, although he knows that dhadi performances essentially differ from that.

Through the prism of Chatterjee's argument cited earlier, we can anticipate in this example some of the practical limits of securing a notion of 'subaltern agency' in a situation in which discourses of religious dharma and not those of ludic entertainment promise social recognition. If the dhadi genre today has become a recognized form of Sikh self-representation, Seetal's recuperative gesture seems to imply a delegitimization of alternative forms of social imagination and public participation. Surfacing tensions in the autobiographical narrative that seek to rationalize historical agency where in fact there is none thus seem to be unavoidable.

If I see merit in this line of thinking, I claim that it still does not provide a satisfactory account for explaining people's ongoing interest in this bardic genre. Seetal saw it as an appropriate form of public participation and presentation, despite these negative connotations.[14] I think this case study illustrates that the refashioning of a pious dhadi performer is self-reflexive in granting recognition to the multidimensional character of Punjabi traditions. What performers reject, I believe, is a moment of being called into an obedient mode of servitude on what they considered illegitimate moral grounds. Whether this is a recognition granted through the autobiographical telling or an appropriate representation of the past event is not what matters in the first place. What matters, I would contend, is that there is a consistency in the performer's overall orientation and habituation to cultural forms of aesthetic receptivity, firmly entrenched in rural rather than urban elite practices. There is obviously a conscious move of moulding the dhadi genre as an interactive space of public debate and presentation through which notions of Sikh pietism and reformist notions of moral conduct are oriented toward the formation of a citizen-subject. But this preference for a Sikh dharmīk way of life does not dispose with cultural and religious plurality as a lived practice.

As I shall point out in the next section, it is the continuity of (musical) apprenticeship in the plural context of vernacular tradition and thought systems that allowed dhadi performers to acquire a position of self-distancing and intervention into the inherited forms of their tradition. Once we turn to the representations of bardic song narratives, this point becomes even more important to consider, as it would be easy to read in these narratives the duplication of ideologies that were current to the day. I argue instead that the transitions necessitated in performative style and genre in a context of religious and political mobilization in the 1920s and 1930s were not merely mimetic of reformist discourse. Certain paradigmatic shifts *within* the generic and interpretative register of representational media allowed dhadi performers to emerge as new speaking subjects and not merely as loudspeakers of others.

The Impact of the Print Media

The emergence of a new 'textual community' of vernacular presses in the late nineteenth-century Punjab was accompanied by significant changes in political economy, education, and religious organization (Talbot 1996). The impact of these transitions could be felt in urban and rural Punjab, even though in rural Punjab the way the public was tied into the wider context of social mobilization and anti-colonial nationalism was still very much dependent on the mediating role of religious authorities such as the *sajjadah nishins* who were in charge of the Sufi shrines.[15] If the public sphere in colonial Punjab was characterized by a multiplicity of religious and secular discourses rather than a singular discursive framework, it is clear that the new print media created new possibilities of knowledge transmission, bringing in more and more people from the rural areas as well. If the emergence of a vibrant printing press was to the favour of the new colonial elites, it was not exactly to the benefit of the traditional forms of public performance. In the process of institutionalizing a modern Sikh community, the shifts in the forms of public debate to the realm of the printed word was clearly visible in the abundant tracts of reformist literature that circulated in the region. As Oberoi (1997) has described, Khalsa spokespersons operated at the front lines of public debate in newspapers such as the *Khālsā Akhbār, Khālsā Samacār* or *Khālsā Advocate*. These journals were monitored by institutions such as the Chief Khalsa Divan, the major ideological organ of the Singh Sabhas before the subsequent establishment of the SGPC in 1925.

Against the background of colonial measures to codify customary law, Sikh reform literature was centrally concerned with the formulation of a Sikh code of conduct that was to be safeguarded against colonial dominance and counter-claims of other religious communities. Accordingly, the overall objective was to petition for new constitutional measures that were to the benefit of the Sikh qaum. To succeed in this, reformists made an effort to canonize Sikh history in appealing and rhetorically inspiring ways. Lou Fenech argues that the Chief Khalsa Diwan was particularly effective in ensuring 'that the Khalsa tradition of martial bravery, selfless sacrifice, and martyrdom were kept alive and vibrant' (2000: 209). Fenech further suggests that the dhadi tradition played an instrumental role in popularizing these discourses.

I am interested here in the connections between the new reformist literature and the oral discourses of popular culture, some of which appeared in print. In colonial Punjab, performative tracts in which reformist and revolutionary ideas were given strong expression were published in great numbers. In addition to the well known Urdu and Punjabi poetry one could add the tracts of the Gadar and Babbar Akali movements, which were produced during the militant struggle of this group between 1915 and 1923.[16] Many of these poetic compilations are interesting to the extent that they allow new insights into how political and poetical discourse converged in the early twentieth century.

In order to show how historical happenings are reflected in such tracts, let me quote a *kabit* (speech-song) from one of the first published dhadi narratives, composed by Sohan Singh Gukewalia. It is set against the background of the Nankana massacre in 1921 that also sparked large-scale protests during the Guru ka Bagh morcha. It reads:

gaḍḍhi yātrā 'c pair ṭakā'iā,	Setting his feet on the pilgrimage
srī nankāne nūṃ	Towards Nankana Sahib
jathedār lachman singh hoyā,	Jathedar Lachman Singh
dhāro vāli piṇḍ jis dā	Who belongs to village Dharowali
jado pās nankāne āe,	As he came close to Nankana Sahib
khabarāṃ pahūṅc gayāṃ	News reached him,
kise dassiā singhāṃ nuṃ jāke,	Someone came to inform the Singhs,
hāl narainū dā	About Narain's intention.
picchhā muṛ jā'u agān nā jā'iu,	'You should return and not proceed!
khatrā jānāṃ dā	Lives are in danger!
luce saddke mahant baṭhāle,	The *mahant* has called his scoundrels.
mās te sharāb uḍḍā	He consumes meat and alcohol,
ka'iyā hatth pastaul bandūkāṃ	Pistols and guns in his hands,
kar morce bandī uh baiṭhā,	He is sitting in an entrenchment,
khālse de mārāṃ nūṃ,	In order to kill the Khalsa.'
jatthedār ne kihā eh saudā,	The *jathedar* then said,
karnā sastā e,	'This is no great matter.
sīs di'ānge duvāre satigur de,	We will bow our head before the true Guru'
enī akhde agāh nūṃ call pae,	Saying this, they proceeded forward
sīs nivā'yā gurāṃ nūṃ	Bowing their head before the Gurus-
sāḍa sidak sikkhī nā jāwe,	The righteous and faithful Sikhs shall not
lāj rakhīṃ bāzāṇ vāliāṃ	be defeated,
khule bār darbār vic vaṛ ga'e,	Save our respect, you owner of the hawk.
jathedār baiṭhā	When entering the open court
tābiā piāriā piāriā	The *jathedar* sat like a humble servant,
duśt narainū ne loharā māriā	And wicked Narain killed him cruelly
	(1964 [n.d.]: 88–9).[17]

The Nankana massacre at Guru Nanak's birthplace took place on 21 July and was among the most bloody events that occurred in the course of the gurdwara liberation movement led by the Akali Sikh in the early 1920s.[18] A group of Sikh protesters was attacked and killed by armed gunmen inside the gurdwara. In the longer version of the composition, this incident and the killings are all portrayed in detail. The above scene describes how Lachman Singh, despite the warnings about the *mahant's*

FIGURE 12: Nankana Sahib, 300th anniversary of the Khalsa
Courtesy Michael Nijhawan

vicious plans, was determined to reach the destination together with a band of self-declared shahīds. We can cull from this example that the combination of forces operating around the 1920s led indeed to a reinvigoration of martyrdom stories in the way they have been traditionally performed by dhadi singers.

How did this happen and what motivation did the performers have in disseminating their compositions in print? First of all, it needs to be recognized that for rural performers in particular, the distribution of written stories and episodes not only appealed because of the popularity of the print media but also because the written medium promised a new form of authorizing dhadi discourses. Local actors, preachers, and orators were certainly not unaware of the transformations taking place in the wider public, and they might well have anticipated new ways to enter the sphere of the written word as authors of Sikh history. The first dhadi tracts surfaced in the 1920s (probably even earlier) at a time when they could be produced and sold at a reasonable cost. Along with many other religious and political pamphlets, they were then transmitted widely in rural Punjab. Even though this might have led to a fixation and authorization of particular reformist discourses in dhadi representations, it also resulted in new modes of public reasoning and an altered self-image of dhadi bards and orators as popular historians.

The appeal of becoming a 'people's historian' is particularly evident in Sohan Singh Seetal's case. Seetal believed he could best serve his community as an individual engaged in the writing and transmission of Sikh history. In his account, Singh Sabha literature occupied a special place and so it is no coincidence that some of the reformist writers, like Kartar Singh Kalaswalia, are explicitly mentioned as intellectual sources.[19] Seetal (1983: 145) mentions at different points his dedication as a writer. His career as a Sikh writer can be traced to his work 'How did the Sikh kingdom fall?' in which he depicts how the internal fractures and moral decline in the royal elite led to the end of Sikh sovereignty in Punjab after Maharaja Ranjit Singh's reign, and a range of dhadi compilations that he wrote in the early 1930s.[20] Seetal's success as a popular singer also indicates that he was a gifted writer.

Note that it is the power and persistence of the written word that attracted Seetal in the first place. This interest is not restricted to the ideological framework of Singh Sabha literature. Thus, Seetal read the Bible, Qur'an, and the Bhagavad Gita as well as some colonial treatises on Sikh history that were available to him. In this fashion, Seetal familiarized himself with the major traditions of religious and historical thought. Provided the Singh Sabha agenda was not so penetrative as to eliminate all other discourses, including alternative discourses on Sikh history and religious reform, it follows that writers and performers like Seetal were not simply acting on a prescribed discourse formulated by a handful of elite actors. Instead, powerful discourses and techniques of representation were applied in ways in which it was seen as consistent with locally emergent forms of public participation.

Baba Deep Singh and the Magic of the New Style

To further develop my argument, I would now like to turn to the discussion of two dhadi texts. Both compositions take as their topic the revered figure Baba Deep Singh, who was a mobilizing symbol for the Akali protesters. The first version is authored by Sohan Singh Gukewalia and included in the reprint of his '*Dhāḍī Haṅjhūṃ* (1964), whereas the second version can be found in Sohan Singh Seetal's *Sītal Taraṅgāṃ* (1993 [1945]). Sohan Singh Gukewalia is mentioned in Seetal's autobiography as one of the dhadi buzurg (elder performers) and as his predecessor. Gukewalia's career as a performer began long before Seetal took up the profession in the late 1920s. The generational

ਸਭ ਹੱਕ ਪ੍ਰਕਾਸ਼ਕ ਦੇ ਸਦਾ ਲਈ ਰਾਖਵੇਂ ਹਨ।

ਨਵੀਆਂ ਨਵੀਆਂ ਢਾਡੀਆਂ ਦੀਆਂ ਤਰਜ਼ਾਂ ਤੇ ਸੋਹਣੇ

ਸੁਵਾਦਲੇ ਨਵੇਂ ਨਵੇਂ ਪ੍ਰਸੰਗ

ਢਾਡੀ ਹੰਝੂ

ਦੂਜਾ ਹਿਸਾ

Sohana Singha

ਪ੍ਰਸਿਧ ਢਾਡੀ

ਭਾਈ ਸੋਹਣ ਸਿੰਘ ਘੁਕੇ ਵਾਲੀਆ

ਰਚਿਤ v. 2

ਸਾਕਾ ਸਰਹੰਦ, ਜੰਗ ਚਮਕੌਰ, ਮਾਤਾ ਸੁਲੱਖਣੀ
ਚੰਦ ਦੀ ਨੂੰਹ ਆਦਿਕ

ਇਸ ਵਿਚ ਬਹੁਤੇ ਪ੍ਰਸੰਗ ਢਾਡੀਆਂ ਦੇ ਗਾਣ ਵਾਲੇ ਹਨ।
ਢਾਡੀਆਂ ਦਾ ਢਿੱਡ ਗਾਉਣ ਨਾਲ ਨਹੀਂ ਭਰਦਾ ਪਰ ਏਹਨਾਂ
ਪ੍ਰਸੰਗਾਂ ਵਿਚ ਢਾਡੀਆਂ ਦੇ ਗਾਣੇ ਨਾਲ ਰੱਜਾ ਦਿਤਾ ਹੈ।
ਰੰਗ ਰੰਗ ਦੀਆਂ ਤਰਜ਼ਾਂ ਇਸ ਵਿਚ ਭਰੀਆਂ ਹਨ ਅਤੇ ਇਸ
ਤੋਂ ਅਗੇ ਤੀਜਾ ਹਿੱਸਾ ਢਾਡੀ ਤਰੰਗਾ ਦਾ ਪੜ੍ਹੋ।

ਪ੍ਰਕਾਸ਼ਕ:-

ਭਾਈ ਚਤਰ ਸਿੰਘ ਜੀਵਨ ਸਿੰਘ

ਪੁਸਤਕਾਂ ਵਾਲੇ ਬਜ਼ਾਰ ਮਾਈ ਸੇਵਾਂ, ਅੰਮ੍ਰਿਤਸਰ

ਪੈਹਲੀ ਵਾਰ ਮੁਲ ੧॥)

FIGURE 13: Dhadi booklet cover, *Dhadi Hanjum* by Sohan Singh Gukewalia
Courtesy Michael Nijhawan

difference is important here, as language and style of expression of both performers differ to the extent that they were not exposed to the effect of the written word in the same way.

Baba Deep Singh's story continues to provide a core narrative of Sikh martyrdom and resistance. As a historical figure, Baba Deep Singh was a contemporary of the tenth guru, Gobind Singh. He is remembered and venerated as a brave warrior who had given up his life during a battle against the Afghan ruler Abdali. If we look at the topical structure of the two compositions that I have chosen for this discussion, we find that there is a significant overlap in recognizing the heroic deeds of Baba Deep Singh. Both dhadi compositions are rather long and comprise two dozen songs each. Gukewalia's text seems to have been rearranged, not from a singular performance, but from various oral presentations.[21] This is particularly clear when, at the end of the print version, different songs are accumulated without any further narrative interludes. Seetal's text, in contrast, is based on a written version of what he called an earlier 'programme'. What interests me here is not so much the story itself, but the change in terms of genre composition and representational technique.

Let us first turn to Gukewalia's compilation. It opens with praises of Baba Deep Singh's achievements for the Sikhs. Baba Deep Singh's proximity to Guru Gobind Singh is the main focus. The Guru bestowed on him the task to create authorized copies of the Guru Granth Sahib. In another paragraph, Guru Gobind Singh demands that Baba Deep Singh should now be prepared to engage in military battle (Gukewalia 1964: 8).[22] The reader is then informed about the lootings and killings of Abdali, which sets the background for Baba Deep Singh's eventual transitions from *granthī* to General (ibid.: 9).

Likewise, Seetal's composition opens with an oratorical section about Baba Deep Singh. His text, however, differs from Gukewalia in linguistic style, number of songs, historical detail, textual arrangement, as well as rhetorical dramatization. Seetal's text begins by situating the story in the context of Mughal rule in the Punjab, for which the appropriate historical data is provided: 'Before all this happened, Ahmad Shah had looted Hindustan three times. The fourth time, he departed from Kandahar together with Muglani Begum, Najibudaula and Badshah Alamgir Mani. He proceeded from Peshawar on 15 November AD 1756 and after crossing the river on 26 November, he reached Lahore on 20 December. He stayed twelve days at Lahore, and then moved to the residence of the local magistrate' (Seetal 1993 [1945]: 5).

Thus, Seetal places emphasis on historical data (using the western calendar) and the wider historical circumstances of Deep Singh's action in the context of waning Muslim rule in the Punjab. We do not find this preoccupation with historical data in Gukewalia's text. Significantly, the only place where Gukewalia provides the reader with such data is in his preface where he uses the Vikram calendar (beginning with the Vikram era 57 BCE). Seetal's zeal for history is by no means restricted to this particular composition. In most of his other texts we find a similarly detailed account of places, names, and historical data.

Seetal situates the character Baba Deep Singh within the historical discourse he has provided thus far. Baba Deep Singh takes centre stage exactly at the moment when the Afghan ruler returns to Punjab. The latter had allegedly committed the sacrilege of destroying the Harmandir Sahib in Amritsar in the absence of Sikh defence. The initial moment is formulated as a motif of betrayal. Baba Deep Singh, in Seetal's rendering by that time the leader (*jatthedār*) of a Sikh *misl* (military squad), is informed about the attack on Amritsar. His rage is dramatically invoked in a passage in which the prosaic narrative gives way to a poetical song-recitation.

(*prasaṅga*)	(episode [oratory])
Eh suṇ ke sherāṃ de dil bhaṛak uṭhe. Ikk toṃ dūjā pahilāṃ shahīdī prāpt karaṇ wāste ti'ār sī. Sabh talwārāṃ pūh ke ti'ār ho ga'e. Turan toṃ pahilāṃ Bābā Dīp Singh ne dhartī te lik wic khic ke ik vār pher lalkār ke kihā:—	When the Sikhs heard this, they got enraged. Everyone was ready to be martyred. They held their swords ready for attack. Before they moved out, Baba Deep Singh drew a line on the earth and once again challenged his companions.
Sākā	*Sākā* [poetic recitation]
lik mār ke dīp singh khanḍha lishkāwe bole: agge līk toṃ uh sūra āwe jis nūn maut kabūl hai, dil nahīṃ ḍulāwe purza kaṭṭ mare nahīṃ kanḍ wikhāwe māre teghāṃ siddhī'āṃ sidhe mūnh khāwe holī kheḍe khūn dī 'Sītal' rang lāwe	Drawing a line, Deep Singh raised his sword and said: Only he should cross this line, who embraces death, and whose heart would not be flattering Who would cut the enemy in pieces, and would not show his back, Who would attack them with swords when facing their eyes, Who would play holi with blood says Seetal (ibid.: 8).

The poetic recitation is indexed as sākā. In the typical form of dhadi song-recitation, verbal aspects of performance and musical accompaniment are combined in each performance to complex poetical-musical patterns. We find the combination of verbal aspects of performance and different musical-poetical genres in all of Seetal's written documents. In this respect, Seetal does not discard the epic style of dhadi performance. Gukewalia and Seetal have reprinted their texts in a way in which it seems in accordance with the oral delivery of the tradition.[23] Narrative sections in prose are each in turn followed by musical-poetical genres such as vār, sākā, baiṃt. The sākā is a traditional genre that is associated with discourses of martyrdom. In the form of print dissemination, the naming of the poetic stanzas thus conveys metacommunicative messages that are informed by the way such topics are received aesthetically.

There are also striking differences between the two texts, manifest in topical arrangement and reconfiguration of oratory styles of dhadi performance. Genres, such as the sākā are inserted in Seetal's compositions so that they make sense within the overarching linear historical narrative. He regards the intervention as rhetorician and Sikh historian as necessary to purify the genre of its mythic and folkloristic associations and to provide it with a modern historical language of Sikh qaumik history. The dhadi songs had to be framed by an elaborated historical discourse that left no doubts about the predominance of the Sikhs as the major agents of Punjabi history—defending the country against the onslaught of the 'foreign (Muslim) oppressors'. This emphasis on Sikh history is reflected in the structure of Seetal's compositions in the space given to narrative elaboration. The narrative sections show almost no usage of formulaic expressions. Instead, the reader is confronted with a refined Punjabi vernacular prose that must have appealed to Punjabi audiences.

Seetal's compositions foreshadowed the new hierarchy between oratory and song that has become characteristic for contemporary dhadi performances on the Sikh stage. Much of the persuasiveness and plausibility of dhadi text and performance in the pre-Partition period rested on the particular narrative form of the historical episode or prasaṅga, which was assessed as providing interpretive space through public deliberation. Seetal differentiates his performative style from the 'old style' of Gukewalia.[24] His emphasis on the 'magic of the new style', as he used to call it, was also mediated by an awareness of the power of the dhadi voice and bodily gesture in oratory. A successful orator needed a voice that captured the listeners. The 'sweetness' of voice (*mīṭhī āwāz*) and its intensity (*hek*) were requisites for the 'new' dhadi genre. If the actual forms of representation and persuasion are decisive for the process through which public reasoning is defined, then it is necessary to discuss the particularities of dhadi style and rhetoric in more detail. I would like to take up this issue in the remaining section of the chapter.

Retaining the Dramatic Style

One of the dramatic peaks in the composition on Baba Deep Singh is the internal dialogue with his destiny at the moment of declaring his willingness to become a shahid. In both compositions, we find a similar constellation of different voices being positioned against each other—a powerful divine agent in the form of fate or death, and Baba Deep Singh. In both versions, the dialogue between Baba Deep Singh and 'destiny' is staged before a large gathering of Sikh followers. In Gukewalia's older version, this dialogue is presented in differently nuanced sākā tunes. It is introduced by a recitation of the events leading to the scene in which the hero is confronted with his destiny (*hoṇī*), showing her arrogance by posing as the superior agent:

tarz sākā maṭṭi'āṃ	Sākā (*maṭṭiā'n* style)
(sawāl hoṇī)	(questioning by destiny)
kahī hoṇī gall hunkār dī,	Says hoṇī, I do not tolerate
maiṃ nahīṃ saindī siṅghā	such arrogance, Singh.
ik ishāre khūn dī,	Just one indication
nain waiṅhdī siṅghā	And a river of blood will flow, Singh;
dal dal suṭdi dalān nūṃ,	Crushed to pieces will be the group
jad paindī singhā	When trouble begins, Singh;
maiṃ pīh pīh kite sūrmeṃ,	I grinded the heroes
ji'ūn maiṅhdī siṅghā,	Like henna leaves, Singh;
jo'e chaṛdī kalā je kisse dī,	You might be blessed with courage
phir ḍhaiṅhdī siṅghā	But things can turn, Singh;
maiṃ bhīsham droṇa	Like Bhisham, Drona and Karana,
karan jahe,	Whom I have taken Singh.
raṇ laiṅhdī siṅghā	Your goal will not be accomplished
tera pūrā paraṇ nā howegā,	I am telling you, Singh.
maiṃ tainūṃ kaiṅhdī siṅghā	

(jawāb bābā dīp siṅgh jī)
(tarz sākā)

ki'ā singh ne hoṇi'e, maiṃ sacc suṇāwāṃ
tūṃ kītī'ān ute jagg de, lakkhām ghaṭnawāṃ
tūṃ māre puuraṇ bhagat ka'ī, baih rauwan māwāṃ
tūṃ mazūmān ton khuh la'ī'ām, māvāṃ di'āṃ chhāvāṃ
tere māre hoṇī'en, rulde vic rāwāṃ
maiṃ kagalīdhar da singh han, shaunh udī thāwāṃ
paihlāṃ āpṇe mārāṃ ton maiṃ harimaṅdar jāwāṃ
bheṭā āpṇe sīs dī, darbār jhaṛāvāṃ

(answer of Baba Deep Singh)
(tune sākā)

The Singh said: Let me tell you the truth, honī;
You have caused many incidents in this world.
You killed people like Puran-Bhagat,
Leaving the mourning mothers [there] behind, weeping.
You snatched the innocents,
Despite the wishes of their mothers
Your intervention caused desolation, honī;
I am a Singh of Guru Gobind's following,
I swear by him
Before dying, I shall reach Harmandir,
Offering my head before the throne
(Gukewalia 1964: 10–11).

Various mythological characters appear in this piece: Bhisham, Drona, and Karna from the Mahabharata as well as Puran Bhagat, the figure of a popular Punjabi oral epic. Honī is addressed as the powerful agent of death and destruction. Baba Deep Singh's voice is challenging the divine agent. The moral legitimacy of divine intervention is rejected and set against the authority of Guru Gobind Singh. This could certainly be read as a deliberate method of contrasting Hindu and Sikh cosmologies. Both are linked with each other at the plane of mythology, but kept separate as sources of self-assertion and normative orientation. And yet, they seem to sneak in the terminology.

We find this element of contrasting cosmological orders replicated in Seetal's text. There are some striking differences, however. Destiny (hoṇī) is replaced by the Urdu word for death (*maut*), which does not bear the same connotation that hoṇī does (even though death remains the female voice in the encounter). On the narrative plane, there is a perceptible move from formulaic recitation to a reflexive and self-conscious style. Instead of adding up ten poetic compositions in the fashion of Gukewalia's text, Seetal's text condenses the dialogue into three verbal exchanges and introduces a new form of oral presentation called *jhok* (swinging motion). The presentation is also self-reflexive to the extent that the dialogue between Baba Deep Singh and death is introduced as the characteristic facet of a poet's exchange (*mushairā*):

Ih sun ke maut taṛaph ūṭhi. Tasswar hai sha'ir da. Ik pāse maut, ik pāse bābā dīp singh, āmho-sāmhne sawāl jawāb karde han.	Hearing this, death fluttered. This is the conception of the poet. There is death on one side and Baba Deep Singh on the other, facing each other in a question and answer game.
jhok	Jhok
maut— *(sun ke gall singh dī bolī maut vaṅgār ke)* *ūṭhi'ā tūṃ nawāṃ sūrmāṃ, tegh sanwār ke* *rolaṅgī praṇ maiṃ tere, rāh de wic mār ke* *ajj takk ko'ī gi'ā nā singhāṃ maiṃūṃ lalkār ke* *na bannh tūṃ dāi'e kūṛ de tur ja'inga hār ke* *ū, nā bannh tūṃ dāī'e khālsā*	death— (Hearing the Singh, death revealed itself) Arisen have you, new hero, holding your sword I shall destroy your life, kill you on the way, Until today no Singh has dared to challenge me; Do not be too sure, your defeat is guaranteed Khalsa, make up your mind.
Dīp Singh— *(dīp sing bole aggon roh de wic āṇ ke)* *lāuni'e makkhā kahnūṃ singhāṃ de nāl jāṇ ke* *sakda nahīṃ rok dhāram rāj, āp wī āṇ ke* *jisde wall satigur uhnūṃ kauṇ dabāwegā* *singh dā ardāsa kītā, toṛ nibh jawegā* *ū, kite praṇ toṛ nibhaṇage*	Deep Singh— (Deep Singh answered in rage) Why do you intentionally strike your head against the Singhs? Dharam Raj in person could not stop us. Who could suppress those who have *satguru* on their side? The Singh who completes the *Ardas* will not be left alone, The promise made will be fulfilled (Seetal 1983: 10).

In Seetal's compositions, protagonists are not only staged dramatically in dialogical interaction with their fellows, enemies, or divine agents, they also appeal directly to the reader-listener. The divine and heroic figures speak dramatically to a present audience; they voice their determination to fight, die, and to endure pain as members of the Sikh community. Once again, we get a glimpse at how the new format of dhadi performance operates on different structural and performative planes, discarding certain features (what Seetal considered the 'epic feel' of the more traditional compositions) and reinforcing other genre characteristics. The rhetorical form of the play of *ṣawāl-jawāb* is frequently used, not just in Seetal's texts. It is not always cast in a particular poetic form; he often uses it in the prasaṅga.

Let me illustrate this by reference to another popular dhadi tract: in a composition in which the original kirtan singers (the rababis) are portrayed, the voice of Guru Arjan Dev is set against Sikh followers who are reluctant or even unwilling to acknowledge these low-caste singers as equal members of the sangat (Seetal 1998 [n.d.]). Here, the dilemma of overcoming caste boundaries within the Sikh community is not merely a question of following the doctrine formulated by the Guru (in this case Guru Arjan Dev). As proposed in the composition, it involves a process in which the actual evocative power of the singers to induce rasa in the participants of the liturgy has to be first recognized by the sangat to be spiritually liberating. This recognition would ultimately lead to the transformation of inherited lifestyles and social distinctions, which, according to the text, were causes for the singer's miserable condition (ibid.: 19–20). The efficacy of such rhetorical devices, therefore, not only rests on the projection of deeply felt self-images but also on the portrayal of contrasting moral world views that account for a process of decision making. As the issue of 'the historical recognition of low caste musicians' suggests, the sangat needs to be persuaded about the claims of belonging enunciated by the low-caste singer.[25]

Cultural Reflexivity in Performative Practice

In this chapter I have refrained from using a classificatory model that assigns a subaltern status to the realm of bardic performative tradition. My discussion has provided some evidence that presumably marginal cultural practices and traditional systems of religious and cultural knowledge transmission were in fact intrinsic to processes of identity formation in the early twentieth-century Punjab. The performers did not aim at forming a subaltern counter-public, nor does it make sense to see in their agenda a reappropriation of orthodox representations through which a particular low-caste identity would be reaffirmed, in the way Gyan Prakash has demonstrated in his thoughtfully written paper on the Bhuinyas.[26] However, I have delineated a process of cultural reflexivity that has become manifest in dhadi performers' interventions in the inherited repertoire of representational languages.

Let me clarify at this point while concluding the chapter that the emphasis on self-reflexivity in performative practice is not meant to let the notion of free will and rational choice enter through the backdoor, simply because this would be required for writing a coherent historiography according to the principles of Enlightenment discourse. The way in which figures like Baba Deep Singh come to be entailed in the unfolding of history, has to do with larger cultural schemes that are generated through habitual forms of engaging in the world as well as with modes of reflexivity. If dhadi performers dramatize Baba Deep Singh as a prominent model of sacrifice and supernatural agency, it poses certain challenges on the writing of minority history in the way Dipesh Chakravarty (2000) has suggested.

Does this mean, however, that, in portraying an interpretive and emancipatory process, I have given too much credit to certain evaluations of individual voice and agency instead of recognizing the performer's submission to powerful discursive strictures? If the larger forces that have shaped the agenda of these men and women are rooted in cosmological orders, then is the notion of cultural reflexivity rather negligible? And does all this imply, as Chakravarty would have it, that we accept the difference of the subaltern agenda as a dialogic voice, even if our own methods of rationalization cannot do otherwise than see Baba Deep Singh, the decapitated warrior, as a figure of mythological status?

My impression is that, without clearly delineating the processes through which subalterns construct and convey such complex forms of agency, we are left with an even more problematic vision of cultural theory that naturalizes the relationship between subaltern identity and religious belief. Chakravarty's insights in the project of writing minority history are extremely valuable, but he runs the risk to lose sight of the various social and discursive connections that make some of these articulations of otherness on the side of the marginalized possible. Without claiming to have solved this problem, my discussion of dhadi vernacular texts indicates that, even though bardic performers situate themselves within a cyclic history of Sikh heroism and martyrdom, it is through particular forms of performative practice and voice that others need to be persuaded about the historical and social validity of certain claims to (supernatural) power.

In this process, much depends on how discourses of accountability and responsibility are projected through performative media upon a specific historical scenario in which audiences find themselves implicated in their everyday lives. It is intriguing to note that people who are usually said to stand apart from elite, intellectual discourse and its modes of historical rationalization have creatively, if selectively, made use of some these rationalizations to articulate alternative notions of historical agency. The image of Baba Deep Singh, the decapitated warrior, therefore has a double location: as the fragmented body it epitomizes what Chakravarty called the 'anthropologicization of historical discourse' (producing differences between subaltern belief and intellectual discourse). Yet in a second and ironic twist, the image exemplifies the transgression of these boundaries in making historical discourse a tool for an alternative project of chronicling and canonizing Sikh history.

Notes

1. Fuchs argues:

   Scheint Chatterjee zunächst die sozialontologische Aufspaltung in zwei Sozialprinzipien zu unterlaufen, indem er sie direkter zueinander in Verbindung setzt und ins Innere des subalternen Bewutseins und der religiösen Bewußtseinssysteme verlagert, so substantialisiert er sie andererseits als eine interne Dichotomie nicht vermittelter und nicht vermittelbarer Modi des Weltzugangs (Intellekt verus Sensualität). In der analytischen Schärfe bisweilen hilfreich, bleibt dabei verborgen, wie Handelnde mit dieser inneren Spannung umgehen und wie diese Spaltung überwunden werden soll' (1999).
2. See the debate between Robinson (1979) and Brass (1979) as an outstanding example of this exchange of arguments.
3. What is predicated here is a neat distinction between elite reform agendas and syncretist practices of the subalterns. While historical agency comes with the former, cultural authenticity belongs to the latter. Oberoi's study is informed by a romanticist view of a pre-modern or pre-colonial 'community consciousness' that functions as a valorized counterpoint of modernity. This line of thought has been instrumental to a broad range of writing in the subaltern school. For more on this point see, Sarkar (2000).
4. See for instance Pandey (1991).
5. By that time, the Sikh shrines were administered by so-called *mahant*s. Some of these administrators were accused of having misused the shrines for entertaining courtesans or gambling. Because the mahants enjoyed the protection and support of the colonial government, the protest movement acquired strong anti-colonial connotations. The movement succeeded in a major breakthrough in colonial legislation. With the Sikh Gurdwara and Shrines Act of 1925, a corporate social body, The Shiromani Gurdwara Prabhandak Committee (SGPC), was established to administer the Sikh shrines, which were hence out of the purview of colonial control.
6. I am fully aware of the potential slippages in reading an autobiographic text as historical narrative. In this chapter I have carefully filtered out

those sections that contain information about the performer's background and certain events in his life. Most of these I could verify in the course of my field research during conversations with some of Seetal's contemporaries within and outside the dhadi community. A further exploration of autobiography as a narrative genre is presented in Chapter 4. For further biographical information see also Sandhu 1997.

7. *Pūran Bhagat*, *Hīr Rānjhā*, and *Sohnī Mahīwāl* are explicitly mentioned as the first stories he enjoyed listening to in childhood. Constituting the core of Punjabi folklore, these legends were transmitted by dhadi singers. They were also available in literary form. Daljinder Singh (1980) mentions Qadir Yar's version of *Puran Bhagat*, *Sohni Mahiwal*, and *Raja Rasalu* as three examples that were sung by dhadis as early as in the eighteenth century.
8. The *Udāsi*s form a sect within the broader framework of the Sikh religion. They are genealogically related to Guru Nanak's first son, who did not inherit the office of the Guru. Seetal (1983: 69) states in reference to the saint: 'He made me eloquent and provided the elementary knowledge (*uhnū maimnūṃ muḍhlā akhar-giyān ditā sī*)'.
9. Thus, Seetal says: 'In the village mirasis recited songs of praise at weddings. They were the best resource for any family's genealogy (*Pindāṃ wic mirāsī te sāmhsī, viāh śādī sameṃ 'kalāṅ' kari'ā karde san'. Kise ghar dī bansāwalī dī jāṅkārī bāre ih sabh toṃ changā sādhan sī*)' (1983: 13). Note that one of his novels has a village *mīrasī* as one of its main protagonists (Seetal 1972).
10. Sikh hagiography records these traditional bards in the figure of Mardana, one of the close disciples of Guru Nanak.
11. '*Maiṃ janāṃ toṃ hī dārmik khi'ālāṃ dā hāṃ.... Maiṃ sāthī'āṃ nūṃ kihā: 'Maiṃ tuhāḍā ā'i'āṃ dā mān kardā hāṃ. Par tussī jande ho ki maiṃ ehe jehe bāhar de gaun waliāṃ nūṃ suṅaṇ wī kade nahīṃ gi'ā. So nāṭak manḍalī wic maiṃ tuhāde sāth nahīṃ de sakdā*' (1983: 113).
12. Ironically, this verse is cited from one of Seetal's own 'folk' compositions (Seetal 1962b).
13. '*Mere vīr! Maiṃ tera dhanwādī hāṃ. Tūṃ maiṃnūṃ ik navī sedh ditī hai. Tūṃ maiṃnūṃ gurū ghar dā ḍhāḍī nahīṃ samjhi'ā, sagoṃ ik 'gaun vālā' hī samjhi'ā hai. Maiṃ ajj toṃ praṇ kardā hāṃ, kī maiṃ jañ sāmṇe khalo ke kade kirtan nahīṃ karāṅgā, bhāv vi'āh 'te nahīṃ jāwāṅgā*' (Seetal 1983: 130).
14. After all, he became a literary person writing novels and popular tracts on Sikh history and even had his own little publishing press in his Seetal Bhavan in Ludhiana.
15. See Gilmartin (1988b) for a detailed discussion.
16. The role of Urdu poetry in Muslim nationalist discourses is discussed in Devji (1993). A compilation of Babbar Akali poetry can be found in Rae (1998).

The role of the Babbar Akali is not further discussed here. This group of Sikh revolutionaries consisted of disillusioned Gadar activists who resorted to militant means to pursue their struggle. The main representative body of Khalsa Sikhs officially denounced the methods of assassination by the revolutionaries, either because they anticipated a hard line by the British or because it was contrary to their idea of spreading the idea of martyrdom as non-violent.

17. All translations and transliterations of the original Punjabi text are by Michael Nijhawan, unless otherwise indicated. Retroflex consonants are marked with a dot beneath the consonant. Long nasalized vowels are marked by ṃ.
18. As Lou Fenech observed, 'examples of horrific punishment and selfless suffering' by innocent Punjabi people, and 'the emotional appeals that accompanied these, inspired Sikhs to leave their towns and villages en masse and make their way to the Akal Takht' (2000: 231). Another crucial mobilizing factor had been the ceremonial honour given to the governor, who was responsible for the massacre, by the mahant at the Harmandir Sahib. This enraged the Sikh community and led to massive protests in support of the Akalis' attempt to replace the mahants from administrative control. The movement was marked by several events that resulted in the death of many Sikh protesters.
19. Kartar Singh Kalaswalia wrote historical poetry (*itihāsakār kavitā*) and is considered to be among the most popular Singh Sabha writers. See Kasel et al. (1998: 440).
20. See Seetal (1944). Apart from the several dozens of historical lectures written on the dhadi genre, other historical works include Sikh Misls and the Punjabi States (1981) *Merī Itihāsak laikcar* (Ludhiana: Lahore Book Shop, 1980), *Sikh Itihās de some* (Ludhiana: Lahore Book Shop, 1981), *Punjab da Ujāṛā* (Amritsar: Mastar Sher Singh, Khazan Singh, 1948). For a discussion of his literary work see Sandhu 1994.
21. Gukewalia's publishers included a special advertisement on the front page of each booklet. '*Dhāḍīs*', it says 'do not fill their stomach merely by singing, they satisfy by means of episodes (*prasaṅga*) that come with the songs.' Obviously, the publishers anticipated modes of reception that were distinct from what is presented in the booklets.
22. 'At the time when Guru-Ji left Talwandi for Nader, he took some followers along with him and said to Baba Deep Singh, "Deep Singh Ji, you stay here as a *granthī* to serve the *Guru Granth Sahib*, but if our *panth* should face calamities, you will fight the enemy as a warrior (*yodhā jarnail*) and sacrifice yourself to set an example for the grandeur of the *panth*."'
23. I do not argue here that modes of textual production and reception would not be significantly different from those of oral delivery. This is simply to highlight that the text testifies to its specific performative format that,

even in its written form, retains some of the specific features of aesthetic evaluation.

24. 'I wanted to proceed on a somewhat different trajectory [than my predecessors, M.N.]. I began to write down the interpretation that I provided after each song. I have understood the secret [*bhed*] that my magic [*jadu*] lies in new style of oratory, not in singing. Thus after every performance I used to write the whole lecture. In this manner I could complete *Sītal Kiraṇā* that consisted of one hundred pages...I followed a totally new style of interpretation [*viākhyā dā ḍhang*]. I would link history with current events and put a mark [*cannā*] on the problems of past and the present. I also used to talk about other religions and histories if required. Audiences appreciated this style very much. I had memorialized many Urdu poems. Tragedy and sorrow I would articulate in poetic verse which stirs the educated mind as well. At the same time I invented some new tunes [*tarzāṃ*]. *Panja Sāhib dī gaḍḍī* for instance became very famous' (Seetal 1983: 148). Translated by Michael Nijhawan.
25. I have observed situations in which these internal differences were put to completely different ends as those articulated in Sikh reformist discourses. Reading Seetal's dhadi tracts one is equally perplexed about how differently he employs such discourses. As I argue in Chapter 4, his presentations are fully supportive of Sikh nationalist claims in the 1930s and mutually opposed to political claims after the Partition in 1947. The representational language of Sikh heroic values, however, remains the same.
26. Writing about the oral epics of outcaste Bhuinya in highland Orissa, eastern India, Prakash (1991) argues that a mere focus on discursive and narrative analysis is insufficient to account for the appeal and transformative power of Bhuinya forms of historical representation. He demonstrated convincingly that the caste hierarchy that positioned Bhuinya as a subordinate group was not, as one might have expected, inversed or mirrored in storytelling performances but mimetically inscribed in their cultural heroes and thus employed in the drama of historical presentation as a form of self-empowerment. In Prakash's rendering, the enacted drama of the Bhuinya heroic past has to be understood as a process of mimesis: 'In participating in this process, the oral traditions neither spoke from, nor envisioned, a field free of power. But while speaking the language of hierarchy and dependent relations, they made it dissonant, thus turning the subordinated existence of the Bhuinyas into something different' (ibid.: 147).

4

The Event as Monument

Reading Sākā Shahidganj

In this chapter I want to concentrate on martyrdom, space, and representation.[1] Discourses on martyrdom work in specific ways to map an interpretive space for social action that is particularly powerful in situations in which spatial forms of ritual worship intersect with political agendas of collective representation. Mythology, claims to cultural and religious heritage, and territorial ritual can be approached as an important nexus of cultural signification in that respect. South Asian history offers genuine perspectives on the transaction between these spatial practices and spaces of representation. Pilgrimages, processions, and various forms of shrine veneration are so widespread that their capacity to mobilize and tie people emotionally to representational sites has not been missed by the major historical protagonists. As I want to argue in this chapter, the manner in which these spaces have been configured are not epiphenomenal to the process of identity formation and conflict. They are, in fact, crucial to an understanding of how people's subjectivities are formed under historical conditions in which the experience of violence assumes a crucial role. This can be clearly discerned in the following discussion of the 1935 Shahidganj incident and the ensuing antagonisms between Muslim and Sikh organizations in the pre-Partition years.

Shahidganj and the Sikh Martyr

Today, the site 'Shahidganj' (literally: treasure or site of martyrs) is visible as a historic Sikh gurdwara that is administered by Pakistani Sikhs and protected as a monument of the religious minority community in Pakistan. Located at the outskirts of the old city, it seems lost in Lahore's urban landscape. It does not convey the significance it acquired when, in the mid-1930s, at a peak of communal politics in colonial Punjab, it hauled Sikh and Muslim agitators to its precincts. The history of the site up to that phase of colonial politics can be sketched very briefly.[2] The mosque was built in the early eighteenth century, that is, in the late phase of Mughal rule in Punjab. Soon afterwards, it came under Sikh control when they gained political power in 1762. The mosque was then closed, because in the eyes of the Sikhs it stood for the atrocities that they had been subjected to at the hand of Mughal and Afghan authorities. The site remained under Sikh control even after a Muslim had claimed his hereditary rights as a *muttawali* to the mosque in the mid-nineteenth century (Gilmartin 1988a: 149; Noorani 2001). The issue only resurfaced during the 1920s and 1930s when Shahidganj became the subject of a legal and political battle between the Muslim Anjuman Islamia and the Sikhs represented by the SGPC. In the course of this legal battle and the political agitations that it entailed, the mosque was destroyed in July 1935 by Sikhs, who perceived it as their obligation to make the site a monument of their history of collective suffering. The destruction of the mosque and subsequent construction of a Sikh gurdwara on the same spot led to the scaling up of agitations and violence in Lahore, until in 1938 the issue was settled in a final court case that denied the Muslim side its rights of access (Masjid Shahid Ganj vs SGPC AIR 1938 Lahore 369).

The contest over Shahidganj is significant for a variety of reasons. It was one of the major incidents in the prelude to Partition in which the major religious communities consolidated themselves in staking out claims over the past and territory. As the dispute figured prominently in the public sphere, be it through agitation, legal battle, or in the agenda of the Punjab Assembly, it lends itself to an examination of the relationship between colonial legislation and religious identity formation in South Asia in the way it has been suggested by Gilmartin and others.[3] The Shahidganj incident can be studied comparatively in that regard, which does not mean, however, that it can be simply equated with the contemporary dispute around the Ayodhya mosque and the aggressive anti-Muslim rhetoric with which the Hindu right poses its claim in an independent Indian state. Most notably, the Shahidganj incident highlights the disputed character of territorial sites as spaces of representation. While in its decision to refuse the claims of the Muslim waqf board the colonial legislation did not distinguish between different forms of private property—claimed as sacred or not—the way in which the public contest over the side was structured, testifies to the sacrosanct character of Shahidganj as a revered space that became the focus of debate and negotiation. As I have argued in the introduction to this chapter, the question that I am foremost interested in has to do with the relationship between discourses of martyrdom and performative practices through which such discourses are mapped on this disputed site, thus creating a new imaginary landscape of national and religious belonging.[4]

In the context of the Shahidganj incident, the pervasive power of Sikh discourses of martyrdom stands out clearly. The rhetoric of martyrdom defined the form the agitation took on both sites of the contest. Sikhs and Muslims alike mobilized around sacrificial discourses and at the peak of the agitation both sides regarded Shahidganj as the materialized proof of their respective claims. Significantly, however, the Sikh struggle could be seen as an extension of their previous and successful attempt to regain control of the major gurdwaras from the administrative control of the colonial government, whereas the different Muslim organizations and representatives who were involved in the struggle had to realize that the evocative force of the martyr discourse was rather short-lived. According to Gilmartin (1988: 163) the realization of internal disputes and disagreements led to the failure of the agitation in the name of the mosque. This in turn helped to bring forth a new idiom of Muslim nationalism: the claim for an independent state.

In the light of the theoretical elaborations provided above, therefore, one of the interesting issues lies in the differences and similarities in which Islamic and Sikh discourses of martyrdom have helped to consolidate group boundaries around notions of territorial belonging. The shahid is a figure that is employed in Sikh and Muslim political discourses to mark the boundaries of each community as exclusive in relation to the other and yet, at the same time, it is a figure that entails a common horizon of religious discourse as well as a shared habitus of ritual practice. It is a rather undisputed fact that the institutionalization of saint veneration in rural Punjab has played into the making of such a habitus as it had been common practice to participate in the other community's major festivals and thus to penetrate sacred space. The Shahidganj incident testifies to this shared habitus, but it also indicates that under the particular circumstances of the early twentieth century, Sikhs rallied far more consistently behind symbols of martyrdom and collective sacrifice than Muslim communities. To better understand this difference, one has to consider what in a Sikh perspective constitutes the central features of martyrdom and why these features were so effective in spurring Sikh popular support on a translocal level.

The Sikh tradition maintains that the concept of martyrdom (*śahīdī* or *śahādat*) is given expression in the deaths of two of their gurus, Guru Arjan and Guru Tegh Bahadur, as well as in a number of heroic martyrs who gave their lives in the period of the early to mid-eighteenth century where some of the worst memories of persecution are located. These memories are connected to places such as Shahidganj. The presence of historic martyrs in Sikh popular consciousness is hardly astonishing, as this history has been transmitted through hagiographic sources as well as Punjabi vernacular literature. It is also commemorated in the daily Ardas prayer as a part of Sikh liturgy. These repetitive acts of commemoration have normalized historical discourses on Sikh martyrdom in a way in which they become generically fused with spiritual concepts expressed in Sikh gurbani. The representation of the ideal principle of martyrdom is based on a hymn composed by Guru Nanak. In this hymn the devotee is commanded to approach God with 'the head placed in the palm of his hands'. Considering the place it occupies in the Guru Granth Sahib, this hymn is most certain to be interpreted as a metaphor for the inner struggle of man against egoism, which is seen as a hindrance to divine experience. Sikh tradition, however, regards the chain of gurus as a continuous representation of the divine. Because some of the gurus gave their life in resistance to Mughal rulers, the hymn came to suggest 'real life' volition for martyrdom, a principle that has been followed by many of the Khalsa in Guru Gobind Singh's following. According to this notion, the self is demanded to move beyond its own human constraints in giving priority to the witnessing of truth beyond all self-centredness, even at the cost of subjecting the self to death. An acknowledgement of this willingness to sacrifice is an essential part of the initiation ceremony to the Khalsa. In contemporary discourse, the image of ultimate sacrifice is most popularly depicted in the figure of Baba Deep Singh who, after fighting the Afghan army, marches with his decapitated head in his hands directly to the most sacred place of worship, the Harmandir Sahib in Amritsar.

I need to point out here that there is an ongoing scholarly debate concerning the status of martyrdom in the Sikh tradition, which is too huge a topic to be adequately discussed here. Considering the easy slippages between purely religious discourses of self-sacrifice and their ideological employment by various political actors to legitimize the use of violence, one has to take strong precautions not to take claims of historical continuity at face value.[5] At the same time, it is also important not just to see the problematic side but also the emancipatory elements in Sikh conceptions of martyrdom which, as far as the early twentieth century is concerned, have been widely recognized as pivotal to an understanding of Indian modernity with its specific couching of secularist notions in religious idioms (Madan 1997: 61; Uberoi 1999: 113). In this context, the gurdwara liberation movement in the 1920s that preceded the Shahidganj incident constitutes a mark in history where the non-violent idiom of Sikh martyrdom in fact acquired a sense of self-emancipation under the colonial rule.[6] Launched by the Chief Khalsa Diwan (at that time the representative body of the Khalsa Sikhs) and led as a non-violent struggle, the movement was overtly articulated under the idiom of *śahādat*, as self-proclaimed 'martyrs of the faith' gathered for large pilgrimage marches to historic Sikh gurdwaras (such as the Janam Asthan at Nankana Sahib), demonstrating a willingness to die for the accomplishment of this specific goal.[7] As the objectives of the Akalis became a matter of great concern for the British, who feared far wider repercussions for the legitimacy of indirect rule and reacted with force, people were jailed and a large number of protestors died so that the historical imaginary of Sikh martyrdom became even more concretized. Through its mass support and demonstrative willingness to self-sacrifice, the gurdwara liberation movement not only achieved its final objective in the Sikh Gurdwaras and Shrines Act of 1925 which assigned the Sikhs the administrative control over their shrines and led to the formation of a corporate social body, the SGPC, it was also praised by Gandhi as the first victory of India's freedom struggle (Uberoi 1999: 115).[8]

The movement was initiated neither as an explicit nor a disguised form of nationalist struggle, but the form it took through the re-enactment of practices of self-sacrifice was not missed by the major religious communities in Punjab, as they became more and more entangled in a new discourse of territorial reordering that took on antagonistic forms in the 1930s. In that sense, there had been a significant shift from the 1920s to the years in which the Shahidganj incident took place. This was the year when separate electorates for Muslim, Sikh, and Hindu communities were introduced by the colonial government.[9] It was also the time when ideas about a separation of Punjab's territory emerged on the fringes of political discourse. Notions of territoriality regained their pivotal importance precisely at a moment in which claims to religious sites proved to be effective in gaining a share in power under colonial law.

This nexus was decisive for the self-organization of the Muslim elites, who felt compelled to react to the achievement of the Sikh Gurdwara and Shrines Act of 1925 with their own claims over sacred territory. Gilmartin (1988a: 150), who has examined the Shahidganj case in the light of the Punjabi Muslims' self-understanding, argues that the Gurdwaras and Shrines Act of 1925 'had important implications for the organisation of religious authority within all the Punjab's religious communities. In fact, although it provided the Anjuman Islamia with an opening to press for the return of the Shahidganj mosque, it had also raised important questions about the character of community leadership, not only among the Sikhs but among Muslims as well.'[10] Gilmartin considers the issue of the Shahidganj mosque as significant because it served as a symbol in political agitations that mobilized the urban and subsequently also the rural Muslims across class differences. If, in the end, the movement did not succeed in this bridging of different interests, it still highlighted the mobilizing force of territoriality and self-sacrifice. This became clear when about two weeks after Sikhs demolished the site and started to rebuild it as a gurdwara, an organized crowd of several thousand Muslims gathered in Lahore, trying to force their way to the contested site. As a consequence of the unrest and the deaths that occurred through police shooting, Muslims would claim their own martyrs of Shahidganj. More than that, Shahidganj itself, which by that time 'had struck very close to the heart of urban Muslim communal self-definition' (ibid.: 149), became an agent of the agitation. This was most dramatically expressed in the court case after the demolition of the mosque, which was filed on behalf of Shahidganj as the claimant. In the next section I will further examine how popular practices of public speech and performance have dramatized Shahidganj as such an agent in the history of martyrdom that had clearly shifted from the inclusive idiom of the 1920s to the exclusivist form of the 1930s.

The Performance of Shahidganj

The appearance of the mosque as the representative of the Punjabi Muslim community was an ingenious approach, says Gilmartin, which 'in effect transform[ed] the mosque from a symbol of the community to being the actual representative of the community in court, a reflection with vengeance of the charismatic conception of the community that had largely inspired the agitation' (1988a: 158). This is to say that Shahidganj figured as an agent of collective Muslim interests precisely at the moment in which a rural idiom of Pir-Muridi relations began to shape the agitation. Does this tell us something about the workings of performative language through which Shahidganj was mapped as a new space of representation? And how would the figure of the martyr mediate between the shared habitus of shrine veneration that is predominant in rural Punjab and the exclusivist idiom that sustained the agitations on both sides?[11]

I want to address these questions from the Sikh perspective by reading a dhadi text 'Shahidganj—The tyranny of Mir Mannu and the Faith of the Sikh Ladies' (Seetal 1994 [1942]) that can be found in Appendix 1 in this book.[12] I examine this text so that it will be possible to draw some conclusions as to how popular notions of martyrdom inserted themselves on people's minds in the given period. I shall argue that the emotional attachment to sacred territory as a pivotal site of moral reinforcement entailed a hidden recognition of the shared habitus of shrine veneration as it temporarily informed the Muslim agitation as well. The exclusivist rhetoric and an underlying assumption about a homogeneous bloc out of which the Sikh community was formed notwithstanding, the rhetoric of martyrdom and territorial supremacy shares many similarities with what could be heard on the platform of Muslim politics in Lahore. At the discursive level of the dhadi text, one could even speak of a reappropriation of selected Muslim discourses by Sikh orators.

The orientation to the other community's model of historical legitimacy and moral authority is clearly indicated in the very first lines of the dhadi composition when the text begins with praises of the martyrs ('Martyrs live forever. They appeal to the living ones and teach them the lesson of perfection'). The voice of the orator directly appeals to the reader-listener who finds himself on an imaginary itinerary to Lahore. The text does not name the place in the first instance, but the allusion to the Shi'ite Karbala tradition powerfully indexes what is at stake in the given episodes.[13] As it was composed and delivered in 1935, the text assumes background information regarding the contested status of the site. It is only at the end of the first song that the author names Shahidganj explicitly ('This is our Shahidganj, in which not one, two, ten, nor thousand, but two or three lakh heads of the Sikhs lie buried. Every little inch of this earth is drenched with our blood').

In the song-texts there remains little doubt whatsoever that the site Shahidganj would constitute a living testimony to the violent deaths the Sikhs suffered there ('This is not a mound of dead bones [*murda haḍḍi'ā*]; in it are many sons [*lāl*] alive'). The song engenders a vivid memory of agony and martyrdom, as scenes of torture are pictured drastically ('many ascended the wheel [*charkhṛī*] laughing', 'some embraced the hot iron', or 'they saw their sons hung on long spears [*nezi'āṃ*]'). Thus carving out a mass grave in the topography of Sikh memory, the claim on Shahidganj is clearly set. The text is very moving and appealing. Its tone of sorrow and pain is strongly evocative. The songs embellish dramatic points in the story, whereas the oratory sections are interspersed with descriptions and idioms portraying the Sikhs as virtuous and brave, resisting forced conversion to Islam.

The grid through which the narrative is structured is indicated in the contrast between maternal love and sacrifice on the one hand, and the Mughal torture wheel on the other ('such mothers would be under these, who saw their fondest ones [*tāre nainā de*] massacred', 'they got made pieces of their beloved children [*dil de ṭukaṛi'ā karvā'e tukṛe*']. Heroic similes among other rhetorical tropes underline this gendered imagery. The prevalence of women's sacrifice in the absence of portrayals of male resistance is quite astonishing. As I have argued in Chapter 3, it might be due to Seetal's attentiveness to the female side of the tradition that he consciously structured the composition in this way. Indeed, there are poetic genres in this text which are rather uncommon on the dhadi stage, such as the chand diund, which is a component of wedding ceremonies, or the shambu-shambu, a lullaby. The lullaby is particularly powerful as it couches the grief of mothers for their tortured children in song aesthetics that convey the deepest sense of intimacy and maternal love. Beyond the author's preferences that might have informed this kind of gendered language, however, it is also clear that the collective sense of injustice and humiliation thus dramatized must have been widely acknowledged for its emotive power.

In the last part of the dhadi composition there is a deliberate shift from the depicted past of suffering to the present context of the demolished site. The oratory section that begins with the *ghazal* recitation ('On the pyres of martyrs fairs will be held every year. These will be the lasting memories of martyrs [*vatan pahī miṇne vāle*]') has descriptions of the demolition of the mosque ('On one side the outside foundation was being dug out and on the other side the [new] wall was coming up.

On that day I saw Sikhs performing devotional services with dedication'). Shahidganj is never referred to as a mosque and the event is portrayed as reconstruction rather than an act of destruction. For the first time, the author uses the first person pronoun when speaking about Shahidganj ('In the year 1935 the old building [*imārat*] of Shahidganj was being demolished for construction of the new surrounding wall; the devotional services that I saw at that time, will continue to shine in our consciousness (*sadā ātmā vic jhalkdā rohegā'*). In the main part of the composition such references would not appear; the true claims would be located in the mytho-historical sources rather than the author's voice. The shift to the first person voice at the end of the text, however, is ingenious as it enables the dhadi subject to locate himself as a witness of this history.

The text ends with poetic lines, in which the dialogic relationship between author/performer and reader/listener is given another interesting note. The reader is confronted with a verbal image (*śabdī tasvīr*) that delineates the itinerary to Shahidganj and the drama of its reconstruction. Shahidganj is being dug out from ruins while the Sikh past of selfless service is re-enacted in the work of the volunteers. [14] The pain of tortures in the past ('Chopped into pieces by the tyrant in the laps of mothers, laying the heads of many sincere [ones], whose heads were being sold, on the bazars of Muslim law') are mapped upon the contemporary scene of restoration. The effect of this conflation of temporal horizons is increased through the insertion of the orator's voice as the imaginary interlocutor at Shahidganj. There he meets the counterpart of the historic martyr in the old woman who is engaged in carrying bricks for the new gurdwara. The ensuing dialogue once more depicts the Punjabi woman's model of self-sacrifice as the seva for the Sikh qaum. The dramatization of martyrdom in this text resonates in most of the other texts that I have consulted, as becoming a shahīd does not occur by mere circumstance but by consenting to one's God-given destiny.

In summary, we can say that at the time of the Shahidganj incident, the performance of Sikh history on the dhadi stage was critical to the expansion of the Sikh qaum over urban-rural differences. While Muslims had turned the Shahidganj mosque into a prosecutor of a court case, the site is dramatized as an agent in a different trial on the dhadi stage. There, with the likeness of judicial and historical evidence, a persuasive claim for Sikh ownership had already been made. Interpreted in this fashion, the dhadi composition situates the addressees in clear relation and in moral obligation to the Sikh cause as against the Muslim side. The mediating role of the dhadi text lies in its capacity to transform the site of Shahidganj into a concretized memory of the Sikhs' vulnerable past. It operates in this manner as a strong reminder for contemporary political claims. It needs to be stressed that the dramatic imagery depicted in the paragraphs above achieves its vividness and efficacy exactly at the moment when a strong sense of place and territorial belonging is given expression on the political platform. For Sikhs this sense of place and belonging was particularly critical at a time when talks about new political and religious demarcations included debates over a separation of Punjab's territory. With Sikhs being demographically in a minority, claims to the past and to origins were significant resources to legitimize claims to territory and political power. As we have seen, this concern was by no means restricted to the sphere of the political and religious elites.

Representation and Violence

One of the striking points in the composition examined above is the manner through which the persuasiveness of Sikh claims is grounded in the moral authority of the martyr as the witness to historical truth. The issue of martyrdom was at the core of Sikh dhadi discourses in the late colonial period. The memory of Sikh martyrdom is spatialized in the history of Shahidganj, a site where the collective fate of the Sikhs was acted out through sacrificial acts. Consequently, Shahidganj could not be allowed the name of a mosque, and Muslim claims in that matter were to be opposed with determination. One of the troubling questions to ask here concerns the intricate relationship between the self and other in making such exclusive claims. As we have to assume that the moulding of a new idiom of martyrdom into the Punjabi vernacular informed some of the cultural attitudes to violence before and during Partition, it is worthwhile to think about how this relationship is apprehended through the very structure of performative form. To further examine this issue, let me turn to a text that will play a critical role in the subsequent chapter as well. It is a compilation of poetic writings by the same author who has composed the Shahidganj text. In this pre-Partition collection *Vahiṅde Hanjūṃ* ('Pouring Tears', Seetal 1962b [1940]: 32–4) we find another text on Shahidganj, a poem that was also written around 1935–6. I will discuss a few couplets in which the contested character of the Shahidganj issue is made very explicit:

Whenever *Śahīdganj* is remembered,
The blood of the Sikhs shall begin to boil [*sikkhī khūn wic ik ubāl āve*],
The mind/inner life shall surge up
And thoughts shall be shaken by an earthquake.
Bīr rasa shall engender a state of mind
So that fire will be flickering in the eyes [*netar agg ḍolhaṇ*].[15]

This paragraph moves around the emotive power of the shahīd. It is not necessarily the calm state of mind attributed to those Sikhs who were said to have triumphed over inflicted pain, but an idiom of anger and rage that is accompanied by an overarching sense of loss and mourning. We find here the popularized idea of the rasas through which most contemporary Sikh dhadi would express the transformative capacity of dhadi performance.[16] The naturalization of this discourse on martyrdom results, first of all, in an attribution of emotional states to the objectified status of memory: the memory of martyrs produces ardent states of mind. This is interesting, first of all, because we have seen that the dhadi text on Shahidganj is not very strong in creating bīr rasa. On the contrary, the dominating tone is that of sorrow and grief: 'Don't mourn as the fresh wound will bleed again', we hear in one of the dhadi lyrics, but still 'the eyes cannot stop weeping.' In contrast to the dhadi lyrics, the poem cited here invests the dominant idiom of Sikh sacrifice with a different aesthetic of martyrdom and violence, one that, ironically, may have been expected to be found in the dhadi text and not in the Punjabi poem with its many borrowings from the Urdu vernacular. Thus, we read in another stanza:

Like a moth that is attracted by the flame [*shamhā dī lāṭ*]
Our heroes will sacrifice themselves full of love
Their hearts filled with faith
From tasting amrit and the sweetness [*guṛhtī*] of bīr rasa[17]

Shall the Almighty preserve *Śahīdganj*
The Singhs will not accept its occupation
Each drop [of blood] will be revenged [*ratt ratt toṃ vikegī*], with the same force. Beware Brother!—there will not be any delay.[18]

The metaphor of the moth that is attracted by the flame is an ancient motif that can be traced to the Sufi mystic al'Hallaj (Schimmel 1975).

It can also be found in the fifteenth century Hindavi text to which I have referred earlier (Orsini 2004).[19] Popularly, it represents the magnetic relationship between two lovers, but in the context of religious aesthetics it expresses the desire of the devotee to eliminate his ego in the longing for the divine. In the poem, the meaning is further expanded to a worldly engagement with particular others who stake their own claims on the site of Shahidganj. The elixir of life (*amrit*) is Sikh baptism and the taste of bīr rasa would transform the present Sikh hero into a person who would embrace martyrdom in the event of a violent confrontation with Muslim opponents. The impact of religious language is quite strong here, not just in the use of this metaphor. The poem speaks of threats and revenge, of blood and counter-action legitimized through reference to the sacrosanct territory of collective memory.

It is intriguing that the linguistic and poetic forms through which such threads are voiced assume closeness rather than the separation of Sikh and Muslim idioms of martyrdom. Borrowings from Persian and Urdu poetic traditions abound. Allusions to the Muslim Karbala tradition in the dhadi text are also strong cases in point.[20] While on the aesthetic and linguistic level, the shahīd is reconstituted as a figure of shared reverence, the textual message draws a clear separation between the legitimacy of Sikh and illegitimacy of Muslim claims. If it is reasonable to argue that the dhadi tradition played an essential role in the process of Sikh community formation in nineteenth and twentieth century Punjab, the critical issue is in fact the relationship between this kind of fictionalization of difference and the shared grounds of expression in the Punjabi vernacular.

Fictionalization is not just a matter of textual representation; it also pertains to a *cultural logic* of representation in which, in actual circumstances of real life martyrdom, the space of the other is penetrated imaginatively. Gregory Starrett (2004: 40–1) argues in respect to the Hamas or Al Qaida suicide bomber, that fictionalization is part of the cultural logic through which the self-chosen martyr is able to manipulate the space of his victim (by fashioning himself in disguise within the lifeworld of the enemy). 'Fictionalizing another's reality', says Starrett, 'requires one to apprehend its narrative form, if not its content, as similar to one's own' (ibid.: 41). This process of 'self-fashioning' through the fictionalization of the reality of the other amounts to a disembodiment of agency (power is submitted to the larger collective or to divine agency) as well as a threatening of selfhood through the martyr's act of transgression. This seems to be the paradigmatic ambiguity of the sacrificial victim in the sense Girard formulated it (ibid.: 42).

With respect to the texts on Shahidganj, fictionalization is no less problematic, as popular culture helps in creating normative models that guide practical forms of re-enactment. At this level of representation, it indeed becomes very difficult to draw clear boundaries between what one would call a heroic drama of martyrdom that is valued in its own terms and violence as a social and political reality. The very process through which a notion of collective agency is articulated in the popular discourses on Sikh martyrdom already contains a problematic notion of violence. In her discussion of the European medieval rhetorical canon, Jody Enders (1999: 165) has laid strong emphasis on this point. She argues that violence is rather the common case, and not just in the context of medieval liturgical representation: 'One of the most important cultural gestures of delivery', she says, 'is the reconfiguration of violence itself as impersonation, imitation, or representation.' Although dhadi discourses are framed differently under circumstances of colonial politics and public agitations, it is still possible to attribute to the 1935 Shahidganj incident some of the intrinsic problems in the relationship between violence and cultural performance. To the extent that historical subjectivity is ensnared in a cyclic version of historical unfolding in which past and present are visualized as temporarily conjunct rather than separated, dhadi performances were indeed of fundamental importance in the re-enactment of the epic scenario of violence under conditions of territorial nationalism.[21] This observation does not necessarily imply that the relationship between Sikhs, Hindus, and Muslims in the many Punjabi villages was oriented toward mutual exclusion. What we find, however, is that the mass public discourse of urban Punjab becomes translated into rural idioms and discourses in which violence is aestheticized and cultural memory reshaped in exclusivist images. Pradeep Datta has argued that it is of crucial importance to examine how in the late colonial period, 'the religious sphere became imbricated with the institutions and desires of mass struggle (1999: 124).' This is what I have tried to highlight in this chapter by focusing on the representation of martyrdom in the Punjabi vernacular public. The ongoing debate over the genealogy of martyrdom in the Sikh tradition notwithstanding, we find in recent history of the Punjab strong indications of how dhadi representations of martyrdom became a shaping force in consolidating group identities around the dramatized image of Shahidganj.

Broader Comparative Perspective

In modern European history, the Kosovo war features as one of the most puzzling appearances of this intermingling between martyrdom, space, and representation, which in turn has been a focus of scholarly inquiry. Thus, Herscher and Riedlmayer (2000) demonstrate how the contest over cultural heritage in the form of religious monuments instigated a process of ethnicization between Kosovan Serbs and Albanians that was in fact decisive to the outbreak of the civil war. Herscher and Riedlmayer argue that the destruction of Muslim architecture at the hands of the Serbs 'has a unique significance in that it signifies the attempt to target not just the homes and properties of individual members of Kosovo's Albanian population, but that entire population as a culturally defined entity' (ibid.: 112). Likewise Albanian resistance singled out Serbian orthodox churches for destruction. The Kosovo case is indeed relevant, as Serbian nationalist discourses have been permeated with a mythology that, according to Longinovic (1996: 370), demanded Serbian self-sacrifice in exchange for the monumental resurrection of the nation. Longinovic argues that an understanding of the dynamics of violence of the war must begin with a historical analysis of the Kosovo myth and its dramatization of sacrificial acts. Longinovic extracts this history from a range of Serbian historiographic and prosaic writings in which the defeat of the epic heroes at the hand of the Turks is woven into a Serbian martyrology. This has far-reaching implications, for it conflates the temporal horizons between the epic past of sacrificial losts and a present in which the repetition of such humiliation must be avoided by all means (ibid.: 374). Even in the texts of a progressive writer such as Ivo Andric, argues Longinovic, the representation of collective suffering as a timeless and monumental epos sustains a discourse in which 'the victim of history develops a national identity based on loss and suffering, around the story of victimization which can be invoked as a sort of political alibi during struggles with its internal and external "others" (ibid.: 381). Longinovic has an important point when he draws attention to these images of victimization. In his reading of Andric's prosaic writings, he finds that the constellation in which the signifiers of communal and national belonging are posed against the background of epic suffering allow for mutually opposed readings of national myth and monument. In these different readings, the history of hybridization in the Balkans can be evaluated positively as a historical, though fragmented, achievement, or negatively as a history of mutual exclusion and sacrificial crisis in which the other community is blamed for one's own misery.

Longinovic explains the cultural dynamics through which martyr discourses insert themselves on people's minds drawing from René Girard's (1977) theory of mimetic violence. In formulating his influential anthropological paradigm, Girard proposed to examine religious phenomena, specifically religious notions of sacrifice, as direct or indirect responses to the problem of violence that he saw as constitutive for social reproduction. Having in mind clear-cut distinctions between traditional and modern societies, he held a holistic notion of culture and society by assuming that, in traditional societies, sacrifice constitutes the primary ritual act needed to cleanse the community of any feelings of hostility and anger that would threaten the connectedness of the in-group. According to Girard, the central objective of the sacrificial act consists in the purification of violence. Violence is in a way 'tricked' by directing it towards a selected victim (the scapegoat or surrogate victim) that would not cause any further reprisal and thus end the potential cycle of reciprocal violence between two rival communities. The surrogate victim epitomizes the dynamics of mimetic othering as it typically represents ambivalent features, partly those of the enemy and those of one's own. The problem begins, according to Girard, when this form of ritual mimesis fails to contain violence, that is, when the sacrificial or surrogate victim does not succeed in bringing reciprocal violence to an end. This failure would be typical for situations of 'sacrificial crisis' (the disappearance of sacrificial rites coincides with the disappearance of the difference between impure and purifying violence), for Girard a characteristic feature of modern conflict.

Modern scenarios of ethnic and religious violence can indeed be shown to entail meaning horizons in which ideas of sacrificial crisis play an important role. Longinovic's study of Serb nationalist mythology is a strong case in point and scholars working on ethnic conflicts in Europe, South Asia, and the Middle East brought forward similar arguments (Juergensmeyer 2000; Mitchell 1988; Starrett 2004).[22] The material presented in this book suggests that, in Punjab too, we need to consider a deeper cultural dynamic of self-recognition and abnegation that has informed communal violence in the region. It seems to me, however, that the Girardian framework with its holistic and psychological metaphors ('mimetic desire') has certain limitations for this kind of comparative analysis. I believe that this is so because the universalistic model of religious violence can hardly be adapted to a conceptual framework in which the agency of different historical actors is taken seriously as a product of sociopolitical discourses. I do not wish to say that the cultural and religious dynamics of violence would play a secondary role. I argue, however, that a refined analysis of the multifaceted intersections of political agendas and cultural representations is necessary to reconsider the role of martyr discourses within these processes. For this, I think, we need to modify the way we look at the relationship between self and other.

Particularly important in that regard is the status of religious sites and the contest over their representational space. Religious monuments such as temples, mosques or churches have of course a strong symbolic meaning. This alone explains why these sites are preferred targets in the context of war and conflict. But to stretch Herscher and Riedlmayer's argument on violence and monument further, it is not just the symbolic character of a site that is at issue; rather it is the process through which a historical unfolding of temporal horizons, an event, is turned into the monument itself. History, nation, religion, all merge in the monument.

The history of Ayodhya and the destruction of the Babri mosque is a clear case in point. The symbolic pregnancy of territorial sites is not consensually agreed upon by the wider public; on the contrary, it is the product of political contest and violence. Gynanendra Pandey's (1995) analysis of the contest over 'Ram Janmabhumi' reiterates this process through a reading of popular Hindu histories on the Ayodhya site. In the popular tracts with their strong borrowing from the epic, the site is reconstituted as the tradition, Pandey argues. Thus, 'the importance of the site cannot be overemphasized, for it stands for religion, community, nation, all rolled into one—the destruction of the ancient temple of Ram Janmabhumi—and returns to this point—the loss of the site—again and again. The loss of this site is, however, more than the loss of a temple: it is the loss of territory, of religion, of nationhood' (ibid.: 386).

I have examined this nexus in a discussion of a dispute around the Shahidganj site in the 1930s Lahore, not at least because his incident has been widely remembered as a prefiguration of the Ayodhya case, even if under somewhat reversed circumstances of colonial rule (Noorani 2001). As Pandey remarks, the parameters of representing the heroic past in this colonial phase of the nationalist movement have not been so radical as to deny the other a place within the space of the emerging nation. This is certainly so in the case of the Shahidganj incident. What is nevertheless interesting to examine is the capacity of martyr discourses in turning venerated sites into spaces of collective representation in which questions of historical agency loom large. In this perspective, I have argued, the Shahidganj issue marks a particular moment of transition from an inclusive Indian nationalist idiom to an exclusivist agenda of communitarian ideology.

Notes

1. Parts of this chapter was presented at the conference 'The Imagined Worlds of Martyrdom' that was organized by the San Francisco Graduate Theological Union and the Department of Religious Studies at UC Berkeley in April 2004. I am grateful to the conference participants for their comments that have been helpful in further developing my argument.
2. For a detailed discussion, see Gilmartin (1998) and Noorani (2001).
3. Noorani explicitly compares the Ayodhya and Shahidganj incident, arguing that Shahidganj represents Ayodhya in reverse:

   > All the elements of the Ayodhya case were present—a mosque in the adverse possession of another community, Sikhs, to whom the site was a hallowed place; its demolition by Sikhs; frenzied agitation by Muslims; involvement of religious figures; Muslim frustration with the courts and determined moves in the Punjab Assembly to enact legislation for the takeover of the site. They all failed. But the situation was not reversed even after the establishment of Pakistan. To this day, when there is hardly anyone to visit it, the Gurdwara Shahidganj stands, as it did before 15 August 1947. This precedent should shame the Sangh Parivar (2001).

4. In this chapter I am mainly concerned with the social dynamics of the dispute that took on clearly exclusivist forms. It is significant to note, however, that despite the increasing tensions that surfaced, the major political representatives of the communities, including Sikander Hayyat Khan and Jinnah, were not interested in reopening the case after its dismissal, because of fears of communal disturbances in other regions.
5. Against the widespread claim that the Sikh concept of martyrdom has remained historically unchanged, Fenech (2000) has argued that the focus on sacrifice for the protection of dharma in the way Sikh martyrdom is understood today might be of rather recent origin. According to Fenech, this focus was the result of late nineteenth century Sikh reformist discourses that have helped to transform the eighteenth and early nineteenth century idiom of heroic death and sacrifice on the battlefield (such as it is expressed in the *Bacittar Nāṭak* related texts) to a generalized notion of the Sikh shahid as witness and martyr 'to the exclusion of all other definitions' (ibid.: 14). Fenech notes that eighteenth century popular ideas of heroic death and sacrifice reveal a 'conspicuous absence' of the Islamic concepts of *śahādat* or *śahīd* as conceptual tools to recapture the glorious deaths of Sikhs as martyrdom. He argues that in those times, Sikhs, like other Punjabis, would pay tribute to martyr shrines because of the various

intercessionary, curative, and preventive powers which the miracle saints and their shrines possessed (ibid.: 154ff.). In this interpretation he clearly follows Oberoi's (1997) example and portrays Punjabi 'popular religion' likewise through largely functionalist lenses. Fenech is certain in arguing that discourses of martyrdom had a specific relevance in the overall religio-political structure of the region. Mystical notions of martyrdom became ingrained into popularized practices of saint veneration that built on ritual transmission of the martyr's shrine's authority and dramatic forms of impersonation through the living descendant of the saint. This system of moral authority was conveyed by complex economic and political relationships between Pirs, local rulers, powerful landlord families on the one hand and the rural population on the other. As an emergent religio-political community, the Sikhs had to struggle with this inherited concept of a territorially anchored form of moral authority and charisma. They also had to struggle with the prevalent Islamic concept of shahid (often in reverence to Husayn. Mansur al-Hallaj, d. 922) that dates back to the tenth century. According to Fenech, in the aftermath of Mughal rule in the region the concept of shahid continued to be closely tied to a public discourse associated with Islam and Husayn's martyrdom, so that it would not become prevalent in Sikh writings. It was only in the nineteenth century that Sikh discourse appropriated the rhetoric of martyrdom in a move to redefine the boundaries of the Sikh community along the idiom of the shahīd.

6. For the history of the Akali struggle see; Mohinder Singh (1978) and Fauja Singh (1998). Uberoi (1999) argues that notwithstanding the different ideological standpoints that differentiated Gandhi and the Akalis, they shared the idioms of martyrdom and self-sacrifice as the central mobilizing force.
7. See Chapter 3 for a dhadi text on the happenings at Nankana Sahib. Many of the historic Sikh gurdwaras were administered by so-called mahants some of whom were known to have committed the sacrilege or misusing *gurdwāre* as 'courtesan houses' or gambling halls. The mahants in turn enjoyed the protection and support of the colonial government, and it was obviously this strategic relationship that provided the protest movement with its anti-colonial connotations.
8. Gandhi's approval is sometimes mistaken as proof of a presumably unified Indian nationalism, which at that particular moment did indeed correspond to the Akalis' objectives. It is true that the notion of self-sacrifice evoked by Gandhi's non-violence corresponded to the way the Akalis conducted their protest. As Lou Fenech points out: 'As the SGPC had adopted the nationalist platform, they began to reinterpret the history of the Panth and the martyrdom of past Sikhs in the light of the new ideas broadcast by the Indian National Congress and M.K. Gandhi. The eighteenth-century Khalsa became, for example, the first group to utilize non-cooperation in India,

non-cooperating with all those who did not have the best intentions of the Khalsa at heart, be they Mughals, Afghans, Hindus, or other Sikhs. The martyrdoms of Guru Arjan and Guru Tegh Bahadur, moreover, became the first sustained examples of passive resistance in the subcontinent.' (2000: 255–6)

9. In the light of the Government of India Act of 1935 and the significant constitutional changes it brought about, Sikhs had consolidated their representative power and many rural Sikhs shifted from the Unionist party to the Akalis who represented their own community interests. This occurred five years before the Muslim League's famous Lahore Resolution in which, for the first time, the idea of Pakistan was announced. From that time onward it was more than a common rhetorical device for Akali politicians to evoke the destiny of Sikh martyrs under Mughal rule, as a reminder that the idea of Pakistan was 'unthinkable' for the Sikh imagination. Although Sikhs participated in discussions about a demarcated Punjab according to religious boundaries, the constitution of a territorial nation state posed an essential problem, because Sikhs could nowhere claim to be in a majority position. Yong (1994) describes the ambiguous situation in which the Sikhs found themselves for the period between 1940–7.
10. In the 1930s, the structure of Islamic organization in the Punjab was seen as too fractured to counter the Sikhs' successful move in reconstituting their religion. Despite the fact that the transformed role of the *'ulema* provided strong claims to Muslim solidarity after the First World War, consolidation of the Muslim community was still difficult to enforce by that time. A major reason was the re-emergence of animosities with rural Muslim politics and the theological stance taken by various factions in the urban elites (see also Jalal 2000, Metcalf 1999). The *'ulema*'s ideal of faith as independent from political authority, based on the awareness of Muslim identity that was symbolized in the Prophet, the Qur'an, and the mosque, rather obstructed the consolidation of political power.
11. The dramatization of the mosque as martyr and the bringing in of the rural Pir Sayyad Zafar Ali Khan to lead the Shahidganj agitation fits in this picture. Without the help of charismatic notions of moral authority, it seemed, the community could not be mobilized in this important cause. As Gilmartin (1988a: 159) points out, the emergence of the rural Pir, who had previously not taken any representative role in the Muslim community and who, as a local intermediary, was considered a 'servant' of British interests rather than a reliable authority in the fight against British domination, was informed by strong ambiguities of Muslim self-definition. Obviously, two different models of emotional attachment to Islamic values paralleled each other, as they were differently institutionalized in the rural and urban landscapes of religious practice.
12. From what I investigated of contemporary performative settings, as well as from what I gathered in vernacular texts, it can be estimated that the

oratory and song introduced an approximately three hour-long performance (19 pages, including 17 musical and poetical compilations in different tunes), in which the history of Shahidganj was portrayed. At the centre of the narrative is the tyranny of Mir Mannu who ruled in Lahore between 1758 and 1763.

13. See for this point Gilmartin (1998: 431). Seetal's oratory is strikingly similar to what is reported in the context of Muslim politics and agitation. Whereas Gilmartin uses a model that sets political rhetoric and everyday life as counterpoints, I would point out how the public and the private converge. As I argue here, the dhadi genre is persuasive because it relates a tradition of rhetorical culture to everyday concepts of piety and popularly shared sentiments of belonging.
14. The name of the song (*gaḍḍī*) alludes to the genre of genealogical narration, and it could well be argued that in actual act of dhadi performance, this was delivered in the style of *kabit*, speech-song, without musical accompaniment. A gaḍḍī ('throne') is normally understood as the place of a historical Guru's successor.
15. *āwe jadoṃ vī yād shahīd-ganj dī*
sikkhī khūn wic ik ubāl āve
dil 'c valvale jāgtar karan paidā
te dimāg de vic bhucāl āve
dharak ā'ūṇ ḍaule, netar agg ḍolhaṇ
bīr ras dā jihā ūchāl āve (Seetal, 1962b: 32).
16. In a conversation with Inderjit Singh Ankhi of Jangpur village in December 1999 this is expressed in the following way: 'If you listen to a story told and sung by a dhadi, about a hero who raised the sword in order to attack those tyrants who inflicted atrocities on the weak, then fervent passion (*jos̀*) will be born in your blood.' (*Jo koyī sundā hai, sūrmeyān dī kāthā, ke kisse zālam ne kisse kamzor de utte zulam kītā, ate sūrme bande ne talwār cuk ke, maidān vic utar ke, us zālam te eh wār kīta. Jadoṃ eh ḍhāḍī kahinde ne, tā uh jeṛī agge vār pher ḍhāḍī gānde hai, te sun ke andar khūn vic jos̀ paidā ho jāndā hai, us waqt.*)
17. Both idioms relate to initiation: *guṛhtī* is the sweet liquid ritually given to a new-born child, *amrit* refers to Sikh baptism which is also symbolized in the consumption of sweet prasad.
18. *'hai kurbānī dī shamhā dī lāṭ ute*
maṛnā vāng patang mashūr sāḍā
amrit khanḍe da, te guṛhtī vīr ras dī
hirdā sidak de nāl bharbhūr sāḍā
mālak rahin shahīd-ganj de
kabzā gair dā sahārde nahīṃ
ratt ratt tom vikegī, nakad uh vī
janū-bhā'ī jī!—assī udhār de nahīṃ

19. In the doha on the Prince and Sahiba translated by Orsini (2004), a musician sings in the voice of the Bhogini: 'Those eyes see which feel love even when not in love, like those moths which come near the flame which burns their bodies.'
20. In Punjab, the concept of shahīd is still couched in the metaphysics of the Sufi path. There are also popular references to the Prophet Mohammed himself, who is sometimes mentioned as the ultimate example of martyrdom by Sikh performers. A popular Punjabi expression for 'he became a martyr' (*nabi dā dand śahīd ho gayā*) is a direct reference to the founder of Islam. The prevalence of Sufi popular martyrologies can be inferred from studies on Sindi Sufi poetry such as in the case of Shah 'Abdu'l-Latif of Bhit (1689–1752), a source of many Punjabi vernacular traditions (Schimmel 1975, 1986). More significant, perhaps, is the case of the *marsiyā* genre. The *marsiyā* is an elegy (poem in memory of someone who died; established literary genre) on Imam Hussein's martyrdom that was traditionally used in the context of Shiite mourning rituals. In nineteenth century India it was transformed into a specific genre of Urdu poetry and has contributed to the perpetuation of discourses of martyrdom within nationalist discourses (Cole 1988: 97; Devji 1993; Rizvi 1986).
21. On the notion of contemporaneity in Sikh militant discourse see Das (1995a).
22. Starrett explores Palestinian and Al Qaida martyr operations and conceptualizes the suicide bomber in a parallel way to that of Girard's surrogate victim. He argues that in the Israeli-Palestinian conflict we find actors that unleash a 'process of mimesis through which rivals develop by means of their competition into monstrous doubles of one another'. Starrett also describes how these Palestinian martyrs undergo a liminal stage in which they dress as the other, thus playing upon another theme of Girard's model.

5

The Vicissitudes of Partition Memory

Literary Genres and the Dhadi Voice

The concern that led my inquiry in the last chapter evolved around the question of violence and representation. I have explored how dhadi performative texts were differently linked to 'real life' scenarios of political violence in the colonial period. If the main thrust of those narratives and discourses consisted in the commemoration of a history of persecution and warfare, the present chapter takes a different turn by looking at what has become absent from the realm of Sikh dhadi performance. For a considerable period of time, I have pondered over the question how to address this issue without simply falling back on a conventional approach in locating the 'original character' of dhadi performance in the various shadings and repertoires of the Sufi or folk performer from which the Sikh dhadi has become separated. Without doubt, the presence of dhadi bards specializing on the *qissa* tradition of (Hir-Ranjha, Sohni-Mahiwal, or Dulla-Bhatti) is attested for in the contemporary cultural landscape of Punjab. Their texts and performances are relevant for the reconstitution of the performative arts on both sides of the border, and in that sense they have become part of the traditional bulwark that has been set up against influence by politics and religion. A reading of the folk ballads as a kind of counter-narrative of Punjabi composite culture is certainly legitimate and also needed. The question that guides my analysis in this book, however, is precisely the relatedness of performative text, religion, and politics. Consequently my interest in the presence of the alternative dhadi voice had to be approached differently. I will demonstrate this different approach here in a reading of texts that confront the history of Partition, a history that is largely absent in dhadi repertoires.

The Partition of 1947 constitutes a caesura, a fundamental rupture in the social imaginary. Its history of violence and displacement reverberates in the realm of Punjabi performative culture, the separation of Sikh and Sufi dhadi performance being just one indication of the large-scale transformation taking place after 1947. The question I am concerned with at this point is the erasure of that history from the dhadi performative scene. Looking at my interviews and collection of dhadi texts and recordings, I was indeed puzzled by the dearth of information in that respect. Probably the only public event in which a few dhadi musicians have been occasionally involved is the annual commemoration of the martyrs' day in the former refugee settlement of Jangpura in Delhi that has been described by Urvashi Butalia (1998: 273–4). The commemorative ritual that is performed to remember the heroic deeds of the Sikh women, who are said to have taken their lives willingly, for the sake of honour in the course of Partition riots that took place in March 1947 in Thoa Khalsa, a village near Rawalpindi, has become something of a foundational myth that has been retold many times through oral, textual, and visual means.[1] The heroic songs quoted in Butalia's account illustrate how collective memory is shaped by martyr discourses as they are constructed and transmitted by Punjab's dhadi bards. The complex history of violence and suffering has been transformed into a story of heroic acts of Sikh martyrdom: women taking their life in the name of family and community honour. Butalia demonstrates in her book how this recasting of Partition violence in such clear-cut images involves a forgetting of other stories that lack any occurrence of heroism. What I expected, therefore, was to find dhadi narratives that would mirror these post-Partition discourses on Sikh sacrifice. However, this was not the case. The oral archive of the dhadi song did not seem to have welcomed the troubling history of Partition in its confines.

The absence of dhadi narratives on Partition opened my eyes to other forms of genre expression that have been produced by Punjab's dhadi performers in the post-Partition period, most notably in the work of Sohan Singh Seetal whom I have introduced in the previous two chapters. By exploring a selected poem, a Partition chronicle, a novel, and some of his autobiographical writings, I shall demonstrate that the silencing of discourses in the dhadi genre has been accommodated by other means of literary expression. I am not suggesting here that these writings function in the same way as most of the Partition stories.

Historians working on Partition have long argued that the division of labour between 'fiction' and the 'historical facts' has led to a distortion of the historical representation of this past. The presence of Partition experience in public discourses has been subdued, the gendered history of Partition violence has been completely erased from collective memory until it resurfaced in the groundbreaking work of feminist scholars in the 1980s.[2] In an important sense, Seetal's texts do not subscribe to this compartmentalization of collective memory and history.

I believe that a reading of these texts is useful to account for the creative lifespan of Seetal the dhadi performer and writer, and more importantly to explore the different modalities of genre expression in the Punjabi vernacular. As sociocultural institutions, genres incorporate in their aesthetic and linguistic framework potentials as well as limitations of cultural expression. The crucial point in thinking about generic differences in that regard is what Mikhail Bakthin (1986), in his famous essay on speech genres, has termed the responsiveness between lived utterance (in everyday speech) and literary discourse. Genre, narrative strategy, and addressee of the utterance are linked up with each other. In the same way that genres reflect an image of an idealized addressee, the listener to a dhadi performance or reader of a history textbook has a set of partially unacknowledged expectations that guide his or her framing of the plot as 'play' or 'historical fact'.

Boundaries between generic expressions can become fluid, however. Creativity in exploiting the cross-over between genre distinctions is among the most important forms of cultural meaning production. In the following sections I will be concerned precisely with these questions: does the pluralization of generic expression tell us something about the possibilities of other discourses and the formation of subjectivity that has so far escaped our attention? Instead of looking at uniform Partition narratives, does it make sense to trace the tremendous impact of the Partition in such moments when the traces of one genre lapse into the dominant framework of another? Let me begin by addressing these questions in the light of Seetal's Partition chronicle *Panjāb dā Ujāṛā* (1948).

Punjab Devastated: A Vernacular Chronicle

On 6 June 1947, the idea of Pakistan was proclaimed and it was further announced that our district [*zilā Lahore*] would belong to Pakistan. Soon afterwards, the idea came up that another commission should be set up to decide over the exact demarcations. As far as possible, our aim was to secure our district from being allocated to Pakistan. We expressed our confidence that our district Lahore and Nankana Sahib would be allocated to India. As could be inferred from the parliament speeches in which the denial of justice against the Sikhs was clearly expressed, the expectations were that the border commission would take the concerns of the Sikhs into serious consideration. At the end, it happened as it had to happen. On August 15, the British transferred the administrative control to India and Pakistan. In the afternoon of August 17, Independence was announced on the radio. The district of Qasur was divided into two territories. Together with Qasur, our village was assigned to Pakistan. India was just two miles away from our village [Qadivind]. Immediately, on August 18, Muslims attacked Qasur. Bela Singh, his wife and children were murdered. The youngest boy was still a baby. But they did not even take pity on the boy. That day, we suffered seventeen deaths. Muslims looted the whole city without any interference of the police. The next day, thousands of Muslims set off from Qasur, starting to loot the many surrounding villages inhabited by Sikhs. Our village was just about three miles away from Qasur. Around three hundred soldiers from the Baluchi regiment were stationed in Qasur. They assisted the Muslim rioters during the atrocities. This issue caused great anxiety in our village. As uprooted Hindus and Sikhs passed through our village, our courage was entirely broken. We had no problems with the Muslim villagers [*gavāṃḍhī*], but problems were surely to be expected from the direction of Lahore, where a large number of bad characters had gathered. On August 20, some households in our village sent off their children and belongings. As the afternoon approached, we received more and more bad news. All night long people loaded their belongings on carts with the aim to leave the village. Sangatra is within four miles reach from our village. That night, my companion and inhabitant of Sangatra, Sardar Puran Singh Ji, stayed with me. He insisted and finally decided that we should leave the village the very next day. He came with his cart on August 21, and we left together with our baggage put on the cart. At that time I was in a strange state of mind. It was not only because I had to leave my home. The real tragedy was because two hundred years earlier our ancestors had taken this village by force from the Muslims, and today we were about to hand over this village to the Muslims and leave from this place. Some of the local Muslims were happy about our departure, yet, as we were about to leave the village, the great majority was very sad. At that time, we did not know that we would not be able to return to the village. Most people thought that after a couple of days had passed, they would easily return to their homes. But day after day, the situation turned worse. Together with my family I stayed around ten days in Sangatra. The rain began on August 22. Sangatra is the last village on the Indian side of the border. Many people from the Pakistani side were stranded there. Hundreds of migrants were sitting outside the rain for the whole night. I was also sitting there in the drizzle. Outside in the rain, one could hear the voices of the crying children—it tormented the heart. The very next day, ten thousand uprooted people gathered around the village.... Within this short span of time I had witnessed many tragedies. What I had experienced in those months could not be weighed by years of experience afterwards. Friendships and relationships were broken and one was absolutely unsettled during this period. I have heard and seen myself that relatives did not give refuge to their uprooted relatives. It is true; people thought that the uprooted could not have been able to preserve their honor. They have become the sacrificial lamb, but.... Wherever people found a place of refuge, in Amritsar, Jalandhar, Ludhiana, Patiala, and other places, I visited and tried to comfort them. Time has taken a turn, the government and territories have changed, but until today the former government employees have kept their positions. Until today their characters remained in the way the British had modeled them. With the transfer of population they too, should have been replaced. The very day I had left my home it occurred to me that I had to write the history of this turmoil. From that day onward I went from district to district to meet my fellow companions in order to write about their condition (Seetal 1948: 5–15).[3]

Sohan Singh Seetal wrote these lines immediately after Partition. They introduce the reader to his *Panjāb dā Ujāṛā* (*The Devastation of Punjab*), an approximately 350 page long chronicle of Partition violence published in 1948. In this hitherto neglected vernacular tract, the dhadi performer and author compiled story after story about the atrocities that occurred during Partition. The book narrates the major political developments that led to the splitting up of Punjabi territory in the style of a history textbook, highlighting the names of political actors and commissions in separate boxes. What follows in the main part of the text is a long narrative in the form of a chronicle on single incidents of violence. Each and every district is carefully listed according to the different *zilās*, *tehsils*, and villages. As the author indicates in the quote above, this comprehensive account is the result of oral history. Uprooted from his former home in a village near Qasur, Seetal moved from place to place, visiting various refugee camps and dwellings. There he listened to the stories of those who had reached the Indian side of the newly demarcated borderline.

Accounting for lost property and lives was certainly a widespread practice during this period. People had an interest to get their names listed so that later claims to territory and property could be legally secured. First Information Reports (FIRs) were produced in the various administrative units in which criminal attacks as well as the names of perpetrators and victims were reported (see Pandey 2001: 74). These documents were not only useful in putting together works such as Gopal Das Khosla's *Stern Reckoning* (1948), a book used frequently by historians to assess the damage of Partition violence, they clearly had a formative role on post-Partition history writing on this event. Seetal's compilation is produced in this period of documentation. It was a time, argues Gyanendra Pandey (2001: 74), in which the 'primary discourses' provided by people's testimony and rumour about communalist violence 'carrie[d] over very easily into the secondary discourse produced by political commentators and memorialists.' *Panjāb dā Ujāṛā* takes part in this process of translation into communitarian and nationalist narratives with their prejudiced attitudes toward the religious other. At the same time, the Punjabi vernacular offers a perspective that distorts this clear-cut picture.

What kind of text are we confronted with here? *Panjāb dā Ujāṛā* does not offer a single frame in terms of a secondary discourse on Partition violence. The narrative is multilayered, characterized by different vehicles of expression—testimony, chronicle, and historical analysis are complicit rather than clearly demarcated. The opening paragraph of the book is noteworthy in that matter, for it mediates between the eyewitness report of how Seetal's family left the village and the reflexive voice of the historian who, in 1948, has in mind an audience to be instructed about the actual contexts of Partition migration and violence. As we shall see, the narrator's voice is certainly prejudiced to the extent that it poses 'our' loss against those of 'the Muslims.' The reference to the 'good Muslim' of the village that poses no threat as against the unknown 'Muslim as rioter' resonates with much of what has been written on such first-hand Partition accounts. The narrator, however, does not stop here. The frustration about Partition is directed against politicians and against the lack of solidarity of his own community. Family members who have been unwilling to accept the displaced are similarly mentioned as patriarchal norms have placed an additional burden on abducted women. First and foremost, the corruption of the political system is strongly criticized. The introductory text yields to a reading of social and gender problems with the Sikh community as the implicit addressee. Irony is a common trope through which this situation is assessed in the narrative. Considering that the narrator has been displaced from his village, it is significant to note that he sees the circumstances of this displacement through similar lenses. Thus, in a long note he articulates how Partition restored historical justice to the Muslims of his village Qadivind who, about two centuries ago, had been expelled from the locality and who now, by historical circumstance, are in a position to reclaim the place. If, in the eyes of the narrator, this does not legitimize the violence 'they' committed, it can still be discerned that he invests the account with a sense of reflexivity and distance which stands in clear continuity with the voice of the historical commentator. The reader has to be reminded that these multifaceted perspectives on the Partition were written long before historians approached Partition history from a critical angle. Without ignoring the anti-Muslim sentiment that runs through the text, therefore, we have to note the attentiveness of the narrator to such a critical reading in the voice of a tertiary discourse of historical reflection.

If the first part of the book tends to conflate the boundaries between primary, secondary, and tertiary discourses, the main thread of the book is that of a chronicle on the disturbances in the various districts of Punjab. Parts 2 and 3 list single localities in which riots took place, many of them prior to 15 August 1947. The last two parts consist of a list of Punjab's major districts (*zilās*). Each section is further compartmentalized in different localities on which the author could gather information. Thus, for instance, we find a report on zila Lyallpur that begins with a report on riots in Chaniut where Sikhs and Hindus were attacked on 27 August, followed by accounts on Lyallpur's Khalsa College and school camp where similar incidences occurred. The narrator then moves further to report on incidences at Gojra, Toba Tek Singh, Samundari, Kamalia, Janjhawala. Violence is seen to spread like an epidemic from one district to the next. In an almost literal manner it duplicates the structure of the rumour of violence, thus fabricating what Pandey (2001: 91) has called the 'rumoured histories' of 1947. This is undeniably the case. What I found interesting in the light of the dhadi texts that I have discussed earlier, is the historicist language that one encounters in this chronicle. To give an example from the Lyallpur section just mentioned, the narrative reads as follows:

In Lyallpur town the mosque and Singh Sabha Gurdwara were very close to each other. The Muslims celebrated the birth of Pakistan with great enthusiasm while on the other spot the Sikhs organized a *nishān sahib* [flag] ceremony, calling loud ovations. The Muslims got very enraged about this incident. The situation was on the knife's edge. The Deputy Commissioner told the Sikhs and Hindus to leave their homes and assemble in camps. The Sikhs went collectively to the Khalsa College, the Hindus to the Arya High School. Similarly, in the neighboring villages all Sikhs and Hindus gathered in camps. Some left from there to India.... No major incident happened in town. The saddest incident occurred at the Khalsa College. A mass of about 1000 Muslims gathered to make their way to Lyallpur. Upon arriving in Chaniut, they began looting houses and some Sikhs and Hindus were killed' (Seetal 1948: 208–9).

The narrative proceeds in this fashion, accounting for incidents of murder and looting, mentioning the loss on both sides. In west Punjab, where Sikhs and Hindus were forced to leave, perpetrators are usually the mass of rioters and the political leaders of the Muslim League as behind-the-scene actors. The situation is different in the accounts of the many 'little' incidents of communal hatred and murder in east Punjab's villages. This is a brief listing of incidents that occurred in villages in district Ludhiana:

Jagraon. People who lived in the many little hamlets around Jagraon were called to assemble. When the Muslims gathered in Jagraon to confront the Sikhs, 3 Sikhs (one of them Kapur Singh) and 350 Muslims were killed. **Hathur**. In Hathur lived the Rangars [converted Rajputs]. They thought themselves to be a martial race. When they met the assembled Sikhs, they attacked cowardly. One Sikh and 30 Muslims died. Others left their houses to gather in a camp in Raekot.... **Ghalib**. There was a fight in the village Ghalib where only about 300 Muslims were killed. Others converted to Sikhism; later they all left with the military to Pakistan (ibid.: 319).

While the loss at the side of Punjabi Muslims clearly outnumbers the casualties suffered by the Sikhs, the former are still held accountable for the violence. This is not the case with other reports where Sikhs and Hindus are held directly responsible for the death of large numbers of Muslims. When on the Pakistani side, the agent is the mass (*vahir*) of looters, on the Indian side we find a similar mass phenomenon, as the narrator refers to the collective body of the jatthas who would launch their attack (*hamla*) on the Muslims. Localities, casualties, and numbers are important, only seldom do we find names such as Kapur Singh of Jagraon, who—I assume—must have been known to the author. In that way the narrative clearly departs from the language of the FIRs. It is not oriented toward legal issues; it speaks to the emotional fabric of one's own community.

If on an overall plane of analysis the narrative considered here is historicist and prosaic, it also has moments in which the feeling tone of the narrative episodes of dhadi oratory come to the fore. In the light of the reformist idiom of the dhadi *prasaṅga* that I have discussed earlier, the boundaries between historicist language and bardic storytelling have indeed become blurred. Thus, while tropes of heroic sacrifice and the imagery of bloodshed are missing in much of the text, there are discernible points where the evaluative language of Sikh sacrifice and Muslim otherness (such as in the case of the Rangars above) erupts in the narrative in the form of fantastic imagery. Consider for instance the following section on an incident in the hamlet Toba Tek Singh:

> There was an attack on Toba Tek Singh, while Sikhs and Hindus gathered there. Some Sikhs were killed on the bazaar and the gurdwara. I heard about a particular painful incident there. A Sikh boy of about 6 years of age was caught by Muslims. Capturing his lower limb they beat him so severely against the edge of a mansion that his scalp was blown off. When Muslims killed children in this fashion, they uttered the crusading cry of 'Long live Pakistan' (Seetal 1948: 314).

Whereas in the long narrative, violence is normalized as a feudal exchange between the three communities, the killing of innocents is considered transgressive, a pathological instance in which the 'true character' of Muslim aggressors comes to the fore. The language used in the section discussed above betrays the claims of writing a neutral account of Partition violence. The narrative spills over in the imagery of Sikh sacrifice that was prevalent in the pre-Partition dhadi texts. As I have argued before, the storytelling genre allows for a dramatization of such imagery in an almost infinite manner. The framing of dhadi performance as a storytelling event on the heroic past enables the consumption of these images, which in their poetic quality seem to generate an experience of their own. Thus, in the composition on Shahidganj only a few comments by the orator were needed to map the transhistorical scenario of Sikh sacrifice upon a particular incident of communal strife in the pre-Partition period.

The situation here is different. In the narrative framework of a vernacular chronicle that covers the contemporary rather than the distant past, evocations of sacrificial acts are limited. Significantly, there is no talk about martyrdom whatsoever. If there is reference to sacrifice such as is indicated in the conclusion and the dedication of the book to 'those who left their lives for the country's freedom' the word used is *qurbānī* and not shahīd. The epic imagery of the vicious other therefore also acquires a different place—it lapses into the dominant narrative of recollection as a fragment, a presence of that other genre of commemoration that has been subdued at the moment of Partition. And yet it constitutes a potent force in producing this narrative of such length. It invests the text at critical points with social energies through which the 'rumorous history' of Partition is translated into evaluative categories and conceptual frames that strike the listener of dhadi narratives as being more than familiar.

Time Has Taken a Turn

In Seetal's chronicle, the border village Toba Tek Singh constitutes a place of transgression, an instance of cruel otherness that is captured in monumental imagery. In North Indian literary discourse, however, Toba Tek Singh constitutes a different site, an allegory for the no-man's land of Partition that is captured in the figure of madness and absurdity. Sadat Hasan Manto's short story *Toba Tek Singh* epitomizes this other imaginary of Partition that, rather than entangling itself in naturalistic languages of sacrifice and otherness, carves out a disillusioned space of loss and mourning that cannot be reconciled with the gesture of historicist recollection. Bishan Singh, the inmate of the asylum who is left wondering about the whereabouts of Toba Tek Singh and who, at the end of the narrative, embodies the in-between place of the border, is a figure in whom the masked truths of Partition reverberate. Manto's *Toba Tek Singh* along with his other Partition stories have been widely recognized for their evocative power in investing the memory of Partition with a subtle voice that lacks verbal pathos. (see Bhalla 1999, Hasan 1993)

In this section I argue that through a turn from the genre of the chronicle to that of the novel, Seetal saw a similar potential to tell a nuanced story of Partition.[4] Turning to his novel *Jug Badal Gayā* (tr. *Time has Taken a Turn*) I am mainly interested in understanding how the prose narrative accommodates themes that have remained excluded from the chronicle and dhadi prasanga.

Time has Taken a Turn begins with the story of the low-caste and physically handicapped Duda, son of a mirasi and a herdsman in the house of a rich landlord's family. The narrative gives an account of a Punjabi village, Varn, depicting in fine detail the complex net of social relations that defined the place in which the Jats played the dominant role. Village life in the pre-Partition years is harsh and does not seem to take pity upon the socially marginalized figures that populate the story. Beside the low caste Duda who features in the first paragraphs of the book, the other main character of the novel is Sardar Lakha Singh, the Jat proprietor and ruling landlord of the village, who has control over a big household, land, and tenants. His alliance with the moneylender Dhane Shah is portrayed as a decisive factor for him to gain access to material and human resources. Ironically called 'Shah', Lakha Singh is the patriarch and manager of kinship affairs that move from his own kin to the arrangement of marriage alliances of his dependent working class which is required to exchange agricultural work for the gift of family alliances. For Lakha Singh, the control over reproductive ties allows him to claim the women he desires. In addition to his first wife Basant Kaur, who is introduced as the nurturing mother, the role model of the virtuous and selfless Punjabi woman, he organizes a second marriage with Swarni who is young and beautiful. People in the village call her Hīr. Her sudden death at a young age reflects the fate of the folk heroine who chooses to die rather than be forced into an unwanted marriage. The 'illicit' affair with a third woman, the low caste Rajo, who Lakha Singh has himself arranged to be married to his herdsman Duda, functions as a turning point of the narrative. From there on, in the narrator's voice, Lakha Singh's chariot began sliding downward. After giving birth to a son Jarnail, whom Rajo conceived from the landlord, the low-caste woman secures her position in the Shah's household, even though she remains formally married to Duda. Unlike Duda, who is completely subservient to Lakha Singh's demand while having a clear perspective of his dependent position, Rajo ruminates and grumbles about the village gossip about her 'illegitimate' offspring. With Partition, however, she is brought in a position to reclaim the debts and force Lakha Singh to acknowledge his low-caste bonds. This happens after the entire family is forced to flee to Amritsar. Upon arriving on the other side of the border, Basant Kaur dies of exhaustion and sorrow. Duda is killed after Lakha Singh has sent him back to the deserted house to secure some jewellery that they forgot to take with them. Rajo survives and her son Jarnail secures a position as a *patwari* in the new administration. Thus taking charge of the allocation of property on the basis of the Partition agreements, Jarnail succeeds in preventing Lakha Singh from receiving the acres of land that the latter had recorded in his name before they left the village. The novel ends on a conciliatory tone when Lakha Singh finally gives in and commits himself to live with Rajo and Jarnail.

At first sight, Partition is not the central plot in Seetal's novel. It rather functions as an epilogue after a succession of episodes in which major characters with whom the reader has been introduced before depart from the scene. I would claim, however, that the death of the two heroines, and the adopted low-caste Duda is a clear allegory on Partition and the loss it entails. The characters of these three figures are lucidly developed in their own individuality and their mutual bonding. Nevertheless, they are also role models, almost archetypal figures that epitomize the valued side of Punjabi rural culture. Basant Kaur appears as the loving mother—vulnerable to the rules of a patriarchal household, yet enduring in her capacity to embrace even those who make her own life as first wife miserable, she is portrayed as the soul of the household.[5] She brings people together through her compassionate attachment and forbearance. The process through which she is shown to accept the demands of her husband's choice of a second and third wife is depicted without any pathos. The narrative's most impressive sections are those in which the reader comes face-to-face with the inner torment of Basant Kaur who has to perform the ritual obligations during the wedding ceremony of Lakha Singh and Swarni. In the course of the marriage ritual, the female barber's voice can be heard to tease the landlord through witty speech: 'With a woman like Heer already in the house, you have another one like Sahiban. Manage another wife for lambardar. No harm even if at the cost of double the jokes' (Seetal 1972: 85). Allusions to the folk heroines are frequent. Swarni in particular meets all the requirements of the Hir figure. She is the virginal beauty, the young woman who is forced to marry Lakha Singh while promised to the love of another. The inner fabric of the tormented female heart, finally, is the meeting point of these women. In the proceeding narrative 'only a character has changed. She had left the stage and another heroine had taken her place.' Basant Kaur's pain is replicated in Swarni's torments, her death on the Muslim bedstead foretold in Swarni's tragic passing away. The heroines' deaths are allegoric for the loss of Partition in that they demarcate a before and after, a time of love and hardship in the Punjabi village household followed by what seems as the temporal erasure of the communities' moral fibre. There is a 'good side' and a 'bad side' to this loss, as Duda and Rajo's story testifies.

First, in contrast to the two heroines, Duda's death represents the absurd theatre of Partition violence. By historical circumstance he followed his master's order to secure some of the landlord's belongings and is killed in this seemingly nonsensical act. If the comic tragedy of this death shows the low-caste subject to be the arbitrary victim of communal violence, Partition is given a different, even positive stance in restoring justice to the formerly dependent low-caste subject in the figure of Rajo. With the loss of family, property, and political influence, the patterns of alliance have become reversed. Lakha Singh has become dependent on Rajo and his 'mischievous-incarnate' offspring Jarnail. He is manipulated in a similar way in which he used to strategically 'care' for his servants and tenants. The social criticism that comes to the fore in this final scene is fully in line with the narrative as a whole. It clearly replicates the social-reformist idiom of the Hindi and Urdu progressive literature in the early twentieth century. In the same manner in which Premchand articulated his critique, social criticism in Seetal's novel is not couched in religious idioms but expressed bluntly in the language of bonded labor and caste hierarchy. To give another example, the introduction of the term Harijan in public discourse is depicted as a mere charade that cloaks the continuing forms of exploitation in the village.[6] Transformative potentials to change the position of the low-caste subjects lie in the rupture of social and economic relations that are brought about with the event of Partition migration.

The Memory of Chenab: Recovering the Poetic Voice

The polyphonic character of the novel has facilitated the return of folk idioms and motifs of Punjabi composite culture to account for the Partition trauma. In this section, I argue that beyond the narrative strategies of the novel and its characteristic polyphony, we can also find transgressive moments, or slippages of generic modalities through which the voice of the witness can be heard. Let me discuss this point by returning to Sohan Singh Seetal's autobiography and the presence of the poetical voice in it.

Autobiography and poetry, of course, assume different modes of receptivity and their directedness to constructions of narrative truth vary significantly. No telling is incidental in the autobiographical genre; it entails a conscious reformulation of life experience and thus constitutes a mode of remembering that is directed toward specific goals in the present. The transformations entailed in the autobiographical narrative can be very different according to the narrator, his or her cultural background, yet the set of expectations and forms of emplotment remain often the same. The poem, on the other hand, is usually considered to create its own reality, reading a poem is an event different from reading a performers' autobiography. The poem's openness to subjective evaluation and its power to touch the emotional self make it unique. Instead of constructing a life course in linear progression of time, it tends to rupture time, temporally propelling the reader/listener out of his sense of time. As I will argue, however, the intertextual dialogues between poetry and autobiography are manifold. The recovery of the poetic voice through the autobiographic voice is a function of reckoning time through displacement. Partition is involved to the extent that territorial tropes and modes of internalization—alien to the expressions in his dhadi compositions—evoke the loss that has meant Partition.

Seetal's post-Partition narrative *Vekhī Māṇī Dunyā* (1983) bears the unmistakable marks of a self-reflexive reordering of biographical time. The life story is set against the background of particular historical referents that are deliberately chosen. It needs to be emphasized in the first place that, in the words of the author, sincerity in narrating the past was a crucial issue. It is stated cunningly in the preface to his autobiography, where he differentiates between the different 'truths' that have to be taken into consideration by the writer:

> Mahatma Gandhi asserts to write the truth in his autobiography. I have in fact no doubt about his truth. Yet, the question is, what kind of 'truth' do we talk about? There is a certain ranking in the different types of truths. One is 'personal truth' [*nijjī sacc*], which is related to our (social) origin, but if we expand this perspective to include the ancestral line, personal truth has in a way also become a social truth [*samājak sacc*].... Furthermore, there is 'religious truth' [*dhārmik sacc*]. To adhere to religious truth is very difficult. It seems that whatever faith we adhere to, we lack the courage to raise significant doubts about our religion, as we fear to be expelled by our brothers-in-faith.... Another is, 'political truth' [*rājnītak sacc*]. Its truth claims are completely baseless. The ethos of politics is to claim superiority over the enemy. If a man takes part in politics, his truth strategies are a matter of ridicule.... The final question is, what should eventually be the guiding principles for writing a [life-] story [*kahāṇī*]. My opinion is very clear in that matter: 'completely abandon the path of lies and stick to the truth. But think carefully what kind of truth is given priority.'[7]

Thus, we can infer from Seetal's introductory words that, at the time of writing his autobiography, he was critically aware about the contested and plural character of truth. He does not offer a final vision of what type of truth should be adhered to in the autobiographic genre, but reading his text, it is clear that 'political truth' [*rājnītak sacc*] is regarded with utmost scepticism. As I shall point out, however, certain ruptures in life, such as the Partition, tend to be flattened out in the narrative recuperation. The interesting point in reading the performer's autobiography, therefore, is not to simply follow his life episodes step by step, but rather by reading the text against the grain of its author's own narrative gesture.

As a cumulative history of the self, the textual structure of *Vekhī Māṇī Dunyā* offers a significant juncture in the middle of the narrative, where Seetal completes his account of his Partition migration and post-Partition resettlement. In the previous chapters, Seetal provided the reader with a fair account of how his family had to depart, in a last minute decision, from their village in late August 1947, when it became evident that the land would be assigned to Pakistan. Departure from Qadivind had to be made in a hasty move, but it went without threats from the local Muslim community whose relationship to the Sikhs is described in terms of friendship and tolerance. The author narrates that during this time he was in a strange state of mind (*mere man dī wī anokhī hālat sī*) and that even prayers would bring no relief. Subsequently, he portrays the difficulties of finding a new home and income in India and of being confronted with yet other hostilities, such as indicated in an anecdote that he assigns to an encounter with a distant relative. According to the text, the latter approached him with the words: 'Now listen you! That time you were propagating the cause of freedom on the stage [*udo 'stage' te banhīṃ khaliāṃ kar kihā kardā maiṃ azādī lainī e*]—tell me, what freedom did you gain anyway?' (ibid.: 165). Throughout this paragraph, we find Seetal in a reflexive attitude with respect to Partition and the kind of personal transformation it required to build a new life. Seetal eventually accomplished this—in establishing his printing press in Ludhiana, saving an income for his family and being relatively independent from patrons.

In the course of this narrative, however, something more essential seems to have been lost that is captured in a scene of remembrance. The scene departs in significant respects from the rest of the narrative. Coming to talk about the progress of his dhadi group after Partition, the narrator embarks on a journey to west Punjab, the landscape of his former travels as a dhadi performer—a landscape that after Partition was now inaccessible to him. In this journey, he traces ruins of a past that are difficult for him to reconcile with. Images of Taiksala and Harappa, the two famous ancient historic sites, and the popular Panj Sahib shrine are all stitched together to an imaginary itinerary. The images he describes are real and unreal at the same time; they are his memories and yet are not owned by him. Seetal is attached to little details, such as the bracelet that, he remembers, helped archaeologists relocate the house of the dancers in Taiksala. Approximately three pages long, the section develops its own temporal and narrative structure, and thus creates a mood that reflects on his state of melancholia. One paragraph I found particularly remarkable reads:

> Remembering those places from which we have departed [*vicaṛ jana*], which we would not be able to see a second time, sometimes torments my mind. Whenever I come to think of *'Panj Sahib' Vaisākhī*, *Katak Pūranāshtmī* at *Nankāna Sahib* and *Joṛ dā Melā* in Lahore [commemorating Guru Arjun Dev's martyrdom] my soul suffers in pain [*taṛap uthānā*].... Once, the *Panj Sahib* committee called us for the *Vaisākhī melā*. We left with a feeling of happiness. On this journey, I crossed the river Chenab for the first time. The water hardly reached to the knee of a person. Small children played in the riverbed. The breast of the river was spotted with little sandbanks. It looked like leucoderma [*phūlbāhīrī*].... Repeatedly it came to my mind that it was this river Chenab in which Sohni drowned. Sometimes the sentiments get out of control. Although I was seated in the disorder and noise of a third class train compartment, I was immersed in loneliness and began to write a poem that is published in *Vahiṅde Haṅjūṃ*. I believe that one's [solitary] place rests in one's interior [*man de andar*], not in the outer world [*bāhar dunyā*]' (ibid.: 183).

What is being talked about in this section is a scene of travelling and discovery. Phrased in remembered scenes of a lost landscape, the section tells us about a man who returns to his interior self, which allows him to write a poem in a turbulent world—a world that causes astonishment. Two tropes used in this section suggest how interiority and the sensual experience of the outer world had been mediated. The first image suggests a metaphorization of time in the river-trope. The dangerous flow of time is covered by a deceptively dry riverbed of voiceless memory that Seetal poignantly terms the *phūlbāhīrī*, a pathological image of skin disease and yet a strangely beautiful image for the world Seetal finds himself in. The allusion of the whole section, however, is a movement from this surface image to the real and incomprehensible depth of the past.

Thus, it is the allegorical space of memory itself that is at stake here. With the imaginary crossing of the river Chenab, Seetal remembers the heroine Sohni who drowned in the river. And he remembers all the *melās* in which he participated. Memory comes back in the form of icons of traditional Punjabi performative culture. It hurts. Seetal describes his state of mind, using a trope of inner torment and longing that is comprised in the word *taṛap*. The connotations of this term are best captured in reference to some of the more common usages in Punjabi and Hindi:

macchī kī tarah taṛap rahī hai—to wriggle like a fish struggling with death.
mā bacche kī yād meṃ taṛap taṛap mar gayī—a mother who dies from intense longing for her children.
premikā premī kī yād meṃ taṛap gayī—the beloved suffers pangs of desire for her lover.

It thus epitomizes an extraordinary form of subjection to painful loss. In Seetal's reckoning, the past lives through his own telling, as a painful reminder of its inaccessibility. It is the reminder of what has been lost with Partition, but on a more encompassing level, it also marks a change in his attitude toward the past as such. The memory scene is sunken in melancholic stupor; this is completely different from his imaginary journeys as dhadi subject. Here, his melancholia is paralleled with a new vision of moral reinforcement in interior religion, cast in the language of Sikh and Sufi devotionalism. If we look again at the paragraph above, we find that Seetal refers to a poem he had written in 1939, which came to his mind while writing his autobiography. I shall read this poem 'back into the future', like a dream that is translated into words whose meanings are yet to be discovered.

Chenāṃ [River Chenab]

Au nadī'e prem-prīt dī'e!
[Tell you love-stricken river!]
Ajj kyōṃ cup kītī vahiṅdī e?
[Why are you running silently today?]
Chale ji'u bharī'ā dil terā
[As if your heart is full]
Par muṅho kuch nā kahiṅdī e
[But not a single word would you utter from your mouth]
Ajj kyōṃ tu bhār ke vagdī nahīṃ?
[Why are you not bursting with water today?]
Kuch āpna āp vikhaṅdī nahīṃ
[Not revealing your real nature]
Lahirāṃ nahīṃ, ghuman-gheran nahīṃ
[Neither waves, nor whirls]
Ko'ī kāndhī bannī dhāndī nahīṃ
[Not the eroded shore]
Jobān nahīṃ, Jobān-mastī nahīṃ
[Not the youth and its vivacity]

Masti dī'ā shokh tarańgāṃ nahīṃ
[Not the playful, energetic waves]

Vidhvā jī'o tere dil andar
[Like a widow that in her heart]

Shā'id ajj uh umāńgāṃ nahīṃ
[Knows no more of those desires]

The opening verses draw an image of deception. The theme is that of love and betrayal. Chenab is addressed in the first person's voice as hiding its real depth and dangerous undercurrent. Several lines describe the dangerous currents and the sheer force of the river as it is described in so many popular stories. The association here is with female *śaktī*. This image is then contrasted with the image of the widow. In the fourth paragraph, the motif of the river is staked out in allusion to a well known epic motif.

Tuheṃ haiṃ jisdi'ān ṭhaṭhā vic
[Is it you in whose strong waves]

Dhubī sī ik muti'ārī nī
[Drowned a lover]

Tere hī kandhe vasdā sī
[Who used to dwell at your shore]

Pritāṃ dā shokh bapāri nī
[Your naughty dealer in love]

Us din tuṃ apne jobān vic
[On that day, in your youth]

Vāgdī sau bhar asgāhīṃ nī
[You ran without effort]

Jad tere kandhe ashak ko'ī
[When at your shore a lover]

Bhardā sī baiṭhā āhi nī
[Sat sighing in desperation.]

Seetal's composition has a wonderful flow and in its refined Punjabi vernacular comprises a form of poetic quality that is hardly matched by any of his other writings. He evokes the drowning of the heroine in the oral epic *Sohṇī Mahiwāl* who, because of betrayal, crossed the river to her beloved with an earthen pot that was sun-dried and thus dissolved in the strong waves of the Chenab, in which she drowned. He also names the heroine in his autobiography, but the measure of betrayal and tragedy is comprehensible in its emotional depth only after reading the poem he referred to. Seetal further elaborates on the theme of drowning and eternal love in the last paragraph. Then, at the end of the poem he says:

Jādū kī ihde pānī vic?
[What is the magic in this water?]
Jihṛhā vī guṛhtī laindā e
[Whoever was initiated by tasting it]
Chaḍḍ jaddī takht hazāre nuṃ
[Renounced the inherited world]
Rānjhe dī manḍī painḍā e
[And entered Ranjha's universe]
'Sītal' Jī, jot muhābbat dī
[Seetal Ji, the flame of love]
Dil mandir de vic jāgdī rahī
[Continues to burn in the inner sanctum of the heart]

The voice of yet another cultural hero is brought up, with the figure of Ranjha, whose tragic love affair with Hir is known to almost every Punjabi child. The meaning of the Hir-Ranjha plot, which allows for a plurality of possible readings stretching from allegories of Sufi mysticism to popular perceptions of the romantic love theme, is rendered in a particular way in this poem. In my reading, the renouncement of Takht Hazara (the historic site where Ranjha's family resided) that I have translated as 'inherited world' carves out an inner landscape of the poet-bard that is both melancholic—a continuation of the loss that meant Partition, displaying a sense of alienation from the vicissitudes of the outer world—and clearly traditional, in its delving into popular Sufi imagery and religious aesthetics.

Partition and New Channels of Communication

Partition has indeed complicated matters for the dhadi subject. In the paragraphs discussed in this chapter, Sohan Singh Seetal—in turning to a range of literary genres—clearly departs from the dominant mode of reckoning the heroic past in the dhadi compositions that I have discussed in previous chapters. The author's voice is confronted with a different landscape of the past with its multilayered voices and unforeseen turning of events. In the movement between the frameworks of genre expression, emotive images of everyday love, friendship, and sociality in village life come to the fore. These images are distinctly different from the epic genre with its many allegories on the heroic spirit of Sikh sacrifice. The chronicle is the only place where this heroic discourse resurfaces, but even there the tendency is that of a complication rather than simplification of the historical account.

From the selection of the verses in the last section, we also learn something about a space of inner tension that has become voiceless or inexpressible in the dhadi compositions. The redistribution of voices among new genres is to a significant extent the result of what the dhadi subject considered the limitations of speaking the language of the heroic. It is a matter of irony, of course, that someone like Seetal legitimized in his own discourse the displacement of Sohni, Hir, and Ranjha from the mould of Sikh dhadi performance. In the course of the Partition, these voices required new communicative channels, as I have demonstrated in this analysis of the Partition chronicle, Punjabi novel, and autobiography.

Notes

1. Scenes of this event have found entry in Bisham Sahni's novel *Tamas* that has also been serialized for national television Sabia Sumar directed film Silent Waters ('Khamosh Pani') challenges some of the former representations by drawing attention to the destiny of a Sikh woman left behind in Pakistan.
2. The hidden side of Partition violence has been addressed in the work of historians and anthropologists, most notably: Das (1995b, 2000, 2001); Butalia (1997), Menon and Bhasin (1996), Mayaram (1997) and Pandey (2001).
3. Translation of this and the following Punjabi texts are by Michael and Veena Nijhawan. Remaining errors in the translations remain entirely mine.
4. In fact, his novels, *Tuṭāṃ Wālā Ku'ā* (1962a), *Icogil Nahir Tak* (1966), and *Jug Badal Gayā* (1972), can be read as a trilogy on Punjab's Partition. A full discussion of these novels is beyond the scope of this chapter. I will concentrate on the last of his novels that has been translated as '*Time has Taken a Turn*' in 1998. I will use my own translations for the discussion of the selected episodes.
5. Seetal's reckoning of these patriarchal relations is rather unambiguous:

   Some unknown bard has composed this line: Thou art my master, I am thine bondswoman. Where this relation of the master and the bondswoman prevails there equality has no meaning at all. Great men like Bhagat Kabir may any number of times term her as the better half, but the bondswoman remains the same so long as she does not rise in revolt to liberate herself from the bondage' (Seetal 1972: 88).

6. In one of the first scenes in which he introduces some of the low-caste subjects, he has the following comment on the 'low caste Sikh' Suba:

   The word harijan had not been coined for the backward classes yet. It is a post-Independence reward after 1947. Such suggestive words are meant to mesmerise the mind as of a child with magic. Clever persons have been aware of this magical effect for long. For all the months of the year, the whole village sent him on errands and in the end by addressing him as rajaji, instead of calling barber, it sought to compensate for all that. Though he would not attach ji with the client's name yet the clever client was particular enough to put emphasis upon the syllable ji...With the advent of Independence, all the low-caste people were designated as harijans. There were no longer the practitioners of archaic religions or the followers of Ravidas or Balmik amongst them.... Lakha Singh's trustworthy worker Suba was called a low-caste Sikh rather than a practitioner of archaic religions or follower of Balmiki. It mattered not that he was neither baptised nor had grown his hair. Sardars did not let him touch their utensils and he could not draw water from their wells either. Even then he was happy for he was called a low-caste Sikh, a claimant to religion. After all he was not regarded ir- or-non-religious. At the time of the census, the lambardar of the village had himself got his name entered as of a low-caste Sikh' (Seetal 1998: 7–8).

7. *Mahātmā Gādhī jī vī āpṇī jīvan-kathā vic sacc bolaṇ dā dā'āwā karde han. maiṃ uhnāṃ de 'sac' bare shakk nahīṃ kardā. Par savāl hai, ki kihrhā sac. 'Sac' dī'āṃ vī kismāṃ han, kuch darje han. Ik 'nijjī sacc' hai, jisda sabandh keval sāḍī zāt nāl hai, par je uhdā amar gavāṇḍhī lokāṃ 'te vī paindā hove, uh nijjī sacc hundiā hoi'ā vī 'samājak sacc' ban giyā.... Us toṃ agge 'dhārmik sacc' hai. Is ute amal karnā bahut aukhā hai. Ka'ī vār jis dharm nūṃ assīṃ mande hāṃ,...usdī kise sacā'ī ute sānū shakā vī hove, is waste sacc kahiṇ dī himant nahīṃ karde, ki saḍe dharma-bhā'ī sānū dharma toṃ khāraj nā kar deṇ.... Ikk hai, 'rājnītak sacc'. Is dā dā'āwā tāṃ asloṃ hī nirmūl hai. Rājnītī dā arth hai, virodhī nūṃ dhokhā de ke, āp jetū baṇnā. Je manukkh rājnītī vic hissā lainda hai, usdā sacc dā dā'āvā karnā baṛī hāsohīṇi lagg hai.... Bas, choṭi qaum vaḍḍī qaum vic mil gayī, jā dūsre shabdāṃ vic vaḍḍī qaum ne choṭi nūṃ khā li'ā, te hazam kar li'ā. So khatrā hameshāṃ vāste miṭ giyā...ākhirī savāl hai, phir kahāṇī likhaṇ vāste kihṛā sidhānt apṇāyā jāve. Merī rā'e hai, ik sada jihā rastā., Jhūṭh toṃ pūrī tarāṃ parhez karo. Sac dā sāth nā chaḍḍo. Par jis sacc dā dūsre ute māṛā amar paindā hove, usnūṃ thoṛā jehaa akhāṃ toṃ uhle vī kar diho* (Seetal 1983: 7–8).

PART THREE

Contemporary Issues
Martyrdom and Beyond

The landscape of contemporary world politics is saturated with images of violence and martyrdom. Suicide attacks have become a routine practice in the war zones of Iraq, where the casualties among civilians rise day by day. Videos of Palestinian suicide bombers in which they justify their acts of sacrifice and murder in terms of a historic victimization of their people are accessible on the Internet. Christian evangelical discourses with a heavy drawing on martyr ideology have also increased astoundingly, Mel Gibson's cinematographic visualization of the tortured Jesus being one of the latest examples of an unhappy alliance between a growing culture of conservative politics and the media industry in the United States. In many ways, it seems, the fetish with the martyr figure caters to forms of social mobilization, sometimes informed by an outspoken or subliminal desire to dominate the other.

The perplexing issue is that the consumption of such images spreads across religious and national boundaries and is perceived in unanticipated ways. *The Passion of the Christ* is a case in point for the film was screened and watched by large audiences throughout the Middle East, where it obviously fitted into a somewhat different space of imagination than in Europe or the United States. In a recent issue of the ISIM Newsletter, Douwes and Herrera remark that in the Arab world, 'the movie was seen as exposing the cruelty of oppressors, evoking parallels, for example, with the oppression of Palestinians by the Jewish state. Very few governments in the region banned the film, and—in a departure from Islamic doctrine—the religious establishment, in many cases, received *The Passion* favourably while overlooking their standard fatwa against the graphic portrayal of the prophets, which in Islam, includes Jesus' (2004: 4).

How does one conceptualize the relatedness of different martyr discourses in the context of political violence and what is to be made of the chain of appropriative gestures through which the martyr figure inserts itself in different social imaginaries? If the new media technologies facilitated the way in which these discourses are transmitted, have they also had an impact on processes of social perception and the construction of martyrdom as legitimate acts of enduring and/or inflicting violence on others?

Before I take up that question, and discuss the relationship between political violence in Punjab in the 1980s and dhadi performative practice, let me begin with a poignant example from the contemporary media landscape in South Asia. I located Figure 14 on a Hindu nationalist website.

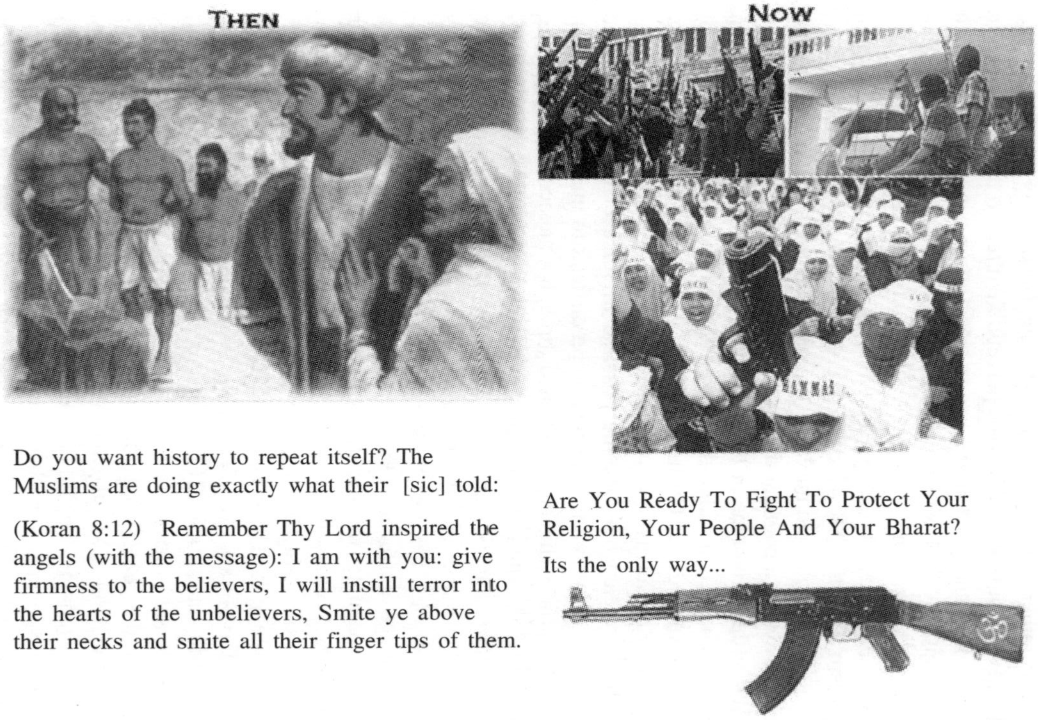
THEN
NOW
Do you want history to repeat itself? The Muslims are doing exactly what their [sic] told:
(Koran 8:12) Remember Thy Lord inspired the angels (with the message): I am with you: give firmness to the believers, I will instill terror into the hearts of the unbelievers, Smite ye above their necks and smite all their finger tips of them.
Are You Ready To Fight To Protect Your Religion, Your People And Your Bharat?
Its the only way...

FIGURE 14: Poster on a Hindu nationalist website

The image depicts a horrific scene of persecution and torture to the left and a number of news photographs of the youth wing of the militant Palestinian Hamas and the Indonesian Hammas to the right. The text below is rather unambiguous in portraying Muslims as persecutors and a dangerous mass of fanatics—a perceptible threat to Indian society. In bridging past and present, the image feeds into a popular discourse on the 'illegitimacy' of Muslim claims to representational spaces within the Indian nation. The image not only articulates a sense of urgency for Hindu right wing activists to react violently against the threat of 'Islamic terrorism' (see the AK 47 rifle), it also constructs a generalized message of the vicious and intolerant character of 'the Muslim' that inserts itself easily into a political rhetoric of contemporary Hindu nationalists.

While the stereotype of the intruding Muslim has consistently been in use in Hindu nationalist discourses at least since the early twentieth century (Amin 2002; Chatterjee 1993; van der Veer 1996), the new technology of imagistic representation is endowed with further potential. It has meanwhile become possible to stake claims on a heroic history of martyrdom that seemed to be difficult to imagine only about a decade earlier. This can be elicited through a nuanced reading of the left part of the image. Through it we can perceive how the place of heroic martyrdom is legitimated precisely at a moment in which the minority discourse of Sikh representations, to which this history obviously belongs, has lost its threatening aspect for the Hindu right.

The image of execution that we see in the montage is part of a series of similar paintings that constitute an important element of Sikh popular martyrology. Some of these I will discuss in the following chapter.

It is not surprising that this caricature has appealed to the Hindu right wing ideologists. There is a double irony behind this appropriative gesture. First of all, even though we have evidence for Sikh hostilities against Muslims, such as I have discussed for the late colonial period, it must be said that in an overall perspective, 'the Muslim' has not figured as the generalized other in Sikh history. Of course, the violations at the hand of Mughal and Afghan rulers in the eighteenth century are vividly remembered but to an extent local castes such as the Rajputs are held responsible for what had happened in that period. Whereas in the 1930s epic imagery of heroic sacrifice at the hand of the Mughal and Afghans were linked to a contemporary contest between Sikh and Muslim nationalists, the same imagery acquires connotative meanings of a different sort after 1984, the year of the Indian Army's attack on the Akal Takht in Amritsar. This was the year of Indira Gandhi's assassination and the ensuing anti-Sikh riots in Delhi, followed by a decade of violence in the Punjab. If images of the sacrificial past of suffering lend themselves to the Sikh viewer's eye today, this is so not because the depicted enemy is the Muslim, but rather because these images have been powerful in creating a sense of awareness of a past of collective persecution. In the 1980s' Sikh militant discourse, this past of Muslim oppression has become analogically related to a present in which 'the Hindu' incorporated that role of the other. The rhetoric of Sikh militant organizations is very clear in mapping this vulnerable past upon a present in which the 'Hindu character' is construed as the new perpetrator. The former ally has turned out to be 'treacherous', effeminate, and lacking the martial qualities of the Sikhs (see Das 1995a: 361). The connotation of the popular martyr image, therefore, has been in significant ways different from the way the contemporary Hindu nationalist website wants to have it. More than that, Das (ibid.: 367) has suggested that there is some reason to believe that allegations against Hindus of being effeminate conferred a subliminal message to the Hindu right. It seems that they inversed these attributes in an attempt to form a militant self-image. Such a move can be discerned from the image discussed above.

In the following chapter, I would like to further explore the potential meanings and interpretive dimensions of the Sikh martyr image in contemporary Punjabi cultural practice. My interest is two-fold here. First of all, I would argue for a differentiated perspective of how the martyr figure is embedded in the social imagery. For this reason and from the particular perspective used in this monograph, I consider it useful to further interrogate the relationship between imagistic representation and (dhadi) performative language. Considering that there is no simple way from imagistic representation to language and vice versa, one of the questions I want to pursue concerns the way in which images of mutilation and pain are both a resource and product of the commemorative function of dhadi oral discourse.

From what I have so far discussed it should be evident that experiential domains tend to be exploited in dhadi performative practice. At various critical points in Punjabi history they have helped to generate a social collectivity of pain and suffering. I have argued before that it is not to be seen as a determinate relationship. However, as practices of dhadi song-recitation have been repeatedly linked to the politics of Sikh self-representation, it is hard to ignore the generative role of dhadi rhetoric delivery in this context. The Punjab crisis in the 1980s provides a useful context for such a discussion. This was a period in which dhadi performance was revitalized in significant ways. It was also a period in which we witness changes in the media landscape (increasing role of the cassette industry) and a certain standardization of martyr iconography in the form of paintings and calendar art had taken shape. It is not a bad idea, therefore, to ask if and how, through the dramatization of mutilated bodies and spectacular display of sacrifice, dhadi performative practice has changed under these circumstances. Is the relationship between the martyr image and dhadi performative techniques parasitic or catalytic? Is the prevalence of painful imagery in dhadi songs simply an indication for an ideological turn; is it a reflection and mourning of this 'real life' of political violence; or does it instill an ethos to endure and transcend painful experience? If, as Starrett (2003: 401) points out, 'the visual has not eclipsed the oral/aural as a mode of religious expression' in societies of the Middle East and South Asia, as I would add, in what ways are both sensory modalities related in Dhadi performative practice?

6

Realignments of Agency

Dhadi Rhetoric and the Martyr Image

I begin this chapter with a discussion of a very popular martyr image, that of Shahid Bhai Mani Singh (Figure 15). Images such as this are displayed in all major Sikh shrines and they circulate in the form of countless calendars, postcards, and posters in the bazaars. This print is taken from a Sikh textbook of the Sikh Missionary College and shows Bhai Mani Singh as a white-bearded Sikh man, who has been stripped

FIGURE 15: Sikh martyr Bhai Mani Singh; illustration by Kirpal Singh

of his clothes, sitting on the ground with his legs crossed. His hair is uncovered and tied in a little knot, indicating that he wears his hair uncut. The white skin of the man contrasts his dark-skinned counterpart who kneels opposite him, holding a huge butcher knife in one hand. The scene of torture depicted in the image can be grasped at first sight. Dress, scenery, and physical appearance denote an image of a well known past of political oppression, the presence of Muslim rule.

A trained eye will see the Muslim cleric (qadi) with a book in his hand (obviously symbolizing the Qur'an) facing the back of the executioner. It is a scene of dominance, a scene of torture in which a single male body is surrounded by spectators and is subjected to having his fingers severed by the knife. The man, however, is portrayed in a firm posture, sitting upright and sternly looking into the eyes of the torturer. At a closer look this contrast is further intensified by the composition of light. Light assumes an important dimension here as the Sikh is touched by sunlight whereas the surrounding figures remain in the shadow.

For Sikhs the denoted message of the image is unambiguous. Bhai Mani Singh, a contemporary of Guru Gobind Singh is one of the most revered personalities in Sikh history because of his heroic confirmation of Sikh faith in the face of torture and death.[1] The incident depicted in the image indicates what he is most passionately remembered for today. Mani Singh is said to have refused to pay an amount of money that was previously agreed upon to get permission for an assembly of the Sikhs. According to Sikh historical record, it was this assembly that was treacherously attacked by Zakaria Khan's army. After he protested against this action, Mani Singh was arrested and produced before Zakaria Khan. Balancing the alternatives of paying the money, converting to Islam, or having his body cut piece by piece by the executioner, Mani Singh chose the latter option.

The stylistic coding of the image comprises some elements that significantly play into what Barthes, in his famous essay on the rhetoric of the image, has termed the connotative or symbolic meaning of the image (1977: 37). The perpetrators in the image are clearly identifiable as a social category: they are the rulers, oppressors, and they are followers of Islam. The physiognomy of the executioner and the surrounding figures is obviously a caricature of Afghan or other Central Asian racial profiles. The eyes are often portrayed with a wild look and disproportionate in size, as are the chin and mouth. The whole body image has something brutish and animal-like. The 'oppressors' are the 'actors of the dark' as opposed to the Sikhs who are 'blessed by divine light'.[2]

This is one of the most popular visual representations of Sikh martyrdom in the modern period.[3] Displayed in Sikh museums in Amritsar, Anandpur Sahib, or Delhi, these images are as much a part of popular perception of Sikh history as they are part of a new visual culture in South Asia. The stylistic conventions of earlier portraits of renowned figures or of battle scenes (influenced by Victorian conventions and produced for display in a royal setting) have in recent times been accomplished by images that depict action scenes in the most graphic fashion. As I have argued before, the paintings are penetrated with relational categories and powerful signs of otherness. The portrayal of subjection by power and the naturalistic representation of the worst kind of pain infliction certainly have relevance for a social collectivity that is consuming and using these images, even for educational purposes as reproductions in today's textbooks elucidate.[4] The way this is done, however, and the manner in which relational categories become linked to the real life other of the present deserves special attention. In this context, dhadi discourses play an important role.

Martyr images are not only transmitted in the form of innumerable print copies, they are produced by figurative language and musical metaphors of the dhadi genre as well (see also figures 16 and 17). This is, of course, a significantly different mode of image production based on poetical imagination instead of visual art or photography. In the contemporary context, however, we find that both modes of representation become intrinsically related. Thus, if we turn to a very popular contemporary dhadi composition on Mani Singh, we find him cited with the following lyrics:

Mirzā

Mani Singh Ji said to the hangman,
Just be cautious to fulfill with obligation
The order given by your master.
It has been honest, well intended, when he said:
'You should be cut to pieces limb by limb
Until the very end you will suffer'
Cut my fingers at each joint,
Do not strike the fist with a single blow.
Wherever my body is conjunct,
Sever it piece-by-piece, you son of a noble!
As you perform the trial of your sword,
My faith [*sikkhī*] will be sharpened by this test.

The personality of the perpetrator (he is described to lack any form of compassion—*jallād de dil wic daī'yā nahīṃ hūṅda*) stands against the unwavering voice and spirit of Mani Singh. In the song, Mani Singh is not passively enduring torture, he actively asks for it. Agency is on the side of the martyr, not the ruler. This is the typical scenario as it informed the Shahidganj text that I have analysed in the fourth chapter. Bakhtin's notion of the epic as a specifically evaluating category that glosses the many tiny historical details and instead focuses on the particular psychic composition of the epic hero has some merit when applied to these sacrificial topics in dhadi representations. What is important to look at here is the way in which the formulaic song-recitation intersects with the historicist narrative in constructing a memory image. Turning to another dhadi song on Mani Singh it is intriguing to see that in this context, it is not just the ideological message that counts. Rather, the entire process of dismemberment, which is depicted line by line in detailed fashion, inspires the resurrection of the historic martyr in dhadi commemorative song:

Gaḍḍī

He then started his work,
First each and every piece of the finger
Was cut with a sharp knife.
Fourteen pieces were severed,
Then came the palm.
The sixteenth blow was inflicted on the elbow,
Then the arm was detached down from the shoulder,
The other arm was treated in the same manner,
Completing the seventeenth piece.
One by one, the feet were dismembered
Until he reached the trunk
Yet, the brave warrior did not utter a cry of pain [*par 'sī' nā sūrme bolī*]
On the face, no sign of agony
In meditating pose
The *samādhī* was not broken.[5]
The *Jāpujī* path was completed.[6]
The life took leave thus
With a strong blow by the sword
The head was separated from the trunk

Textual analysts often ignore that formulaic language embodies a tacit recognition of its actual power and persuasiveness in a performative space. The performance of dhadi songs is not to be understood as a mirror of an absolute and idealized past. In the *gaḍḍī* cited above, each instance of dismembering yields the composition of yet another poetic song-line; each severed limb paradoxically adds to the sense of wholeness and transcendence of the Sikh ethos that is depicted in Mani Singh's character. It can be culled from the several compositions that I have discussed so far, that the image is central to the conception of dhadi representational practice, in that it gives concreteness and symbolic plentitude to particular historical events and experiences that mere literal representation would not achieve. If we move from the conventional image of Mani Singh to the engenderment of such an image in dhadi compositions, we find that the symbolism in the image is multiplied by linguistic tropes and sonic images. Mani Singh has an active voice in this image. He challenges the executioner and we hear him reciting a Sikh prayer (*jāpujī*) while enduring the torture of his body. He does not utter any expression of pain (*par sidakī ne 'sī' nā ucārī*), a sign of his imagined fearlessness and capacity for endurance as instilled through the prayer. Before I discuss how this engendering of martyr images can be understood in the context of political violence, I want to make some theoretical observations on the relationship between rhetoric, image, and pain.

Imagistic conceptions of performative practice are not to be seen as derivative from a referential language system based on an abstraction from the sign as the sensual mediator between concept and percept (Wagner 1985: 17–18). The fact that imagistic conceptions of dhadi performative language tell us something about the relationship between rhetoric, image, and pain can therefore not be surprising. Historians (for example, Enders 1999; Fenech 2000) as well as anthropologists (Caton 1990; Starrett 2003) have investigated this relationship thoroughly, showing how the complex processes of symbolic coding mediate between the perceptual or experiential world of the individual and the world of language and culture.[7] Fenech (2000) notes in his study on Sikh martyrdom that the Sikh reformists of the early twentieth century saw in the rhetoric of martyrdom a great potential to create a more intimate relationship between Sikhs and their historical heritage, popular performative culture being among the central activities through which this was to be achieved.[8] Starrett (2003: 411) notes that the modern theory of rhetoric departed from the ideal of communicating ideas, instead exploiting the tonal and visual means of rhetoric delivery to influence the passions. This thrust is clearly perceptible on the dhadi stage. We can observe here that symbolic approximation is mediated by body images that are passionate, as they consist of a graphic depiction of inflicted pain. If it is true that neither the experiential world nor social collectives are directly accessible as objects (Fernandez 1986), but only by means of representational media and practice (where they are objectified), then it seems to me these images play a formative role within cultural processes that mediate both ends of the spectrum, the experiential and the social imaginary. Dhadi song aesthetics amount to a realization of such an imagistic perception of the world, in which the image of pain has acquired the rank of a mediating metaphor.

Pain, Rhetoric, Image

If metaphoric predication is crucial to an understanding of language and culture, does it then also have implications on how we understand pain as a cultural topos? The 'dolorism' (Le Breton 1995) in the representations of Mani Singh discussed above is indeed very graphic, yet it needs to be stressed that this kind of dolorism is considerably different from discourses in Christianity where the self-infliction of pain as religious purification and castigation is not only prevalent, but also historically embedded as a widespread religious practice, at least in the early Christian tradition. Self-castigation as means of salvation in addition to the endless debates on pain as a signifier of the divine voice as it is attested in the book of Job are virtually absent from the Sikh cosmos. In what ways, then, is the body in pain transmitted in Sikh discourses shaped by a different cultural understanding of pain?

For a beginning, let me briefly elaborate some issues within scholarly debate in that matter. Since pain is, by definition, a phenomenon that collapses the distinction between mere bodily or emotional-cognitive experience, authors like Scarry (1985) have presumed pain to constitute a world without referential anchorage—without intentional object, to be more exact.[9] This kind of theorizing reflects an understanding of pain as incommensurable with culture and language. Those who suffer pain, it is argued, cannot rely on the representative function of everyday language to convey their pain, because of the very destructiveness of the pain inflicted (ibid.). Indeed, it might be legitimately argued that the experience of extreme pain, such as the pain of torture, resists ordinary, everyday language and experience, and thus creates worlds unintelligible to others or even to the own self (Daniel 1996). The danger of being exiled in such a 'province of pain' (Jackson 1994) is without question very real, not only in the course of violent infliction of pain but also, for instance, in medical contexts of chronic pain. For the individual, pain is the most powerful creator of social contexts, as it leaves no doubt that his or her experiential world is threatened in its very existence (Allué 1999; Le Breton 1995: 138). This does not explain, however, the persistence of arguments that deny pain a voice in culture and language (also see Das 1997).

Crapanzano has addressed this problem in an article in which he argues that European academic and popular discourses (based on Herderian language philosophy) tended to focus on the incommunicability and privacy of pain precisely because such a fundamental rupture could create a bridge between signifier and signified, between the object and the word (2000: 227). He challenges Scarry's assumptions not because she would hint at the moral scandal of pain, but because she would embark on a mystified notion of the origin of language in painful experience (ibid.: 229). Scarry suggests the naturalness of the body or bodily experience, which from an anthropological standpoint seems to be highly questionable indeed. Furthermore, her arguments not only preclude an understanding of the 'body' as a cultural construct, by conflating body and 'body', notes Crapanzano, she also masks the rhetorical power of 'body' and 'pain' within academic discourse, or language ideology for that matter (ibid.: 224).

It is indeed often overlooked how closely rhetoric and pain are related, even within the European or Judeo-Christian tradition itself. The above-mentioned book of Job provides one of the alternative visions from which to interrogate the relationship between language and pain from a pre-Cartesian world view. As a foundational text on human suffering and pain, the book of Job has evoked considerable theological and philosophical reflection (see also Le Breton 1995). One of the major reasons has been the enigmatic character of suffering: perceived as a sacred incision, pain and suffering become a paradox in Judeo-Christian thinking to the extent that the question of *what* exactly is being witnessed by Job's suffering remains opaque (Good 1990).[10] Whereas it is not possible to fully reconstruct the original cultural setting and genealogy of the Job text for purposes of comparison, we are better equipped with examples from medieval Europe, such as are provided in the martyr cults and liturgical sermons of the Christian tradition. Enders' work on the musical and rhetorical conceptualizations of language in medieval liturgy (1990) and, more importantly, her recent publication on the medieval theatre of cruelty (1999) provide surprising links to the subject of this investigation. Enders focused on the relatedness of rhetorical theory and practice with discourses of violence in the rhetorical domains of invention, memory, and delivery. Drawing on a vast range of medieval documents such as liturgical scripts, drama plays, educational treatises, and juridical rhetoric, she argues that the bloody and pain-inflicted body had become the ultimate space upon which medieval rhetorical process was inscribed—both in the virtual and performative dimension. 'In memory, and in the veneration of Christ's body,' she points out in a section on mystery plays, 'there was no comparable conception of the body as "private and incommunicable", contained in the body of the sufferer's body' (ibid.: 102). Much of her historical and literary evidence virtually opposes the central concept of incommunicability and privacy, underlying Elaine Scarry's work on the body in pain.

Enders does not end in criticizing a current theory of pain: her argument is germane to cultural theory in general in that she provokes us to rethink the place of violence and pain in cultural aesthetics, particularly in the function to link memory (*inventio* and *memoria*) with performance (*actio*). On the one hand, she provides ample evidence that the scholastic conceptualization of memory and invention contributed to processes by which violence became discursively regulated and normalized as an essential feature of European medieval rhetoric culture (ibid.: 79–80). On the other hand, and by expanding the perspective to reception ends, she argues that aesthetic strategies that were associated with a 'rampant imagery of bodily mutilation' (ibid.: 173) were far more common in the public sphere than one might be led to believe.

In this respect, let us have a closer look at how she conceptualizes the martyred body as one of the pivotal figures in the transition between rhetorical imagination and memory to the sphere of public enactment. The analytical hinge upon which her different excursions in that matter converge is what she traces in classical rhetorical theory as the *imagines agentes*, that is, verbally, musically, or pictorially displayed thought images that become 'real' and vivid through rhetorical delivery or performance. Rhetorical theory emphasized that rhetoricians' main objective would be to construe images in such a way as to adhere as long as possible in memory (ibid.: 67). For this reason it was crucial that images became agents. They had to be engendered in dramatic and even musical fashion to be heard and to be persuasive.

In the context of medieval martyr cults, in drama and forensic rhetoric, these images are bloody. To a significant extent they consist of martyred and tortured bodies that are depicted in great detail. These bodies are not mere phantasm; they bear strong resemblance with those bodies that were the object of coercive methods characteristic for medieval politics. Enders concludes that the drama of the memory image was parasitic of real violence and that its persuasiveness was based on inherently violent matter (1999: 66). Rhetorical speech and drama consisted, so to say, of violated and dismembered human bodies. Similarly, in Chapter 4, I have discussed a text in which we not only find a storehouse of martyr narratives, but also an oratory voice that directs attention to songs as if the audience is to view an image (*sabdī tasvīr*). The reader/listener is meant *to see* rather than to listen to the dhadi song. The singing of bodily mutilation depicted in the contemporary dhadi song (on Bhai Mani Singh) also acquires its rhetorical power through bloody images of torture and agony.

Some clarifications need to be made before I continue to speak about the relationship between pain and agency in this context. First of all, I would argue that the central role of desire in the material studied by Enders and its ambiguous relationship to pain and violence is not of fundamental importance in the context of Punjabi culture.[11] A *desire* for pain is not only alien to Sikh or Sufi value paradigms and cosmological ideas, but also largely absent from the different cultural traditions in Punjab. Second, I do not suggest analysing contemporary dhadi discourse as a pre-modern folk form that resonates with European medieval culture. I have argued that dhadi performances of Sikh history must be read in the context of an emerging Indian modernity, not as a remnant of a medieval past. If heroic imagery is a characteristic feature of epic genres, the way it becomes entailed in modern identity politics surely turns it into a modern phenomenon. This does not rule out the need to pay close attention to the conceptual continuities of representational techniques and their aestheticization of violence. Such has been Jody Enders' concern, and I should be similarly aware about such possible linkages in the context of Punjabi cultural history. Considering that Punjab has been struck intermittently by foreign invasions, religious conflicts, and widespread forms of political violence and persecution, at least from the eighteenth century onward, we might not go wrong in assuming a certain historical depth in that matter. Against this background, I would also like to stress that I am not concerned with the scholastic tradition of rhetoric that for good reasons has been identified as an essential tool in political and religious communication, as well as in judicial torture in medieval Europe (Asad 1993; Foucault 1979).

Instead, I am considering a point that has been purposely bracketed and named in a footnote by Enders as the question of 'why, when, and how popular anxieties about violence exert themselves in response to precise hegemonic structures' (1999: 10). In the light of Enders' reasoning, this is a point of utmost importance, as she is not only concerned with the commemorative function of the torture image, but with its linkages to actual events of violence in the public. Thus, she says:

> The way in which drama assaults, dis-members, and re-members, through vocalization, enactment, imitation, and impersonation harks back to the theatrical register of the theory of torture. The rhetorical connection between the dynamic memory scene and the delivered discourses of forensic oratory is the

FIGURE 16: Cassette cover, 'The Story of Bhai Taru Singhji'
Courtesy Michael Nijhawan

virtual and verisimilar spectacle of torture. In memoria, which imagined the infliction of pain upon human bodies, the interplay among wounding, birth, destruction, and resurrection is seconded only by that between virtual and actual violence. In *actio*, the enacted outcome of inventional and mnemonic systems, there is a real moment in real time when real bodies come alive before other real bodies (ibid.: 109).

We have to ask, therefore, how hegemonic structures of political violence in the 1980s have informed the commemoration and enactment of martyred bodies in dhadi performance.

Borderland Insurgency

It is against the recent backdrop of political violence in Punjab that the rhetoric of the martyr image can take on one of its most potent functions. It is here that we can examine how images acquire an agentive dimension that impinges on social action in a contested political field. Considering that the images discussed above do not constitute an ahistorical cultural topos that would be incidental to any discussion of agency and historical transition, but are instead mediated through particular, violent historical processes, it is indeed crucial to examine dhadi rhetorics against this background.

This is not the place for a full discussion of the circumstances that led to the crisis situation in the 1980s (see Jeffrey 1986, Jodhka 2001, Pettigrew 1995, Gurharpal Singh 2000, Thandi 1996). For readers who are not acquainted with the violence in Punjab, however, let me briefly summarize what happened. The common wisdom until the 1980s imagined Punjab to be a prospering region and the Sikhs to be a community firmly integrated into the Indian nation. This belief was shattered in its very foundation when anti-nationalist rhetoric and the exclamations of an independent homeland of Khalistan were articulated by a powerful religio-political movement that turned into a militant insurgency in the course of successive critical events in the political landscape of the 1980s.[12] The genealogy of this situation is indeed complex, but a significant juncture is certainly to be found in the early 1980s when the Congress party (then representing the majority of the Hindu population) regained power in Punjab. This occurred at a historical moment in which state hegemony over the region was enforced by legislative and coercive measures. Since president's rule in the late 1970s, these measures were strongly opposed by Sikhs in Punjab. The economic and political impact of these measures has been sufficiently dealt with. One

FIGURE 17: Cassette cover, 'Khuni Saka' (Songs of Blood and War) *Courtesy* Michael Nijhawan

issue that has to be emphasized, however, is the communalization of the political spectrum by branding claims of the Sikhs as anti-secularist or separatist (Gurharpal Singh 2000: 108). At the same time, significant changes in the political landscape of the Sikhs occurred as the Akali Dal lost influence and internal clashes between different political factions proliferated (in particular between the orthodox Dal Khalsa and the Sant Nirankaris). This destabilized political landscape and the persistent atmosphere of popular mobilization provided the ground for a charismatic religious leader to emerge and to re-emphasize the questions of Sikh nationalism. Jarnail Singh Bhindrawale, or 'Sant Ji' as his followers revered him, was educated in an orthodox religious institution of Sikhism, the Damdami Taksal which, significantly, is associated with the martyr Baba Deep Singh and the Sikh militant tradition. His role as a charismatic religious leader was crucial, as he 'was able to revive a vision of Sikh nationhood by drawing on the rich pool of Sikh religious and historic symbolism that cut away the ground from moderate Akali politicians' (ibid.: 110). To the extent that this was based on concrete experiences of injustice, an overall sense of moral degeneration in the political sphere, and internal dispute in a religious group, it was a characteristic situation for the emergence of a fundamentalist interpretation of history and religion. Bhindrawale appealed, in powerful ways, to many rural and young Sikh men to oppose what he perceived as the ultimate threat to Sikh culture and religion—the 'treacherous Hindu government'. He eulogized the use of violence as legitimate means of resistance in his speeches that circulated widely on cassettes, as well as in the many sermons and religious congregations over which he presided (Das 1995a; Puri et al.: 1999). Dhadi performances of Sikh heroic history in this context were of essential importance and certainly helped to create a mood of resistance and a willingness of martyrdom among Bhindrawale's followers. All over Punjab, but specifically in the Majha region in the northwest of the Indian Punjab (still the stronghold of Sikh dhadi bards) dhadi performers were known to participate in political congregations. Several dhadi performers told me that they knew Bhindrawale personally. His speeches and charismatic appearance obviously had a strong appeal to marginalized Sikhs in the villages. Although it is far from true that all dhadi groups participated in the movement, or even shared the militant's views on violent resistance, a great majority of them would perform at Bhindrawale's and his follower's congregations in this period.

The situation deteriorated in early 1984, after the Bhindrawale group occupied the vicinity of the Akal Takht in Amritsar. When rumours of killings and weapon supplies circulated, and negotiations with the government failed, the situation turned into an open violent confrontation between the Indian Army and Bhindrawale's group that was by then declared a separatist threat by the Indian state. The army attack in June 1984 (known as Operation Blue Star) and the following outburst of violence has been written about extensively. A heavy military force first bombarded the sacred vicinity of the Darbar Sahib and Akal Takht. After a fierce battle with the well organized militants, the army entered the inner domain with tanks and armed forces. The battle resulted in the death of Bhindrawale and his followers, but also in the killing of many innocent pilgrims and in the visible violation of sacred Sikh territory. Consequently, the great majority of Sikhs, who were previously indifferent or even opposed to the objectives of the movement, felt shocked by the events. Many Sikh soldiers even deserted the Indian Army, some of them to become followers of the militant movement.

The year 1984 evokes the most horrible memories of Sikh persecution in previous centuries. After the assassination of Prime Minister Indira Gandhi in October 1984 by her two Sikh bodyguards, anti-Sikh riots in Delhi and other Indian cities subjected Sikhs to the worst imaginable forms of communal violence (Das 1990). In the course of these happenings, it was not difficult to understand why the militant movement which emerged at the margins of Punjabi society, was hitherto invested with a much stronger support base. It could now draw on a widespread perception that violence that was targeted against 'perpetrators and betrayers' was at least an acceptable, if not a necessary strategy to defend the integrity of the Sikh community. In the decade to come, Punjab was in the hands of militancy and police counter-insurgency. This became manifest in the form of bomb attacks, killings, torture, and imprisonment of suspected 'terrorists'—all in all a situation in which feelings of insecurity and uncertainty proliferated all over the region. The great majority of suspects and deaths constituted young Sikh men who wore the external symbols of a baptized Sikh (*amritdhārī*), many of them belonging to rural Jat lineages. As soon as rumours spread that ordinary Sikh or Hindu citizens were associated with either side of the conflict, families and communities were in danger of becoming subject to militant operations or police intelligence forces.

In this situation and because of their known association with the Bhindrawale group, dhadi performers were confronted with hazards of public speech. In a time when the mere appearance of a young, bearded Sikh wearing a turban was sufficient to fulfil the criteria of a suspected militant, the public voicing of Sikh heroic songs and passionate oratory could hardly be ignored by the state. I came across several stories according to which performers were taken to police stations, harassed, forced a commitment to stay away from public events or even tortured. One of the stories that widely circulated in the dhadi networks dealt with the death of Harjeet Singh Sarang, who was killed in a staged encounter by Punjab police forces in 1987.[13] When people began to investigate Harjeet's case, and rumours reached the police that his father would propagate it, the latter was repeatedly arrested on his way to attend congregations and religious functions where he was supposed to perform. He was also arrested when a religious ceremony to commemorate the death of his own son was about to take place. The warnings to abstain from public appearance and from speaking publicly about his deceased son were not to be mistaken.

This was by no means an extraordinary situation. There is a current anecdote that articulates, ironically, that there did not exist something like a neutral commemorative voice of dhadi. Thus, it is said, the police once interrogated a singer because he was eulogizing the two Sikh bodyguards who killed Prime Minister Indira Gandhi. When questioned, the man was laughing and said that he was simply singing what someone else had told him. The policemen, however, were infuriated and imprisoned him for three years. The pun relates to the derogatory image of the 'stubbornness' of villagers to the same degree that it indicates the sheer arbitrariness that reigned during the 1980s. On a general scheme, it has to be observed that songs and speeches about the most recent Sikh martyrs (militants and others killed in gunfight or staged encounters) were disappearing from the scene, long before they could become popular, although some cassette recordings were circulating among households who supported the movement. Even at the occasion of commemorative events that are held in the name of those who died during the Punjab crisis, direct allusions to the time of militancy are scarce. In course of my current fieldwork on the Punjabi diaspora community in Germany, I attended several dhadi performances, most of which dealt with the recent events in Punjab. One of the most popular narratives, it seems, is the 'martyrdom' of 'Sukha' and 'Jinda', the two young Sikh men who assassinated General Vaidya, one of the main protagonists of Operation Blue Star. In these performances, every little detail of their action is vocalized, beginning with their preparations of their motor cycles and ending with the actual killing of Vaidya. The heroes would not show any sign of weakness or apprehension, even if they were to be tortured to death by intelligence forces.[14] Sikh militants are turned into Mani Singhs and Baba Deep Singhs. Pettigrew (1992: 101) also reported about dhadi texts on the Sikh militants. In an eulogy on Labh Singh, a well known guerrilla fighter of the Khalistan Commando Force (KCF), for instance, the singers compare his act of sacrifice with that of Baba Deep Singh who fought against the Afghan army. The texts collected by Pettigrew are based on rigorous dualisms between the 'Sikh cause' and the 'betrayal by the Hindu state'. Performers also do not hesitate to draw further conclusions in terms of violent counter-action against those who persecuted the Sikh.[15]

But what about the potential of the popular martyr image to transcend an experience of powerlessness and subjection to violence. If figurative and incisive oral language achieves a certain effect in a situation in which the dhadi tradition comes precariously close to the support of militant ideology and violence, does this also have a 'curative' effect? Where does this effect materialize? Thus, in her recent book on expatriate Khalistan militants, Cynthia Keppler-Mahmood quotes from a conversation with a former militant. His account is about how he first experienced the pain of torture while being kept in prison:

> In our daily prayers, we remember all our Sikh martyrs during the Mughal period, those who went through terrible hardships.... I used to think, 'What type of people were they?' and while I was in the movement there was sometimes a little thought in the back of my mind that if the time came, would I be able to behave as those brave Sikhs, my ancestors, did? But finally, when I went through it, it was not me but those other Sikhs who were sustaining that. It seemed they were taking the pain with me. I felt then the satisfaction of knowing that with Guru's grace I was able to pass the test of being a Sikh (quoted in Mahmood 1996: 37).

The religious ideology of pain that is evoked in this citation is that of the historical Sikh culture heroes, taking the tortured body's pain along. We can estimate the importance of the engenderment of historical martyr images such as Bhai Mani Singh's for the ideology of the Khalistanis as it sustains the discourse of Sikh militancy. If, as Mahmood figures it out, 'resistance to perceived injustice is an existential stance for the militant Sikh, something one does as meaningful in itself' (ibid.: 196), pain in torture would be reinterpreted as something meaningful—as a test of being a true Sikh in the way Bhindrawale cloaked the militants' martyrdom operations in his speeches. The mystical concept of self-erosion necessary to merge with divine grace is thus taken literally as a script for self-sacrifice: the grotesque dismemberment of Bhai Mani Singh as an imaginary space of pain endurance.

This ideology is very problematic insofar as it caters to the gendered discourse of selfless sacrifice that not only disregards incidences of non-heroic suffering but also negates the intricacies of the movement with its own internal antagonisms and ambiguous motivations. However, the sense of self-disempowerment that is expressed in such statements entails a different understanding of pain and agency that is worthwhile to consider. Mahmood says that in the utterance lies a potential to counter the hegemony of the torturer's world, which is otherwise defined by its power to narrow down the world of the victim (ibid.: 201). It serves to define a situation in the active mode—the consent to being martyred—which otherwise would be painfully passive. Read in such a fashion (that is, leaving out for a moment the question of the person's own complicity in violence), the rhetoric of the dhadi images sustains a notion of pain as agency. This is of course different from studying the everyday processes through which victims of violence communicate their experience of torture and pain in their immediate social surrounding (see Daniel 1996 or Feldman 1991), but the concept of pain as a kind of action (resisting, 'passing the test'), even if ideologically framed, needs to be looked at carefully.

Asad (2003) has recently argued that notions of disempowerment might be as important to consider as notions of self-empowerment when thinking about agency. Asad raises a point, which I think has significant ramifications for my discussion of dhadi rhetoric. Rather than considering pain and suffering as passive states of an afflicted body in a way which is the very other of what we usually have in mind with the secular idea of the rational agent, he suggests thinking of pain as an active relationship, a habitual engagement with the world in which we live. For him, the domain of the passions has as much to do with a theory of agency as, say forms of subaltern rebellion. If we try to understand pain as a kind of action, a form of relationship through which to know the world and 'not just as the thing that is inimical to reason' (ibid.: 67), it must then be assumed that the voluntary subjection of the self to pain and death is not just an aberration of distorted minds or a socio-psychological mechanism in the way Girard would have it, but a complex form of self-extension. Martyrdom, then, could be understood in the framework of a theory of extended agency. Most importantly, Asad suggests that music and musical metaphors serve to structure the experience of pain as a culturally constituted domain, rather than a private experience. It is no coincidence, then, that dhadi performative practice is particularly prone to structure such pain experience through its various theatrical, rhetorical, and non-discursive forms. We therefore have to look at the *imagines agentes* as they are produced in dhadi discourse in their aesthetic dimension. The soundimage of the sarangi with its lamenting tone, or the vocalization of the *hek* by dhadi singers among other performative facets that I have described earlier, all play into the structuring of experience at the level of *actio*. Representations of martyrdom and pain in the dhadi tradition are not 'merely commemorative' for that matter. It is also not the case that they would 'contain no vision of a future society' as Pettigrew (1992: 85) once put it. In my opinion, Asad's (2003: 92) point that the performance of pain tells us something about the epistemological status of the body and its moral potentialities functions as an important corrective against the functionalist view.

Dhadi Rhetorics and the Time-Space Nexus

One of the agentive dimensions of Sikh dhadi discourse, it has been suggested in the previous section, is its capacity to map out the body of the martyr as a spatial and temporal category. The moral ambiguities of this process are more than evident. The iconicity of pain has been a formative element in the process of remembering a past of suffering that acquired a new immediacy under the hegemony of political violence in the 1980s. I have indicated in what ways this iconicity of pain becomes the space for particular kinds of action. More importantly, however, I have argued that the intricacies of real life pain and dhadi mnemotechniques are mutually reinforcing each other. With each new death, it seemed, the immediacy of martyrdom engendered in dhadi oratory and songs acquired a more realistic note: 'Real moments in real time when real bodies come alive before other real bodies', to repeat Enders' (1999: 109) formulation. This immediacy was enforced and shaped by orators and musicians who were capable of creating persuasive analogies between the experiences of torture and persecution, such as depicted in Mani Singh's image with the contemporary situation. As I have argued before, such analogical moves were important as they helped to bridge critical differences between the two historical moments.

A photograph collected by Human Rights sources depicts a young Sikh man who was captured by the Central Reserve Police. This image depicts a policeman who is about to slap the young Sikh, who has been stripped off his turban. In the background you can see a turbaned policeman silently watching the scene. Such images circulate from hand to hand and are easily accessible on Khalistani websites.[16]

The photograph of the young Sikh prisoner shares the sense of degradation and oppression epitomized in the Mani Singh painting. It differs from the latter, however, in two important respects (apart from the different artistic and perceptual conventions on which I will have more to say below). The face of the prisoner, as one might expect, expresses fear and repulsion, which is quite different from the stern look of Mani Singh. Furthermore, the composition of the surrounding figures is significantly altered, as a Sikh police man is among those who watch this humiliating scene. The connotative meanings in both visual representations, therefore, change dramatically. They involve a shift from the supreme act of heroic sacrifice to a sort of humiliating passivity of the Sikh prisoner within the same parameters of brutal pain infliction. The differences between both images must be understood against the background of the different stylistic conventions and technologies of image production. As Barthes has pointed out, a photograph is very differently penetrated with signs than is a painting. The painting is dependent on a discontinuity in the image that itself constitutes connotative meaning, whereas the photograph 'can not intervene *within* the object' (Barthes 1977: 43, emphasis in the original). As Barthes further argues:

> The type of consciousness the photograph involves is indeed truly unprecedented, since it establishes not a consciousness of the being-there of the thing (which any copy could provoke) but an awareness of its having-been-there. What we have is a new space-time image category: spatial immediacy and temporal anteriority, the photograph being an illogical conjunction between the here-now and the there-then (ibid.: 44).

I would argue that the dhadi discourse shares its main feature of representation from the painting while it draws at least on one important aspect of photography. It shares with the painting the stylistic and rhetorical means to intervene in the object of representation and to create connotative meanings through that intervention. At the same time, we can understand it as 'photographic' to the extent that it creates a spatial and temporal linkage between depicted object and the present of political violence. The ambivalence of this double location can also be discerned from the more recent occurrence of dhadi videos in which this 'photographic' aspect is stretched to its furthest extent possible.

In the early 1990s a new form of dhadi representation through visual media could be observed. With the advent of cassette culture and with the booming video industry in Punjab, I found that dhadi performers have turned to recording their song performances for market distribution. Recognizing the potential of the new media has not been without ambiguities, for on a general scheme this development has not really been to the benefit of the tradition. The influence of the new media in the form of the radio, the cassette, and more recently the video, has been instrumental to the decline of more traditional forms of folk performance and patronage to which the dhadi tradition would belong. Dhadi bards were at first apprehensive about these transitions, but more recently it seems that at least some of them have adopted new technologies of representation to gain access to an expanding local and global market. One of the reasons why performers are eager to get funds to produce a videotape is because it provides the opportunity to reach addressees who would not attend gurdwara or festival performances in their private settings in Punjab. It also allows creating new linkages between Punjab and the Sikh diaspora. Videos produced in Punjab circulate among households and gurdwaras overseas, and they are good visiting cards for being invited to tour the diaspora communities. This alone is a strong motivating factor for many young performers to enter the tradition. Similarly, dhadi performers who were already abroad, use the video to transmit messages in the opposite direction. Ideologies of the Sikh homeland are nowadays flowing from the diaspora to Punjab. Video images that are recorded in the vicinity, for instance, of the Stockton gurdwara in California thus conflate temporally and geographically discrete moments that come to coexist within the same imaginary space of the Sikh diaspora.

As an example, I refer to a video that was shot in the vicinity of the gurdwara at Manchiwara, featuring a well-known dhadi performer I worked with. It is noteworthy, first of all, that the orator is never shown together with the musicians in the video edition. While dhadi song lyrics are audible in the background, the story is told through a montage technique in which the orator is portrayed in front of the historic sites in which the story is historically placed. The viewer is presented with images of the dhadi orator in front of historic gurdwaras and popular martyr shrines in addition to pictures of the Punjabi landscape that index the places of historic battles and martyrdoms. The camera frequently moves from a wide angle shot to a close-up, focusing on the face and again expanding the focus to show the bodily gestures of the orator. For each new song that is introduced, the camera moves back to the musicians in the congregation hall.

With the shift from oratory to song, the scene changes to the inside of the Sikh shrine where the spectator is presented a scene from the actual musical performance and the assembly of those gathered for the performance. The next episode is then shown in rich imagery. In this fashion, the video production succeeds in enhancing the performative effect of dhadi oratory. In comparison to the dhadi texts that I have discussed in earlier chapters, one can notice that the videos exploit the rhetorical strategy of visualization in a much more dramatic fashion. The montage of images allows for a conflation not only of the past and present, but also of spaces of religious worship and other topographical sites such as the martyr shrine. In that sense, dhadi representations can easily incorporate different elements without causing much of a paradox.

While the video productions enforce the 'photographic' dimension and what Pinney has termed the 'proximal empowerment' (1997: 173) through which persons, objects, and images acquire a sense of authenticity and authority, they simultaneously tend to lose the hold of the orator-position on the stage, the latter being able to directly intervene in the dialectic process of listening (see also Starrett 2003: 417). The video*wālā*s are cautious enough to include sequences from the actual dhadi performance in the video. This conveys a message about the legitimate place of dhadi performers in the Sikh community. However, in the eyes of many performers this looks like a minor concession.

The contours of the overall situation are therefore not so clearly etched. At the same time when dhadi oral performance has come to be regarded as integral to Sikh gurmat and particularly so against the background of the Punjab crisis in the 1980s, appropriations of dhadi aesthetics through visual and sonic innovations seem to carve away the ground upon which the more traditional dhadi performance would be based. This is not only the case for the video production, there are also new tendencies in diaspora-based music forms in which dhadi sounds and song-lyrics become absorbed in a new urban music culture in which the dhadi performer has only a virtual presence.[17] Among the network of dhadi performers with whom I have worked, therefore, the new video and audio productions are both welcome and regarded with some suspicion. Performers recognize a potential danger of getting out of touch with real-life audiences, thus losing the possibility to monitor face-to-face interaction in performance. Meanwhile, they have also recognized that their engagement in the years of the Punjab crisis has not led to a full compensation of their earlier neglect as low-caste Sikhs. The way the performative community responds to this issue of recognition is addressed in the following and final chapter.

Notes

1. It deserves notice that one copy of the Guru Granth Sahib that is now at the Sikh institution of the Damdami Sahib is linked to his name.
2. The light metaphor is indeed very crucial. It is a stylistic convention, but it also resonates a religious concept according to which saintly figures meet the end of their human existence in a stream of light that connects them to the divine abode. The first remembered Sikh martyr, Guru Arjun, for instance is believed to have immersed in light after he suffered torture. Similarly, all historical Gurus are portrayed with a halo as a sign of their blissfulness.
3. Fenech (2000), who refers to this artist in his work on the Sikh martyrdom tradition, even assumes that a person like Kirpal Singh might have been inspired by popular representations of martyrs as engendered in the dhadi genre. See McLeod (1992) for a discussion of popular arts in Sikhism. The distribution and circulation of painting by means of new print methods began in the early twentieth century, at a time when the postcard gained worldwide recognition as a new form of media and communication.
4. The image of Bhai Mani Singh is also included on Sikh websites or the digitalized Sikh encyclopaedia. The reception of such signs of otherness is further channelled and enforced by the linguistic messages that accompany these images in form of short historical treatises in which the figures are named and the story given a historical date and setting.
5. The *samādhī* refers to the practice of sitting in the meditative lotus posture, holding one's breadth in order to concentrate on the passage to death.
6. *Jāpujī* is one of the daily Sikh prayers.
7. The origins of this line of thought are often traced back to the German philosopher Wilhelm Dilthey and his processual perspective on what constitutes 'an' experience (*Erlebnis*). Dilthey made the important observation that experience constitutes temporality, as each remembered experience is always reflective of past and future and thus discontinuous with the flow of life (Bruner 1986: 9). I do not engage here in a discussion of 'experience' as valuable analytical category. Certain epistemological problems do arise as soon as one shifts from the exposed scenes of cultural performance to the less articulate and blurred scenes of everyday life. As my argument is embedded in a context of public performance, however, I focus on the key role of enacted images and representational media and assume that these have at least a structuring effect by mediating human experiences through accessible cultural categories.
8. See my discussion in the last chapter.
9. Scarry's book on the body in pain has been particularly influential in post-modern American scholarship, ranging from literary criticism, to which her own work belongs, to philosophy and anthropology (Daniel 1996).

10. It captured my attention that the book of Job is one of the oldest examples of the rhetoric of pain. The text is based on an ancient model of rhetoric culture. The structure of the text, consisting of a combination of prose and poetry, arranged in dramatic fashion as a battle of words between Job, his comforters, and the divine voice, indicates its orientation toward dramatic recital. The pain-sufferer Job, punished by divine intervention, is staged as the main orator. We find him able to persuade his interlocutors about the insufficiency and moral ambiguity upon which their inherited concept of pain would rest. He fails, however, to persuade himself. Sharing certain formulaic features with oral literary traditions, the text epitomizes historically embedded cultural and religious ideals as well as specific rhetoric styles in which cultural concepts are communicated and playfully imagined. Some interpreters trace the textual body to Mesopotamian literature that was written in the style of 'wisdom literature', whereas Good (1990: 10) rejects the claim, pointing at the underlying assumption that 'wisdom literature connotes a uniform style of proverbial narratives that is not characteristic for the book of Job.' Whatever course this ongoing discussion will take, we are safe to assume that it is one of the most profound examples of the rhetorics of pain that is historically accounted for. The reception of the book of Job over the centuries also accounts for the fact that it was based on a different notion of representation, not in the sense of mimesis of objects in language but, as Lamb has phrased it cogently, as a 'struggle between two subject positions competing for the right to speak forcefully in the first person' (Lamb 1995: 11).
11. The notion of pain is central to Sufi mysticism, but in this case too, pain is attributed to divine incision and the experience of the divine word and not to any form of human desire for pain.
12. For a genealogy of the idea of Khalistan see Grewal (1998b).
13. Harjeet Singh was the son of a well known dhadi performer in the region. At the time his dead body was discovered, people witnessed disfigurements—signs of torture that the young student had to endure in police custody. Eyewitnesses who saw him while he was in police custody declared that he was in such a bad shape that he could not recognize the visitors anymore. Human rights reports on Punjab have documented sufficiently the torture methods used by some police forces that resulted in such misery. These included electrical shocks on the genitals, beating the feet with bamboo sticks, rape, burning of the skin, or the crushing of thighs with 'the roller' (a wooden cylinder, weighed by people standing on it). See Human Rights Watch (1991, 1994). For interviews with torture victims see Mahmood (1996). Axel (2001) writes about the metaphorization of the torture discourse in the Sikh diaspora.
15. Pettigrew also raised this point in her paper on Sikh dhadi (1992: 86). I have earlier pointed out Pettigrew's shortcomings in framing the genre exclusively in Sikh categories. In the framework of the Khalistan movement her

arguments are important, however, because she was among the only authors drawing attention to the role of representational media and their function to mediate between the individual and social collective. In this chapter, I draw on some of these observations but place them in a wider analysis of rhetoric, pain, and music in the context of political violence.

15. Pettigrew recorded performances by Gian Singh Surjeet, who did not seem to be familiar with the generic forms of the dhadi genre, much more so, however, with the political objectives of the militant movement. His oratory makes direct references not only to the atrocities experienced by the 'Sikh nation' (attack on the Akal Takht), but he also eulogizes the decision of Labh Singh to join the KCF and 'to teach the oppressors a lesson'. In various song parts, all composed immediately after the events, political discourse is indexed in names, dates, and direct references.
16. Mahmood cites this image as one of the most humiliating photographs shot during the political crisis of the 1980s (1996: 11).
17. A good example is the CD 'Defenders of the Faith (Dharam de Rakhwale)', produced by the Immortal Productions label (a musical offshoot of the British Organisation of Sikhs Students). Virinder Kalra (2005) argues that dhadhi melds almost too well with the political rap music which is now a phenomena of many urban centres, so that it could be argued that the emotional power of dhadi is enhanced by the infusion of urban beats. However, Kalra argues, this second point begs the question, to what end is this emotional energy put, when the contexts of listening are unpredictable and often incommensurable with the pronounced political aims of the project. For a detailed discussion see the forthcoming article by Kalra & Nijhawan in the journal *Sikh Formations* (December 2006 issue).

7

Interpellated Subjects and Formation of the Dhadi Sabha

The capacity to circumscribe the situation of the speech act is jeopardized at the moment of injurious address. To be addressed injuriously is not only to be open to an unknown future, but not to know the time and place of injury, and to suffer the disorientation of one's situation as the effect of such speech. Exposed at the moment of such shattering is precisely the volatility of one's 'place' within the community of speakers; one can be 'put in one's place' by such speech, but such a place may be no place
Butler (1997a: 4).

What is the place of dhadi performers in contemporary Punjabi society and the Sikh community? With their turn to Sikh religious language and self-representation, as I have delineated in previous chapters, have they achieved a different symbolic identity? In what ways are the performers today socially and ideologically recognized and how can we read their performative acts in the light of 'being hailed' into existence?

To find answers to these questions, the present chapter investigates contemporary discourses in the dhadi performative scene. For a variety of reasons, I prefer to use the term 'performative scene' rather than 'folk singers' or 'group of Sikh dhadi musicians'. Speaking about a performative scene, I have in mind a dynamic field of social relations and performative action that is not sufficiently described by defining particular motifs and intentions held by a group of performers. I am interested here in the kind of internal and external relations that constitute the contemporary Sikh dhadi subject. In previous chapters I explored how relations between religious reformists, political formations, and dhadi performers have changed according to historical circumstance and changing forms of aesthetic reception. In this chapter, my main focus is the process through which the subject of the dhadi performer is constituted in language. The focus on language is neither reducible to the meanings of transmitted messages nor to their illocutionary effect. It has to do with processes of social recognition and subjectification. Thinking about such practices of subjectification, it is important to recognize the power of naming. Performative acts of naming and self-identification emerge out of particular forms of interaction between dhadi performers and the society at large. Dhadi performers are named by others in stigmatizing ways and the performers respond to this mode of address. As I want to show in this chapter, injurious words and modes of social recognition become discursively appropriated in the dhadi performative scene, that is, in contexts of everyday conduct as well as in the ritualized forms of dhadi song performance.

A simple reading of the cultural texts of dhadi performance is avoided here. I have chosen to analyse the performative elements of dhadi speech and song in a way in which their reflexive character is highlighted rather than their narrative contents. The notion of reflexivity that I employ in this context links Judith Butler's work on performativity with anthropological approaches to the study of ritual and performance to the extent that the latter have been influenced by practice theory. Anthropologists who are interested in the relationship between power and agency have by and large agreed that social actors have a capacity for reflexive self-monitoring even under circumstances in which ideological or economic constraints are formative of social experience (see for instance Keane 1997a; Ortner 1984, 1999). Unlike Giddens (1979) whose notion of reflexivity as self-monitoring has triggered critical inquiry in sociology and anthropology in recent years, anthropological approaches have held a different notion of culture and subjectivity, one that is not confined to the discursive processes through which people rationalize their actions. This is particularly important to consider in contexts of religious conduct where it is not just the elaborations on religious doctrine but moreover the practical engagement in ritual and other forms of ceremonial practice in which various forms of agency and reflexivity materialize.

The emphasis on 'religious reflexivity' resonates with a wide range of anthropological scholarship, starting from semiotic approaches in which the self-referential character of ceremonials and other symbolically pregnant acts is emphasized, and continuing with performative approaches that relate the notion of religious reflexivity to the theme of identity formation, something which is of direct interest for the topic addressed in this chapter (see Nijhawan 2005). Højbjerg has argued that 'religious reflexivity implies more than a critical attitude to the assumptions concerning religious ideas and actions. It relates more generally to the issue of imagination, understanding and consciousness, and the presence, absence, and diversity of meaning' (2002: 4). In his introductory paper to an edited volume on the same topic, Højbjerg further argues that it is not enough to link reflexivity with the communicative and metacommunicative devices that relate performative practices with processes of group identity formation in the way it has been proposed in a broad range of ethnolinguistic and performative anthropology. Both aspects must be addressed, yet specifically in contexts of ritualized practice, such as the practice of ritual song performance, there is a further self-referential dimension that lies in the very form through which practices reflect back upon the actor.[1] This consideration of religious reflexivity does not replace questions of efficacy (a 'classical' issue for performance studies), but draws attention to the possible connections between actor and the form that the enacted ritual takes (see also Houseman and Severi 1998). Following this trajectory, we should not take for granted a shared cultural and religious background of practitioners but instead focus on degrees of ambiguity and cognitive dissonance that people experience in the very act of performing rituals.

Applied to the context of my own study on dhadi performative practices, I would argue that it is precisely the question of ambiguity where relational approaches to the study of ritualized practice and theories of subject formation can be productively related. Ambiguity matters because on the one hand, dhadi performers engage in a field of cultural production in which they rework the ambiguous connections between two aesthetically distinct, yet discursively connected forms of ritual song performance and ritual prayer. On the other hand, they are connected through this practice to a culturally mediated and historically emergent field of power in which they acquire a particular social identity.

This chapter draws on my ethnographic data and describes situations in which contemporary dhadi performers struggle to relate a discourse of social recognition to an inherited practice of public song performance. In the performers' eyes, this connection appears to be based on a degree of ambiguity precisely because their enactment of dhadi texts constantly evokes tensions in performer-audience interaction and in various modes of self-recognition. Degrees of ambiguity are not only crucial to how dhadi performers commit themselves—as active participants in religious ceremonies—to various Sikh normative symbols. Ambiguity here is at the bottom of a process of embodiment through which the dhadi subject is recognized in performative language. Let me first turn to the cultural scene of the dhadi association in order to be in a position to further explore the theoretical approach outlined above.

What is in a Name: The Dhadi Subject after 1947

In late November 1999, I was attending a meeting of the Srī Gurū Hargobind 'Ḍhāḍī Sabha, a local association of traditional Sikh orators and bards in a small town near Ludhiana. I had become familiar with this group of cultural performers in an earlier phase of my fieldwork. Most of the performers live in and around the town of Ludhiana, where I also found many occasions to observe their performances that were held in small groups of three to four persons at local festivities and gurdwaras. Attending the regular meetings was particularly instructive for studying the process through which the dhadi performative community reorganized its local patterns of relations. I have argued before that the the dhadi community is a community in the making that, before and after Partition, has realigned its pattern of affiliation with the Sikhs. Broadly speaking, the forms of religious participation that were earlier defined by a broader context of popular saint veneration (due to the large number of Muslim bards), shifted to a more exclusive form of representing Sikh religious and cultural values. Partition is indeed a watershed in this process of reconstitution of the performative scene, as it led to an entire transformation not only of the patronage system, but also of the public image of the dhadi format.

The nationalization of Punjabi politics and the politicization of religious boundaries had two major consequences in terms of dhadi patronage in India. First of all, shortly after Partition and in the wake of the Punjabi Suba Morcha, Akali politics emerged as a major player of linguistic nationalism and religious revitalization of Sikh identity. This had an ultimate impact on processes of dhadi self-definition. What began in the pre-Partition years as a process of mutual recognition between Sikh political representatives and cultural performers (see Chapter 3) resulted in large institutions taking up the role of the local patron in the postcolonial period. Second, due to anti-Muslim sentiments around the event of Partition, the participation of those few remaining Muslim performers in political or other congregational gatherings was commonly seen as inappropriate. It was only later in the 1970s that the few remaining mīrasī performers could acquire a new role within a system of state patronage with its folkloristic agenda (Nijhawan 2004).

Strong demarcations emerged between performers associated with the religious institutions of the Sikhs and those who tried to benefit from the secularly defined patronage of folk arts by the state (their patrons were mostly associated with the Congress party). The division implied a reconstitution of dhadi performative space. One of my fieldwork interlocutors, a hereditary Muslim performer whose family did not migrate during Partition, made this point very clear in our conversation. He mentioned that in the 1950s his family was denied access to the local gurdwara. Consequently, Muslim bards refrained from performing registers associated with the Sikh gurus, concentrating on the few remaining Sufi festivals, many of which have become politically appropriated and transformed as folklore. With the exception of Maler Kotla, the former princely state that was spared much of Partition violence, the crossover between religious affiliations was seen as even more inappropriate. Different from the colonial period—as I have shown in the last chapter—where the rejection of such folk performance was articulated in a reformist idiom and under different conditions of cultural plurality and caste politics, after Partition it implicitly worked against the social category of the remaining Muslim performers. Musicians of low caste origin had to clarify their position. Another musician, with whom I was acquainted from the very beginning of my fieldwork, told me that he stopped performing certain repertoires such as Punjabi oral epics in the early 1950s. At that time, as a young performer, he decided to be baptised as a Sikh and to focus on Sikh religious narratives such as required by the new patron. With the breakdown of the old patronage system, the pressure was indeed high on musicians. The choice was one of abolishing dhadi performance or seeking full affiliation with Sikh institutions which, all political pressures notwithstanding, could also offer a positive and largely non-folkloristic self-image of the dhadi tradition.

Partition thus led to a redistribution of performative styles and repertoires and to a stronger emphasis on narrative repertoires with religious content. In the group meetings that I have attended, I have hardly heard any explicit reference to these issues. If at all, issues of religious conversion and memories of the immediate post-Partition years would emerge in the course of private conversations with elder musicians and there, most of the performers that I have met describe what happened as a natural decision. Public gatherings of the dhadi sabha, however, allow for a more complex understanding of this large-scale process of transition.

Voices that Hail the Subject

Social relations that define the dhadi performative scene are distinctively egalitarian, despite the internal asymmetries that are characteristic for the teacher-disciple relationship. During a group meeting there are little constraints on speech and opinion making. In their gatherings performers were engaged in communicative practices that, first of all, were clearly set apart from the highly formalized modes of stage performance that I observed at public events. The sabha meetings opened a discursive space that was tied to the Sikh normative paradigms and yet assumed a different subject position as will become clear in the following. First of all, I could discern from the conversations and my own observations that this group of performers was in a truly awkward position. In terms of bodily appearance performers were clearly recognizable as baptized Sikhs, having their turbans tied in a particular fashion and displaying the religious symbols of the Khalsa such as the *kirpān* which they would wear on top of their white *kurtā*. This marked body, however, entered language in a way in which hidden meanings of otherness and alternative imaginations of social belonging were given emphasis. Dhadi performers were painfully aware that the embodiment of Sikh normative values, exemplified in their everyday conduct and performative practice, has not resolved their continuing struggle for social recognition within the wider community of the Sikhs. In the following I would like to turn to the articulation of this embodied opposition as it was enunciated in the sabha meeting.

It was a sunny November day, so the participants assembled at a place outside the local gurdwara. The place was convenient and incidentally just big enough to host the four dozen people who arrived in order to appoint a new spokesperson (*pradhān*) of their association. The event was considered an important step to promote the collective agenda of the dhadi sabha. With the early winter fog dissolving and the sun breaking through, I found myself chatting with a group of performers, when the first speakers began to address the audience with welcome notes. Other speeches soon followed in which the celebratory tone suddenly seemed to pave the way for open criticism. Sant Singh, a

FIGURE 18: Discussions at the Dhadi Sabha meeting
Courtesy Michael Nijhawan

well-known performer in the region had the following to say about two important political and religious organizations:[2]

Am I not telling the truth if I say that the Shiromani Committee and the Shiromani Akali Dal expect that we commit ourselves to their cause? That we would prepare their ground [*unhāṃ dā assī 'ground' taiyār karānge*]? We crunch the stones on the ground [*assī 'ground' vic roṛ cukde hāṃ*]! We mould bricks from earth! We do everything! But with their cowardice they do not even recognize how clear this ground has in fact been made. They also know that we are upright people [*pakke log*], but tell me, up to today what kind of help did we receive from the Shiromani Akali Dal and the Shiromani Committee people?

The performers present uttered words of confirmation and support. Sant Singh used metaphors of construction work and labour that sounded familiar to those present, many of whom previously worked as dependent labourers. In his oratory the rhetoric of labour was applied to performative and ideological functions of the dhadi profession. It is not just the work of hand and gestures in musical and oratorical practice that is talked about here; the language of 'moulding bricks' indexes a process of narrativization and oral persuasion through which the common man's mind is 'prepared' for accepting Sikh religious beliefs. Sant Singh portrayed the labour of oratory and bardic music as a sweatshop of cultural and religious production that has been erased from official memory. For the majority of performers I have worked with, the economy of signs that pertains to dhadi performative language is seen as a suppressed site of productivity, politically censored by the state in times of insurgency and marginalized by society in the contemporary context. Yet, it is exactly through this economy of signs that the process of social reproduction is sustained in the performative community.

The meeting of the dhadi performers was characterized by an immense orchestration of different views and opinions. The point raised by Sant Singh, however, found widespread support. Gurbaksh Singh, another performer, was even more explicit in portraying the situation as one of complete disrespect and disdain:

> *Vahe Guru Ji ka Khalsa, Vahe Guru Ji ki Fateh!* We come together here today because of a very important issue. We restless people, we dhadi, I say that we have become orphans [*yatīm*], washing someone else's underwear [*kacchere*]. Do you understand? We wash them for the Sikhs, and still nobody would appreciate our deeds.... With our limited means of serving others, have we ever refused to serve the master tea and milk? Did we ever attempt to change our affiliation?... There has been a need for us to find a place in this world [society]. In whatever way we can achieve this, with the help of our new president...we must be aware that they will just add a tail to it and name it their own. Whomsoever we elect as the president, it is for making us one, so that every Singh amongst us will be helped.

It was the tone that distinguished between 'us' and 'them', dhadi performers and 'the Sikhs'. It is interesting to note how this difference becomes manifest in this oral presentation. First of all, take the metaphor of washing the underwear (*kachairā*) for the Sikh patrons. It alludes to dependent labour and at the same time draws on a popular idiom that names dhadi performers as those 'with the worn out underwear'. The kachairā is one of the five bodily symbols (the *kakār*) that characterize the ritualized body of a Khalsa Sikh. To say someone has worn out kachairā is a demeaning remark on his presumed immorality and fallen status. Appropriated as a signature of social orphanage, the stigma of washing other's underwear is invested with a self-reflexive, ironic twist—a twist that, in Butler's (1997b: 3) reading, is at once turned upon the self and away from it. The kind of subjectivity produced in these dialogues is cast in the language of servitude to the Sikh patrons and institutions. Note the idiom of serving tea and milk, which alludes to intimacies of social interaction and which must be considered basic forms of politeness in everyday conduct in Punjab. One could argue that performative practice, even in its critical reformulation, still incorporates the overall structures of domination and subjugation. The cultural specificity of this language of servitude, however, is such that it enables performers to stake a claim upon the master—the absence of particular gestures on the part of the patron is read as a double negligence, a lack of social recognition and a deficiency in terms of economic and cultural reciprocity. This can still be read within a theory of hegemonic relations. Yet, at a closer look it also opens a space for identity formation that is reflexive and affirmative, one that exceeds social stigmatization. I would argue that this affirmative potential lies precisely in a process of religious reflexivity: the reckoning of emancipatory potentials of Sikh religious language and normative models that are associated with the institutions from which one seeks recognition.

It can be inferred from what I have discussed so far that people are engaged in processes of rationalization and objectification of the religious traditions and practices they inherit (see Højbjerg 2002: 8). This process of rationalization is mediated by a discourse on social identity, in which religious symbols are contrasted with a social stigma. In the case of the dhadi performative community, this process has a particular historicity that I have indicated in earlier chapters: the coming into existence of a social subject that is at once granted recognition and yet, at the same time, threatened by a stigmatizing call. The coming into existence of this subject is defined through a process of apprenticeship of performative forms—a mastery of words and gestures that sets the subject in direct relation to a dominating discourse in the moment of its constitution. I argue that it is through the recognition of this notion of mastery that a process of distancing becomes possible.

Historians and anthropologists engaged in writing on ritual, power, and agency have repeatedly confronted this paradox of subject formation. Ortner (1990) as well as Bell (1992) argue that people realize their creative and transformative power through processes of acquiring mastery and discursive resignification of culturally stipulated schemata and norms, even under the most repressive forms of political domination. Performative language assumes a central place in their argument to the extent that the re-enactment of conventionalized forms of speech and the submission to particular forms of social authority alludes to a reflexive position toward those forms, a path of conscientiousness, 'as a way to gain a purchase on identity' (Butler 1997b: 129). In the introductory examples, this 'purchase on identity' results from a linguistic mediation of two different sets of bodily metaphors, each signifying a different subject and social memory. The transparent body of Sikh religious identity markers intersects with a hidden, labouring, and recognizably low-caste body that, in its embodied dimensions, is one of otherness through which this performative community experiences itself as marginalized and subjugated. It is significant to note, however, that the 'call of recognition' that hinges upon a stigmatized body is not responded to in terms of subversion or open resistance against a powerful other. Voices of dissent are cast in a language of reciprocity between patron and performer, not in a disjunction between dhadi practice and Sikh patronage. Furthermore, as I have pointed out, voices of dissent draw their moral legitimacy from Sikh normative concepts, not in opposition to them.

In drawing attention to such issues, my aim is not to suspend notions of 'misrecognition' of the 'what' of what ritual practice does beyond peoples' strategies and intentions. The objective is rather to examine the extent to which religious reflexivity and the evaluation of particular cultural and religious aesthetics are instrumental to the production of a new dhadi subject. Especially in praxis theory, it seems to me, the conceptual move in placing religious language on the side of ideology and power through which people are subjected within a hierarchically structured environment has been a hasty move, probably at the cost of overlooking the western model of religious ideology operating here, and certainly by ignoring the emancipatory potential of religious *doxa*. The objective in this chapter, therefore, is to rethink the place of religious reflexivity in the encounter of the socially marginalized with dominant religious institutions.

Scenes of Reputation

Among the dhadi performative community, religious language has become the pivotal form of self-assertion and in this way has helped to shape a new performative framework through which the genre appears as a recognizable form of a religious public sphere in Punjab. In the following section, I first discuss the role of religious language as a mode of structuring the internal scenes of reputation and moral accountability in the dhadi network in which I have conducted fieldwork. As I shall argue towards the end of this section, the processes through which matters of internal fracture and self-improvement are negotiated are significant beyond the immediate context of this particular performative community. From what is discussed below, we can draw conclusions on how religious notions of self-discipline constitute the speaking subject in a wider social context that, in the eyes of the performers, currently lacks morality and thus appears to them as a site for contestation.

It is the word 'politics' that captures these evaluations of public conduct. For the people I have encountered, this word bears all the negative connotations of economic inequality, excess in consumption, bribing, and individualism that, for them, characterize a loss of morals among the emerging middle class and the class of politicians. As far as 'politics' is concerned, the common assumption is that it also structures the internal workings of institutions such as the SGPC, or the Akal Takht.[3] 'Politics' also relates to the fissures between spoken words and assumptions of speakers' sincerity. People voice their concern about named and unnamed public figures (performers, preachers, politicians), who would display the outer symbols of Sikhism but lack the inner qualities that distinguish a pious Sikh (*gursikh*) from the hypocrite. Issues of sincerity and intentionality in speech as they are enunciated in such conversations are sometimes assessed in terms of an idealized realm of subject formation in the individual interior, but more importantly it is the observable form of everyday conduct that counts in this matter. If 'politics' has destroyed the equilibrium between speech acts, forms of intentionality, and social transactions—in the way suggested in the introductory example of failed reciprocity between patrons and performers—it follows that the cure of the basic social ills is also not confined to an accusation of individual failure. Yet, to the extent that it can be culled from the discussions in the performative scene, it is only by means of self-discipline and self-improvement that a new body politic can be imagined. Notions of religious self-discipline are made explicit when the performers evoke images of 'proper speech' and pious conduct—notions that are modelled according to the principles of the Sikh *rahit maryada* and its prescribed practices of praying and ritual. In that sense, the dhadi sabha articulates its vision of community in distinction from the structure of political patronage and in accordance with the spread of specific standards of pious behaviour of the gursikh.

Precisely because the notion of a new or reformed speaking subject necessitates an active engagement of self-improvement and discipline—that is what the performers articulated—it is necessary to look more closely at the actual processes of interaction through which actors acquire a new sense of the self, a new identity.

For the performers I have worked with, matters of self-improvement are closely linked to matters of reputation. Reputation alludes to the actual processes of internal differentiation in a performative scene. It is an established category in performance studies that relates to 'the informal, consensual evaluations by which performers judge one another's competence and relate to one another in a social network' (Gerstin 1998: 387). According to Gerstin, matters of reputation have to be considered as key sites of identity formation. Questions of aesthetics, competence, and social belonging are constantly reworked and concretely related to performative practice (ibid.: 397). This can be observed in the networks of dhadi performers. For instance, I heard strong opinions on actors who would call themselves dhadi but, in the eyes of the performers I worked with, would lack the necessary performative and rhetorical skills that distinguish dhadi performers from other Sikh musicians and preachers (*parcārak*). Reputation in the dhadi performative community rests on skilled apprenticeship and thus on the capacity to display musical competence, historical knowledge, and rhetorical skills, in particular the appropriate forms of body language and voice modulation that distinguishes the performative genre from others.

Reputation also alludes to a broader notion of social recognition. For the performers I have worked with, it is religious discourse that provides the argumentative structure through which social change and new social visions are aspired to and materialized in the social world. For them, the question is not solely how to couch a social and political agenda in religious language or ideology, but to consider religion itself as the means to challenge the status quo of power relations and social stratification.[4] Let me explain this in the light of the discussions as they unfolded in the Sabha meeting.

Unlike many other meetings that I have attended, the congregation of the dhadi sabha was an event of particular importance, due to the fact that a new pradhān had to be appointed. This occasioned a series of speeches delivered by the former and new president and a variety of other participants who were interested in putting specific claims on the agenda. For the purpose at hand I shall concentrate on a speech delivered by the former spokesperson of the group, Charan Singh. In his oratory, he succeeded in bridging internal disputes that had surfaced previously among the different groups attending the meeting. When

Charan Singh got up to address his audience, it was after more than one hour of intense group discussions and so he felt compelled to respond to several issues raised by previous speakers. In his opening lines, he emphasized the generational gap (bear in mind that this entails recognition of a presumed loss of religiosity) and the new requirements of being a Sikh performer:

When we assemble here to reconstitute our dhadi sabha, our primary concern is the present generation that follows the footprints of the ancestors. Not only the present generation, we also have to consider coming generations, younger performers who are shooting up [*āun wāle jeṛhe sāḍe puṅgār rahe ne*]; and who will have to move this caravan [*kāfla*] forward.... It is a difficult task, of course, but one thing is quite clear—through hardship human beings can get their task accomplished [*Ah ik shai zarūr hai, ke bande mushkalāṃ de nāl, te bande hī prāptiyāṃ karde ne*].

Far too long, argues Charan Singh in the first part of his speech, have quarrel and suspicion prevailed, partly because of the entanglement with 'politics' and partly because of envy towards performers who have achieved a better social standing than most of those present in the meeting. Thus, what can be observed in his oratory is a reflexive stance toward notions of group solidarity that have been historically undermined by the structure of patron-client relations.[5] Strategies of consolidating the performative community in terms of a collective agent have to be based on other resources. For Charan Singh one of these resources was the rural, unemployed youth. A crucial point in the discussions was the propagation of their cause among the rural young population. There was, however, a certain amount of ambiguity in this notion of 'the youth'. The issue of the youth evoked the danger of a social ban, but at the same time it held the promise of gaining strength through recruitment, as can be culled from the next quotation of the speech:

And I said [addressing the last speaker], A. Sahib! After I have considered it thoroughly, when we bring the entire dhadi community on a single platform, will we form one big sabha. You should propagate this to the youth of today [*tūṃ ajj dī 'youth' vic ih bhand kar de*]! You indicated that, by provoking the youth, or propagating this dhadi-art among them, it could be harmful to us [*sāḍī ḍhāḍī kālā hānī-khārak ho sakdī*] and could lead to another censorship on dhadi performance. Yet, I think that if our dhadi tradition would proceed on that path, prohibition would only mean encouragement for them [the youth]. We can make this work.

Cloaked in idiomatic terms a variety of problematic issues are expressed here. One of them is the association of the English term 'the youth' with militancy.[6] This term is closely associated with those who, in the course of the Khalistan movement, joined militant squads, sometimes even without supporting the political cause that defined the core of the movement. But as we have seen, Charan Singh is arguing that there is no other way than to strengthen recruitment efforts of rural, mostly illiterate youth, giving them opportunity in religious education and by that means cultivate their taste for the aesthetics of dhadi performance. On the other hand, he also takes care of integrating the old and often illiterate participants of the meeting whom he calls respectively the *buzurg*: 'We should always cherish our respected dhadi elders in our hearts [*unh layī sāde hirday vic hameśā 'respect' rahnī cāhidī hai*]. See, if they had not raised their voices like lions on the stages, today's children would have lacked the faith and devotion [*inhā de andar kaḍi wī śradha paidā nahīṃ honī sī*] to serve the community as dhadi.' Through such praises of the elders' honour, he manoeuvres through discussions on education and illiteracy, which might have devaluaed their contributions. This balanced way of speaking is regarded as highly appropriate for a spokesperson and ultimately adds to his reputation.

Part of what was at stake during this meeting was the reconfiguration of the performative community through processes of debate and persuasion. Although the nature of the speeches was usually colloquial, specific formal elements such as taking recourse to poetic verse and reported speech allowed speakers to demonstrate their skills in argumentation and social knowledge. The lack of economic and social resources seems to be outweighed by the cultural power imbued in public speech. Solidarity can never be taken for granted and all kinds of rhetorical devices are resorted to in order to sustain the community of the performers. Certainly, what cannot be ignored is that these actors have incorporated conceptions about persuasive conduct in their everyday lives. In order to understand how dhadi performers gain reputation within their performative community, one has to cautiously analyse the various linguistic practices through which a speaker like Charan Singh is capable of persuading others, even at the moment when he was to be replaced as the main representative of the sabha.[7]

These strategic elements notwithstanding, I have cited these quotations in order to think about processes of religious reflexivity that transcend certain individual intentions and modes of persuasion. The figuration of religious tropes alludes to the discursive shifts through which a new collective agent imagines itself to be authenticated by a religious cause. Let me clarify this point with a further citation from Charan Singh's speech:

> Maharaj has given orders, and we should obey these. And with the Guru blessings [I shall say]: 'If you improve yourself, then you will be able to reach me. And after you accomplished this task, you have the whole world at your disposal. If you continue following the Guru, then the whole world will belong to you [*āp sanwāre maiṃ mile, maiṃ milyā jag hoye, je tū merā hoye rahe, tā sab jag terā hoye*].

In this quote the orator takes recourse to a Sikh normative framework in which the ultimate principle of pure speech (*gurmat*) emanates from divine authority. On the one hand, the pronunciation of these moral issues has a strong binding effect. Considering the difficult socio-economic conditions under which dhadi performers accomplish their profession, the reconfirmation of values that transcend the practical necessities of contemporary patronage are seen as particularly powerful and transformative. On the other hand, it is precisely because of the discrepancy that exists between such principles of pure speech and the actual practices that constitute the everyday affairs of the dhadi performative scene, that an argument on the actual meaning of religious doctrine is instigated.

The issue that looms here, I believe, has to do with the formation of a speaking subject through religious notions of duty and morality. This emphasis has informed the reformist agenda of the pre-Partition years, but has acquired completely new meanings in the post-1984 context, in which the ruptures between Sikh institutions and dhadi performers are openly negotiated. In this respect, I would argue, the dhadi tradition constitutes a space for public deliberation that shares features of religious reform agendas such as have been described by Asad (1993, 1999) or Hirschkind (2001) for the al-da'wa movement in Egypt. Hirschkind demonstrates in his work that religious virtue constitutes a domain of ethical discipline and a 'non-discursive background of sentiments and habits' (ibid.: p. 5) that has become formative of modern Islamic practices of public reasoning. The disciplining power of ethical speech, Hirschkind argues in his analysis of the Quranic practices of da'wa, is an overarching objective 'that takes public deliberation as one of its modalities' (ibid.: p. 4). Da'wa in written and oral form became popular because it constituted an alternative form of public engagement in opposition to the state-controlled media. Beyond this political context, however, it is also a preferred 'conceptual site wherein the concepts, public duties, character and virtues of an activist Muslim citizen were elaborated and practiced' (ibid.: p. 11). From the point of view of the pious, one is made a Muslim citizen as a consequence of an engagement in da'wa practices. Da'wa, argues Hirschkind, renders the private public and politicizes individual choices, 'subjecting them to a public scrutiny oriented around the task of establishing the conditions for the practice of Islamic virtues' (ibid.: p. 12). Hirschkind points to the specific historical conditions under which such processes have unfolded. These are ultimately tied up with processes of modernization and nation building, yet they also remain 'structured by goals and histories not easily accommodated within the space of the nation' (ibid.: p. 5). The emphasis on the formative rule of the religious virtues is therefore based on a dialogical model of persuasion and public debate that cannot be subsumed to the logics of the modernization argument: religious orthodoxy and ethical discipline do not preclude but stipulate public debate.[8] This emphasis seems to confirm a statement that dhadi performer Kamal Singh expressed in a private conversation on his motivations to perform in public. He said:

> Whether it is in honour of Guru Maharaja or not, wherever we dhadis will go, our talk will be about Sikh history, about the principles of Sikhism. We'll talk about *gurmat* [Guru's precepts, principle teachings]. We present *gurmat*. We will deliver what the Gurus prescribed as 'duty' and taught as religious truths [*huqāṃ*].... Rather than speaking about those who disregard the principles of the faith, our presentation is about the ethos of being Sikh [*sikkhī*], about the history of Guru Maharaja, the history of the Singhs, about the principles/doctrines of *sikkhī*. Whatever place, as long as there is an assembly of listeners [*sangat*], we shall give voice to dhadi vars.

In this quote too, the speaker comments on how the actual process of dhadi performance needs to be grounded in disciplinary notions of religious duty through which the transformative character of a performance ought to be channeled. It is at the same time a comment on how the performer's agency is extended through an incorporation of particular words in concrete practices of song performance.[9] The merit of Hirschkind's argument, I believe, lies precisely in relating the disciplinary and emancipatory aspects of religious language and practice through which historically situated actors articulate themselves as publicly responsive citizen-subjects. The crucial difference to the dhadi performative scene, however, is that the latter is clearly shaped as a cultural institution that has an ambivalent secular orientation. The persistence of this cultural mediation in addition to the social image it entails, I would argue, has made it difficult for dhadi performers to pursue an agenda that would be shared by a large number of similar minded religious reformists. Even if their main focus is the presentation of gurmat, as the above quotation suggests, their public conduct is still framed in terms that sets them apart from those who practice Sikh sacred language (gurbani) such as the kirtan ragis.[10]

Scenes of Betrayal and Moral Accountability

The subjection to Sikh normative values not only accounts for the complex dynamics of internal organization within the performative community, it also sets the parameters around which public performances unfold. Public performances occur as a part of the daily liturgy at the gurdwara, at the occasion of community events such as the *shahīdī* niwas which are held to commemorate the death anniversary of a Sikh martyr, and at various folk festivals. Whereas in the religious contexts there is a relatively stable set of expectations and evaluations of dhadi narrative and musical genres, the 'duty to perform gurmat' enunciated in Kamal Singh's words has a different connotation when applied in festival contexts. Here, secular evaluations of folk music and ludic entertainment frame the performative event.

Popular imagination of Punjabi folk culture has sustained a broadly defined category of the dhadi singer that encompasses forms of non-religious bardic expression, such as the performances of the Punjabi oral epics. The standard expectation of most people present at such a festival occasion would be that the performers simply adapt to the required circumstances and perform songs that are to the audience's taste. As I have argued, however, the sabha members seek to overcome the social implications of this framing, as it categorizes them as folk bards in the service of a cultural discourse to which they do not want to subscribe anymore. I will demonstrate in the following sections how dhadi performance mediates the tensions between these sets of expectations by first considering the citationality of voice in the performative event, and second, by looking at processes of voice embodiment.

Dhadi Discourse in the Space of the Mela

From among the many occasions of public dhadi performance that I could observe in the course of my research work, I have selected a presentation that was held at a folk festival (mela) in Ludhiana in memory of the venerated local poet and patron of the arts, Mohan Singh. I refer to this particular event because I was both acquainted with the organizers of the event as well as with the performers.[11] The spatial arrangement of bardic performances at the Mohan Singh mela was rather informal, the duration of each performance being restricted as each group was allotted 30 minutes on the stage. It was expected that, through oratory and song, the dhadi performers would contribute to the memory of the deceased poet. A degree of discursive predictability has therefore been inherent to the staging of dhadi performance. Under the special circumstances of the commemorative event, the Sikh dhadi performers become part of a setting in which the enunciation of claims of historical truth meets certain formal and stylistic requirements of stage performance before an audience that is mostly familiar with the legacy of the patron for whom the festival is held. The way the performers achieve a sense of authority and voice in the given performance has to be considered against this context.

During the two-day event of the Mohan Singh mela, the dhadi darbar was staged as the opening event along with other Punjabi and Rajasthani folk performances. Around 150 listeners were sitting on the ground relatively near to the stage where the performers were seated. When it came to their turn, Kamal Singh and his colleagues began tuning their instruments and introduced their performance by praising Mohan Singh's achievements, followed by general allusions to 'Punjab's heroes' and the need to remember their deeds in the present day. As the orator of the jattha, Kamal Singh then specified the topic of his talk—the story of Sham Singh Attari. The latter is a well-known general who served under Maharaja Ranjit Singh until the middle of the nineteenth century. He is remembered by Sikhs today because he gave his life during the first Anglo-Sikh war in 1846. This battle took place in Sabhraon. The importance of this battle lives on as a myth on the presumed betrayal of Sham Singh Attari. Sikh memory has it that Sham Singh was called to the battlefield by two companions, known as Teja Singh and Lal Singh, who 'treacherously' left the battlefield and tricked Sham Singh into a hopeless situation in which he was cornered by a superior British force. The story is therefore significant at different levels. First, it amounts to Sikh heroism and discourses of martyrdom. Second, it engenders the issue of betrayal within the in-group of the Sikh panth. In this case, betrayal led to the defeat against the British and thus to the end of Sikh rule in Punjab.

The structural feature of betrayal is too familiar a topic to be left in the distant past. Take for instance, the first verses: 'there is injustice on the Earth, as it happened in Punjab', 'friends turn into enemies, inciting injustice', or 'the fatherland is threatened from slavery'. Although these verses relate to the historical narrative on Sham Singh Attari, the idiom of betrayal has strong connotations on the current political situation. The notion of betrayal and injustice resonates with the discourse of post-Khalistan politics, in which politicians—local and state level—are often described as corrupt, being interested in personal gain rather than in improving the condition of the people. I have cited similar statements as a part of daily conduct among the dhadi performative community in the first section of this chapter. In contrast, the performative texts, did not explicitly name so-called betrayers (*gadarāṃ*) of the present—neither in allusion to the political realities of the 1980s (Congress or Akali Dal politicians), nor to the present context of the mela event (local politics and patronage).

Other modes of linking past and present were produced in the narrative sections of the dhadi performance. By taking Sham Singh as an exemplary model, the orator succeeded in staking out an ideal character of Sikh moral virtues as it is implied in the notion of martyrdom as a testimony to religious truth:

> Since hundreds of years, millions of people come and leave this world every day, but rare are those sons on earth whose name, bravery and deeds get written down in golden letters on the pages of history. Thus, a poet's life endures; it does not get extinct from this world. And the martyrs have become immortal; the world will never forget them.

By associating the poet (*śa'ir*) with the martyr (śahīd), Kamal Singh drew an interesting allegory: a timeless truth is incorporated in the poem, in the manner that Sikh martyrs incorporate a universal, moral truth. The heroes have left their names 'in golden letters on the pages of history'. What can be inferred from such instances is how a modern concept of historical consciousness is constructed in a given performance. And this is, indeed, a very common facet of dhadi song performances. Through the allegory between śa'ir and śahīd, the narrative plot becomes recontextualized in the given circumstances of honouring the poet Mohan Singh: the orator demonstrated eloquence in praising the life of Mohan Singh and at the same time quoted from Mohan Singh's popular poems to elaborate on the notion of a Sikh ethos.

Reported speech that occurred frequently throughout the performance thus helped to heighten the contrast between notions of betrayal and martyrdom. One could get a sense of this in the jattha's dramatization of Sham Singh's death on the battlefield. Again, it was through the citational character of dhadi presentation that crucial concepts like the heroism of the Sikhs was dramatized. Sham Singh voice was staged as follows: 'You brave ones! Guru Gobind Singh [*kalgiyāṃ wāle gurū pātshāh*] is present here today to witness the wonder of your bravery. Let us repeat once more the battle of Chamkaur [*camkaur dā sākā*].' Since Sham Singh discovered that part of the Sikh forces fled from the battlefield, there was no hope for victory. What would be his answer? Reference to the famous battle of Chamkaur, during which many of Guru Gobind Singh's followers were 'martyred' on the battlefield, left the audience reassured that the hero would not retreat, but face his destiny with a willingness to lay down his life. The contrast between the immoral betrayer and the moral Sikh hero could not be more apparent. The reference to the Chamkaur battle further demonstrates how, within reported speech, different mythohistorical events of the Sikh past become conceptually related.

The contrast between motifs of betrayal and moral virtue is also given emphasis through the acting body during performance. When the story reaches its climax and Sham Singh calls his followers to embrace death on the battlefield, Kamal Singh raises his voice as if he himself would call for the beginning of the battle, thus indicating to his companions to sing Sham Singh's song. The performance ends with another of Mohan Singh's poems, in which the immortality of śa'ir and śahīd was again emphasized:

And, while presenting two lines of Sardar Mohan Singh, I want the audience [*sangat*] to honour the eminent patrons of Punjabi culture, Jagdev Singh, to Sardar Parman Singh and Sardar Gurbhajan Singh. They have selflessly promised to broadcast the heritage of Punjab's favoured poet, for whom since 21 years this mela is being held. Professor Mohan Singh has written two marvelous lines in his poem 'Nurjahan'. And, according to 'Nurjahan', Professor Mohan Singh heard a voice in a dream: 'The way you have valued my poetry and dropped on my grave a few tears//The same way people will weep in your memory and drop countless tears' [*Merī śā'irī dī jis tarhā qadar kar ke, merī qabar te gire ne cār hanjūṃ//Aiwain ronā tainūṃ wī yād kar ke, lok giran ke beshumār hanjūṃ*']. Today, Punjabis are shedding tears in memory of their favourite poet.

Through such praise, the audience is not only reminded about the continuous need to remember the poet Mohan Singh, the bards also project an image of their own group as socially significant. Eventually, the orator expresses his gratitude to patrons and audience, reminding them to honour Mohan Singh as an arbiter of a particular moral commitment expressed in his poetic verses. The form of bardic speech as it was enacted during this event certainly accounts for the de-authorization of individual voice that seems to be characteristic for bardic discourses throughout North India. In the context of the dhadi performance, however, this deferral of agency also has a force in staking claims on historical validity and the moral accountability of the contemporary patrons. The praise of the patrons in the last paragraph follows social conventions and can be seen as an appropriate statement to the liking of the patron. Yet, in a nuanced reading, I would argue, the speaker issues an implicit critique of the organizing committee in reminding them about what he considered to be Mohan Singh's legacy.[12] It is a legacy of the 'heroism' of Punjabis, reframed in terms of religious concepts of self-sacrifice and moral virtue. Obviously, this issue has become secondary to the political and social agenda of the folk festival that was organized around local election campaigns. We can say with some plausibility that the dhadi group's evocation of Sikh normative language was also directed against what they considered moral failures *within the Sikh community* as they materialized in the present context of folk patronage. This is something that was not missed on the part of the festival organizers, as I was reassured in our private conversations.

If the example above provides evidence of how socially prescribed narrative plots are recontextualized within the framework of a ritualized song performance, it also shows that the dhadi performers do not simply function as 'loudspeakers' of particular patrons and ideologies, as a common understanding of their profession would suggest. Performative practice enables speakers to work upon normative discursive structures in a way in which social differences that have traditionally defined the patron-client relationship are assimilated into a more encompassing notion of morality and religious piety. These notions of morality and religious piety are at once tied to the doxa of Sikh religion and yet reflexively linked to actual manifestations of identity politics. In the contemporary context of dhadi performative practice, religious language appears to be a major resource of social emancipation. It promises new forms of community solidarity and participation in the wider public. However, the appropriation of such religious principles of self-improvement is never fully under control, not only because the relations of power that subject the performers in a position of dependent labour are still disproportionately effective, but also because the bodily act of voice production that places the performers in a context of relations with their social and cultural environment, is never fully controllable.

Interpellation and Voice

In linguistic anthropology, voice is usually conceptualized as the combined acts of formulating and delivering a speech (Keane 2001: 268ff). The linguistic approach is useful because it allows us to analyse specific speech situations based on cultural models of speaking, subjecthood, and agency. In this chapter I have analysed such different modes of voice production in the dhadi performative scene. I have also argued that the dhadi voice implies a notion of performativity that transcends discursive structures. The dhadi voice has a recognizable feeling-tone and acquires a particular aesthetics in this capacity when cultivated in particular genres of song recitation. The musical image of voice production is more than metaphorical in that regard. It literally ties the dhadi performers with the members of a face-to-face community.[13] The relatedness of linguistic interventions and non-discursive practices places the dhadi subject in an ambivalent position. It participates in a broader discourse of self-emancipation and yet the claims to concepts of religious reasoning seem to be contradicted by actual forms of interpellation. In fact, the issue that looms here is the relationship between religious language and interpellation.

Althusser's theory of interpellation that has been instrumental to a critical theory of subject formation does not offer a clear perspective in that matter, as he tends to place religion as ideology by the side of the powerful voice by which the subject is hailed and thus given birth in language. Butler (1997a) has argued that this concept of religious authority is itself an ideological construct and, I would add, thus hardly useful to be expanded cross-culturally, specifically if notions of personhood and attributions to divine or non-human agency and voice essentially differ from western conceptualizations. However, Butler's critical expansion of Althusser is very instructive. As it turns out, her main point of criticism against a theory of interpellation is not positioned against Althusser's basic premise, that is, the observation that subjects are inaugurated in language 'through a prior performative exercise of speech' (ibid.: p. 39). Her scepticism concerns the figure of the divine voice that is implied in Althusser's example of the turn toward the law exemplified in the policeman's voice. The notion of voice has featured as a critical point in Althusser's theory of interpellation, and it is precisely the meaning of voice in the theory of subject formation that Butler sees in need of revision.[14]

One of the main points in Butler's argument is the dormant model of religious ideology in Althusser's model. Thus, she argues: 'Althusser inadvertently assimilates social interpretation to the divine performative. The example of religion thus assumes the status of a paradigm for thinking ideology as such: the authority of the "voice" or ideology, the "voice" of interpellation, is figured as a voice almost impossible to refuse' (ibid.: 31). Attributing such power to the voice of authority that names and brings the subject into being is problematic for Butler precisely because it serves to disguise the discursive procedures of subject formation. According to her 'interpellation must be dissociated from the figure of voice in order to become the instrument and mechanism of discourses whose efficacy is irreducible to their moment of enunciation' (ibid.: 32). Citing Foucault's theory of power, she counsels against the tendency to see the subject as the one who would 'exercise sovereign power of what it says' (ibid.: 34).

One could imagine that in Butler's work on hate speech this is indeed a critical point. The crucial argument against legal discourses that tend to 'isolate the "speaker" as the culpable agent' to be punished, is a focus on the repetitive character of speech acts. 'The speaker assumes responsibility precisely through the citational character of speech. The speaker renews the linguistic tokens of a community, reissuing and reinvigorating such speech. *Responsibility is thus linked with speech as repetition, not as origination*' (ibid.: 39; emphasis added). If the voice-centred theory of interpellation is based on a mistaken view of speech as origination, can there be an alternative perspective of interpellation based on a model of voice that is constituted through reiteration and repetition? Is the subject's role in the act of speaking not also dependent on a mode of recognizing the ways in which the boundaries between inner and outer voices are constantly transgressed? And is the figure of this fractured voice not in fact appropriate for conceptualizing the paradox of linguistic injury that, according to Butler, can be redirected against the 'venue of power' (ibid.: 12) through which it circulates?

In the light of the material discussed in this book, there is no clear-cut answer to these questions. The possibilities of speaking in the dhadi voice against a venue of power are certainly limited, as the conditions of social marginality continue to shape the dhadi performative scene. Yet, what can be learned from this study is that the relationship between voices that hail the subject and voices of performative enactment have tended to emancipate dhadi performers at the social margin rather than further subjecting them to the command of ideology.

Notes

1. For this point see Houseman and Severi (1998).
2. After Partition in 1947, these two institutions have emerged as the major patrons of Sikh dhadi performers. The SGPC is a particularly important institution, as it administers the Sikh shrines, appoints religious representatives, and manages the internal affairs of the community.
3. These evaluations are by no means restricted to the group of dhadi performers. Take, for instance, the voice of a representative of the Sikh Missionary College, a religious institution that educates youth in religious disciplines and doctrines. Asked about the connections between the college and some leading institutions of the Sikh panth, the answer was: 'We indeed have relations, we are receiving recognition and they even respect us. They know that we are preaching. But we would not get any help from them. They want to flatter us, but this is not according to our principles. We have one condition: If someone wants to enter politics, he has to give in his notice and depart from our institution, only then he can do it.' This is a small section of a longer interview that was conducted by my research assistant, Khushwant Singh with the president of the Sikh Missionary College, Harbhajan Singh, in October 1999, Ludhiana. Khushwant studied the educational agenda of the Sikh Missionary College and how it appealed young rural Sikhs. The interview was broadly designed however, and covered topics that we shared in our research projects. Harbhajan Singh is a well-known figure in the context of Sikh religious institutions, so that his evaluations can be said to acquire a certain depth and authority.
4. For this point see Juergensmeyer (1982: 269) as well as Fuchs (2000).
5. The sabha members find themselves in a situation in which they cannot rely upon the solidarity of these eminent performers who have better access to educated elites and key actors within the religious institutions. The reputation of these individual performers is seen as disproportional to the actual benefit they have brought to the performative community as a whole.

6. People would normally use the Punjabi term *muṅḍā*, but Charan Singh made frequent use of English words.
7. The question of whether or not Charan Singh had to resign is circumstantial to the point raised here. My emphasis here is not on a man of reputation who was more or less successful in deferring attention from his eventual loss of status.
8. See also Asad (2003).
9. I am of course not confusing here the performative process of a storytelling ritual with its discursive re-evaluation in the fieldwork encounter. The exploration of ritual performance as 'scenes of encounter' (Keane 1997a), as I have demonstrated elsewhere, can only make sense in a properly contextualized ethnography that takes into account many situational and historical factors that I cannot investigate further at this point. The argument I would like to pursue is a step removed from this kind of performative analysis, yet it is closely tied to the kind of subjectivities that result from a participation in the actual performative scene.
10. Kamal Singh's talk about the 'duty to perform gurmat' occured in a fieldwork situation from which there grew an empathic and mutual understanding between us. I see in his statement a comment on the complex conditions and entailed risks of actual performances that I could observe. The performer ponders here about possibilities to come to terms with the institutionalized conditions of public performance that are always defined by a relatively stable set of expectations and evaluations held by particular audiences. In the case described here, Kamal Singh speaks about how notions of folk music and ludic entertainment framed the performative event in which he and his group participated. As I have argued, the sabha members recognize the institutional effect which is usually a negative one, as it continues to categorize them as low-caste, mirasi bards. Yet at the same time, they perceive a potential to alter this set of expectations that adhere to the repetitive acts of a singing performance.
11. For a discussion of dhadi mela performance see also Appendix 2.
12. I have had long discussions with the performers about their opinion on folk festivals and their organizers. My argument is based on these conversations and on my own observance of the festival in 1999.
13. For this point see also Krämer (2002: 337). I have argued in the previous chapters that there is a distinctive way in which dhadi performances are recognized aesthetically and socially. Although dhadi performers do not use a complex grammar of facial expressions and meaningful gestures, as it is known from Indian drama, as singers and musicians they are still engaged in a manner in which the movements of the hand, the modes of voice production, the play of gestures, and the symbolic meanings displayed by the body in terms of dress and posture, constitute recognizable performative aesthetics that share common features with various other

forms of dramatic performance. The aesthetic evaluation of a 'good' dhadi performance entails the perception of these visible signs of facial expression, gesture, and bodily movement.

14. The efficacy of discourses of power, Butler (1997a: 31) argues, has to do with the historicity of conventionalized acts, that is, with the citationality of various speech acts, rather than with the figure of the divine voice that, according to Althusser, brings the subject into being through a singular act of naming. Similar to the religious practitioner that finds the culturally stipulated ritual act ready to be enacted, in Butler's view the speaking subject is not the originator of the discourse through which it is socially constituted: there are scenes of encounter that 'underscore the way in which the name wields a linguistic power of constitution in ways that are indifferent to the one who bears the name' (ibid.).

8

The Making of a Border Genre

More than three decades ago, Arendt (2000 [1970]) warned her readers in a widely acknowledged essay about the dangers of what she called 'pseudoscientific' discourses on violence. Reflecting on the worldwide political crisis in the Cold War era, Arendt was sceptical about the implicit assumptions of current political movements and state policies. The strategic employment of violence was often uncritically propounded in leftist ideologies to be a legitimate form of political action. Arendt saw the legacy of this line of thinking in nineteenth century philosophical and nationalist traditions and their implicit assumptions about violence as being vital to life, humankind, and revolution. She also anticipated the coming decades of ethnic nationalisms that would be characterized by the destructive force of political violence in many postcolonial societies.

What had previously dodged the purview of scholarly analysis that is, the dynamics with which violence exhorts itself on postcolonial societies, ethnic and religious groups, has not only become visible in dramatic ways but has also resulted in an altered understanding of how scholars approach and conceptualize the notion of violence. At least since the 1980s, anthropologists have devoted much effort to understand violence as an enduring universal problem for humankind that threatens localities and social fabrics in their very foundations. Yet, unlike what was suggested by Arendt, anthropologists have had good reasons not to infer from the universal manifestation of political violence a singular or oversimplified notion of violence as it is indicated in the instrumentalist definition provided by political analysis. Quite the reverse, scholars have found that violence is formed, experienced, and narrativized according to the different cultural traditions, regional histories, and forms of sociality to be found in such complex civilizational contexts as for instance in South Asia. The analysis of dhadi narratives and the discourses that link the performative practices of dhadi storytelling with violent events in twentieth century Punjab have been written from such a perspective.

Violence and the Border Genre

By placing the social history of a Punjabi performative tradition at the centre of this work, I have essayed a historical anthropology of violence that unfolds around a discussion of critical events in Punjab, the contested border region that since 1947 is divided into Indian and Pakistani territories. I have suggested investigating the twentieth-century history of the dhadi tradition in its own terms, as a 'mirror' and 'window', to use a popular phrase coined by A.K. Ramanujan (1999a). I have done so in order to understand the impact of violence on the social and cultural world on the one hand, and the creative potential of individuals and groups entailed in these events on the other.

The impact of Partition on the dhadi tradition and the self-definition of its practitioners led to the emergence of what I would call with Paredes (1993) a 'border genre'. I use the term in a slightly different manner than Paredes, as I am less interested in *literal representations* of border discourses, and more concerned with the *resignification of the performative tradition as a whole*. In that sense the idea of a 'border genre' reverberates Stokes' (1992, 1994, 1998) work on urban Arabesk music. Stokes demonstrates in what different ways border subjectivities are shaped by overlapping political discourses and cross-border antagonisms in the public sphere of modern Turkey. Similar to Stokes' work, the relationship between discursive constructions and aesthetic evaluations of music and performance has been pivotal to my analysis.

I have demonstrated that the inherited language of martyrdom and violence in the dhadi tradition at times sustained political cultures of violence. Dhadi performers, particularly in rural Punjab, have been engaged in relating particular historical representations to projects of collective self-definition that were at times violently opposed to other political formations. In each of the historical scenarios that I have explored, it did not make sense to frame dhadi texts and performances in terms of entertainment and expressive culture as separable from political discourses. This does not mean that I have subscribed to the view that these performers inspired audiences to commit violent acts. Nor would it be adequate to say that they were solely and entirely engaged in political discourses. Rather, I have demonstrated that representational practices entailed violent events. And this entailment, I have argued, tells us something about how violence is translated in cultural and social life.

In this context, a focus on discursive analysis alone is insufficient. The religious and performative aesthetics of the dhadi genre (articulated in popularized concepts of emotions) have been of particular importance. Precisely because violence and suffering do not lend themselves easily to verbal representations, the sonic dimension of the dhadi genre has had a particular appeal in translating suffering and pain into collectively shared forms of aesthetic experience. People in Punjab have assumed the dhadi voice to be capable of transforming feelings of rage, anger, sadness, and grief into particular aesthetic forms in which these feelings were give a particular *gestalt*. Instead of recollecting historical accounts, therefore, my objective has been to understand the inner dynamics and meaning structure of these key events in relation to language and performative practices.

To write a social history of a performative genre thus meant on the one hand investigating a chronology of related events, as they represent particular moments in the development of a performative genre over a period of almost a century. Institutionalized in the form of an oral tradition that is handed down over generations, the dhadi genre traces a genealogy of recognizable conventions, cultural attitudes, narrative repertoires, and musical-poetical grammar. My text has been organized around case studies in which I offered a perspective on the continuities and discontinuities in the representational forms and practices of the dhadi genre. At each historical juncture, I focused on the particular relationship between representation and issues of self-identification through the dhadi tradition, framed by a discussion of dominant political discourses and key events. With the microscopic focus on the representational forms of the dhadi genre at different historical junctures, my goal has been to show that the dynamics of violence had a strong impact over what direction the social use of a performative genre took. And, as pointed out at length in my discussion, it is not just the 'strategic use' of the genre in various social settings that is at stake, but moreover the recognition of the genre and its practitioners as a part of a larger social collectivity—an issue which was contested and constantly renegotiated. In conclusion, I have tried to follow a line of thought that sees the social in terms of alterity and historical emergence. To present this in the form of a social history of a performative genre seemed particularly interesting, for it allowed accounting for the different temporalities of critical events, the various forms of historical consciousness, and the changing relationship between social actors, genre, and social collectivity.

Genre and Community

Let me restate my argument that the performance of a particular genre and narrative repertoire, though socially recognized and attributed to a particular collective identity, is never entirely defined by this relationship. Throughout the text I have suggested approaching the relationship between genre and community in non-folkloristic terms; I have regarded the presumed identity of the dhadi genre in terms of group 'ownership' with some scepticism. The analysis of how people relate or differentiate themselves from a social collective or community by means of performing a particular genre is in itself an important question for cultural analysis. As pointed out by Ortner (1990: 85), the relationship between actors and their cultural repertoire has to be conceptualized as a kind of 'elastic distance' rather than a determined structural relationship. In the course of my discussion I have demonstrated how performative genre and community are related in concrete encounters. In these encounters it could be discerned how people enact cultural patterns in creative ways and in that fashion were also capable of dissociating themselves from dominant identity formations.

I have pointed out that in the early twentieth century the dhadi performers attempted to create linkages between dhadi tradition and the discourse of Sikh identity politics in making the genre suitable for public Sikh self-representation. I have described how in the course of the reformist movements in the early twentieth century, performers sought to change the narrative repertoires and the social image of the genre so that it could be meaningfully related to an emerging Sikh political community (qaum) with its new institutions in the colonial- and nation state. By focusing on this reformist agenda in the 1920s and 1930s I had several goals. First, rural Sikhs had their own vision of how reformist religion and traditional idioms of piety, sociality, and public performance had to be brought into perspective. This move was enabled by the political and social dynamics during these years of social mobilization and political unrest. These resulted in a proliferation of public gatherings and performances in which dhadi performers could participate and acquire new roles as proponents of various protest movements. And maybe most importantly, they could emerge as 'people's historians' to engage in the pre-Partition public sphere. Second, the impact of reformist and nationalist discourses, the subsequent dismissal of ludic forms of dhadi performance, and the almost exclusive relocation of the dhadi tradition within Sikh gurmat, did not come without a sense of loss and ambiguity. The ambivalence inherent to the relationship between the dhadi tradition and the Sikh community has not really vanished and it is clearly expressed in the way Sikh performers relate to their self-image in a language of neglect and social marginality. As I could witness during fieldwork, Sikh dhadi performers have expressed their disillusionment with the political agenda of their patrons. Although the genre has acquired an unambiguous format in the sense that the self-representation and performance on the stage succumb to the normative paradigm of institutionalized Sikh religion, self-representation of Sikh dhadi is cast in a language of difference in relation to the representative body of the Sikh community.

While I am sometimes led to use the term 'Sikh community' rather indiscriminately, I have tried to problematize the notion of community in the sense of shared culture at 'different levels of identification' (Flueckiger 1996: 177; see also Chatterji 2004). Following Flueckiger, we can of course locate different levels of identification of genre and community, such as indicated in the community of the Sikh dhadi performers, the 'folklore community' of Punjabis who are familiar with the traditional performers, the religious communities that reject certain genres as secular forms of ludic entertainment while claiming other genres to be part of the religious tradition, or different communities in the diaspora setting, where first, second, or third generations of Punjabi migrants and differently tuned to folk, Bhangra, religious, or other kinds of music. Yet, as already pointed out, I did not intend to interrogate the notion of community in order not to classify different regional or cultural forms of collectivity by reference to performative genre, but rather by staking out performative genre as a field of social praxis and interaction. In this sense and because of its composite cultural and social picture, Punjab is a region that has been crucial to the study of community formation in a relational field of power.

The multilayered linkages between genre and community can also be grasped through Juergensmeyer's (1982) distinction between the dharmik (custom, social obligation, pious conduct), panthik (religious community with its emphasis on spiritual lineages), and qaumik (political religion, community as 'nation') dimension of religious practice in

Punjab. This model of differentiation is useful to the extent that people become affiliated with particular forms of community life by placing different emphasis on these orientations. References to 'religion' are neither restricted to this three-fold model nor do persons always draw a clear line between one or the other. Yet it gives us some idea as to how religion is practiced as a way to relate to others (see Fuchs 2000). The qaumik orientation has been a dominant mode in framing the dhadi genre in terms of the collective voice of the modern 'Sikh nation'. I have shown, however, that dharmik orientations were similarly important in reinforcing a differentiation between a religious language and the politics of religious institutions and representatives. The performative community of Sikh dhadi singers in the sense of a self-reflexive, institutionalizing body of a collective union (*sabhā*) has, for instance, only emerged during recent years. One of the most important claims brought forward against Sikh patrons was that performers perceived themselves in dharmik terms, that is, they perceived their legitimate place within the Sikh gurmat tradition on the basis of their proclaimed pious living and moral conduct as Khalsa Sikhs. It is on these grounds, rather than by mere political affiliation or a self-understanding of a 'service-caste' of a particular patron, that they have claimed social recognition.

Religion and the different modes of piety and religious conduct given shape through public performance have thus constituted a decisive moment in the history of the dhadi tradition. Sikh religion provided a discourse in which it is placed in a continuity of communal affiliation. As a religion that places emphasis on equality and the dismissal of class and caste distinction, Sikhism has appealed to performers at the social margin of Punjabi society. Juergensmeyer (1982) has observed this trend of 'Sikhization' (in allusion to M.N. Srinivas' concept of Sanskritization) in the social movements of twentieth century Punjabi history. Yet, I have also pointed out that the dhadi genre has retained particular attitudes and aesthetics that were related differently to various other genres. The memory of an alternative cultural form, I have argued, was equally influential in shaping the social image and self-reflexive understanding of dhadi performers in twentieth century Punjab.

Genre and Agency

I have approached the question of agency from different perspectives. First and foremost, I have argued that the supposedly structural marginality of so-called subaltern subjects is insufficient to problematize the notion of historical agency. While orientalist scholars and folklorists—although sympathetic to 'indigenous culture'—refrained from studying performers' own agendas altogether, more recently scholars interested in popular culture and folklore have emphasized the subaltern agency of such groups as opposed to elite formations in South Asia. Acknowledging the marginal status of many of these traditions, I have objections against a dichotomous representation of popular and elite groups. The two models of the subaltern consciousness as either culturally autonomous or derivative of elite formations (see Fuchs 1999) have not been useful to account for the problem of marginality in the dhadi performative scene. In the first part of the book, I have argued that non-elite rural performers knowledgeable in religious exegesis and historical discourse could acquire an eminent role in Punjabi culture and politics in the role of dhadi musicians and rhetoricians. The case studies that I have offered provide evidence that presumably marginal cultural forms and traditional systems of transmitting religious and cultural knowledge could be meaningfully employed in acquiring agency as a modern Sikh subject in the early twentieth century.

The question of agency is also not restricted to matters of individual and human agency. To stay with the perspective offered by the subalternist school and its critics, the nature of human agency seems to be itself the problematic issue. Rosalind O'Hanlon (1988) argued that in the attempt to recuperate the subaltern subject, the subalternist school has reintroduced 'the classic figure of Western humanism—the self-originating, self-determining individual, who is at once a subject in his possession of a sovereign consciousness whose defining quality is reason, and an agent in his power of freedom' (ibid.: 151). Dipesh Chakrabarty (2002) has argued in somewhat similar manner that the project of writing minority histories necessarily faces epistemological problems by ignoring or accounting for, forms of agency that are ascribed to non-human actors.

This discussion has implications for the present study, for as I have argued, there are different layers of agency involved in dhadi performative practice, depending on whether focus is placed on the internal structuring of the performative community (patron-client relationship, ideas of authority and accountability due to the ustad-shagird relationship in each and every dhadi Jattha), the authority of the text (questions of authorship and efficacy of words often attributed to sources beyond the particular performer), or the overall power structures in which dhadi subject remain marginalized or subaltern. If we were to speak of subaltern agency at all, we have to consider, as I did in Chapter 3, how this form of subaltern agency is historically emerging in its complex assumptions on matters of accountability and responsibility on the overall societal level.

In performative contexts, the issue of agency has to be differently approached. I have argued that Sikh dhadi performers represent themselves as part of the heroic history of the Sikh qaum: in gesture, voice, and body language they become an icon of the represented history. Authority and authenticity on the stage are created by forms of depersonalization. Yet, authority as a consequence of representing a particular public image remains partial and unrecognized if performers cannot persuade audiences that they are without self-interest and fully committed to what they represent. And here, as I have indicated, we can locate some of the problems resulting from the dissonant memories implied in the dhadi genre. Rather than assigning agency to the actual participants and referents (that is, the jattha, sabha, patron, and so forth), in a given context of cultural performance people delegate agency to the represented figures in the enacted stories. The gurus, heroic figures, martyrs, and poets are considered to be powerful agents, such as I have described in the case of the martyrs Baba Deep Singh or Mani Singh. These figures are staged at particular historical moments where Sikhs were being inspired by their heroic deeds and mastery of spiritual practice, to the extent that they had subjected themselves to endure extreme forms of suffering and pain. Thus, when these voices are dramatically staged by performers, and analogically projected by means of rhetorical devices into a contemporary situation of social crisis and conflict, the heroes become prototypes of an ethos and pathos that seem to be lacking in a 'fallen' social world.

I have also indicated that the way agency is assigned to the heroic martyrs can take on forms of collaboration and complicity with cultures of violence that is not aspired to by the dhadi performers. I have described how in recent years, in the aftermath of bloodshed and militancy in the 1980s, dhadi bards have re-emphasized the aesthetic mood of stillness, combined with a discursive orientation toward the politically 'neutral' commemoration of 'authentic' Sikh history. Importantly, differences are drawn within the same discourse of religious aesthetics and performance. After many performers have become the targets of police interrogation and once becoming subject to suspicion and social neglect, the dhadi performers I have worked with emphasize matters of responsibility on the stage in a move to regain control over the representational forms of dhadi. Notwithstanding the adequacy of such reinterpretations, what can be inferred from this is what Keane (1997a) has described in a different context as the hazards of representational practice: agency is not something solely attributable to ontological entities, be it humans, groups or other agents. It is the matter of complex processes of enactment, interpretation, and the contestation over meanings available in discourses that are at public disposal.

APPENDIX I

Sākā Shahidganj

The Tyranny of Mir Mannu and the Faith of the Sikh Ladies[I]

Sohan Singh Seetal

੧ੴ ਸਤਿਗੁਰ ਪ੍ਰਸਾਦਿ ॥

Who says death wipes out human beings? Those who die for their country are amongst the living ones. Having left, they still appeal to the living ones and teach them the lesson of perfection. Go to Lahore! As soon as you arrive at the station, a certain site will touch your heart. This is the *Karbalā* (Sahidganj) of the Sikhs. The moment you pass to the inside, your eyes will first have the glimpse of the memorials stored in the glass cupboards [*śīśe dī almārī*]. What is it?

Baiṃt

This is not a mound of dead bones [*murda haḍḍi 'āṃ dī*]
Many sons [*lāl*] are living here
Countless women [*satwantiāṃ*], husbands in these mounds,
Countless mothers' beloved sons [*lāḍle*]
Laughing, they ascended the wheel [*charkhṛī*]
Some embracing the hot iron
Some 'lions' [*sher*], playing in the lap of their mothers
Were butchered [*churī zulam dī nāl halāl ko'ī*] by the knife of tyranny
Also, such mothers would be under these
Who saw their fondest ones [*tāre nainā de*] massacred
Cut to pieces their beloved children [*dil de karvā'e tukṛe*]
They had to accept defeat and humiliation

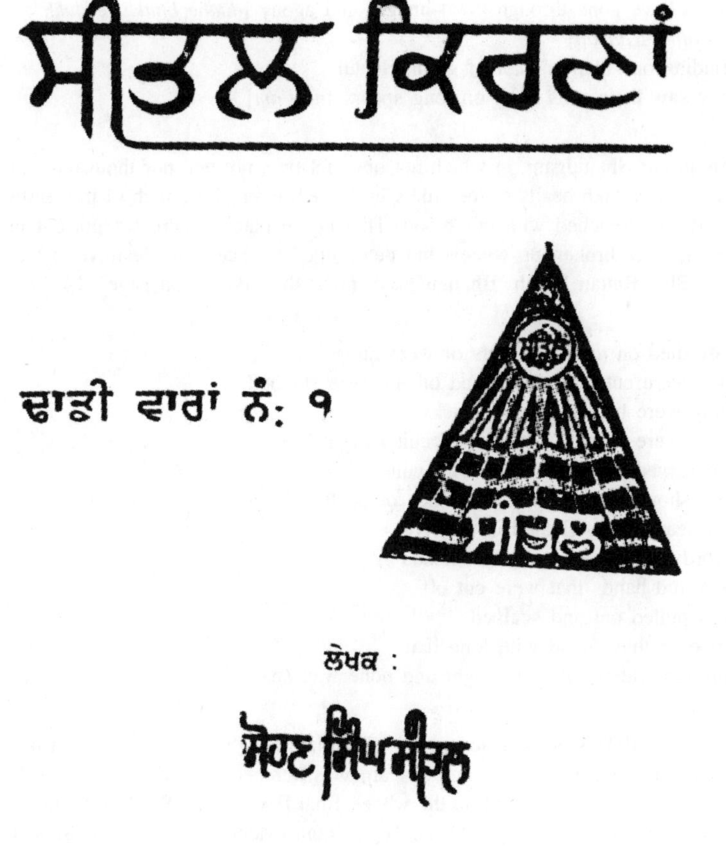

ਸੀਤਲ ਕਿਰਣਾਂ

ਢਾਡੀ ਵਾਰਾਂ ਨੰ: ੧

ਸੀਤਲ

ਲੇਖਕ :

ਸੋਹਣ ਸਿੰਘ ਸੀਤਲ

ਮਿਲਨ ਦਾ ਪਤਾ :

ਸੀਤਲ ਪੁਸਤਕ ਭੰਡਾਰ

ਸੀਤਲ ਭਵਨ, ਮਾਡਲ ਗਰਾਮ, ਲੁਧਿਆਣਾ—੨

ਮੁੱਲ : ● ਰੁਪਏ

FIGURE 19: *Sital Kirana*, front jacket of Dhadi booklet
Courtesy Michael Nijhawan

They would have lived with a chop of barley
Would have gone through great hunger and agony [*ḍāḍhe bhukh te dukh uṭhā'e hosan*]
Grinding one quarter *man* of grain, Seetal[2]
They saw their sons hung on long spears [*neẓi'āṃ*]

This is our Shahidganj, in which not one, not two, not ten, nor thousand, but two or three lakh heads of the Sikhs lie buried. Every little inch of this earth (dhartī) is drenched with our blood. This is the place, where we got cut in pieces, were broken on wheels but determined to face their destiny. Listen, what Bhai Rattan Singh 'Bhangu' says in 'Path Parkash' on page 214:

They died on torture wheels or were hung
They were cut into pieces and others were stabbed
Many were beaten up with sticks
Many were drowned or pulled behind the horse
Suppressed, trashed, killed with guns
Who should count these thousands of deaths?
Like leaves they floated in the river
Swords that blew away their heads
Legs and hands that were cut off
Eyes pulled out and scalped
Whoever they found with long hair
Children, elders, all got caught and none was spared

Yes, indeed! This is the place where Bhai Mani Singh's limbs where cut into pieces, where Bhai Taru Singh's scalp was scraped off, where Bhai Diala Singh (Shemrewale) turned on the wheel, Bhai Hira Singh (Ramgar Namgal), Bhai Sarup Singh (Khudian), Bhai Tega Singh (Mehtab Kotia), Bhai Saddan Singh, Bhai Takra Singh, Bhai Bahadar Singh, Bhai Garja Singh, Bhai Bulaka Singh (Kang), Bhai Paharra Singh, Bhai Wazir Singh (Majita), Bhai Mehtab Singh, Bhai Shabeg Singh and Bhai Shahbaz Singh (Jambar), Bhai Hakikat Singh, Bhai Mehtab Singh (Mirankot) and many others were sacrificed for the country (*desh qurbān hu'e*) bearing severe tortures. It was at this site, where Mir Mannu tested the conviction of the Sikh ladies.

Numerous were those who sat on the throne of Lahore, but Mir Mannu was the one to come last. He ruled Lahore for nearly 5 years and 7 months, from April 1748 up to 4.11.1753. Under his governance this tale of the Sikhs gained popularity:

Mannu is our sickle, we are his plant.
The more he cuts us, the more we shoot up

Prices were fixed for each Sikh head. Vagabonding soldiers went on murdering—such was the daily routine. Muslim history records that Mannu took two ser of Jañu (sacred thread) every day by force.

This continued for considerable time. I want to present you a particular incident of Mir Mannu's time. Mannu is sitting on his throne. He has sent the (mobile) troops to find the Sikhs. Who waits in front of Bhala Singh's sword?

Vār

As the ruler of Lahore, Mannu
Blew the sword of tyranny on the Sikhs
Sending his patrolling army
To wipe away the name of the Sikhs
Time after time, Mannu used his sword face to face with the Sikhs
But who can bear the resistance [*chāl*] of the 'Sri Sahib',
The Turks were not able to succeed.
When nothing was left to defeat the Sikhs
Another strategy was found
His thinking [*matt*] was defeated by egoism, says Seetal
The heart lost its connection to God

When Mannu realized that it was not as easy to fight with Sikhs on the battle field as he thought, a cowardly idea sprang to his mind: 'If you want destroy the garden, you better extinguish its offspring. It's easier to hunt their kids than to quarrel with the Singhs.'

Sākā

Defeated by the Sikhs, the army went back home.
They were again prepared to confront them
Setting up their camps at Mulanpur
Mannu, Moman Khan, infuriated as they were
They plundered the Sikh houses
Babies, Children and Sikh ladies, all were arrested.

From different parts of Punjab (predominantly from the Mulanpur area), elders, children and women were arrested to be sent to Lahore. The person behind this tyranny was the vice leader of Mannu, Moman Khan. Look how the innocent ones are brought to Lahore.

Pūran

After arresting all the children and women
They were sent to Lahore

Caught by the sword of tyranny
It became the trial for the innocent ones
Calling themselves justified rulers
They forgot the justification for their cause
Mannu put the virtuous ones
Before the sword of tyranny
Arresting them upon their arrival in Lahore
They got tangled in strings of sorrow
They could bear this lesson, says Seetal
For they got their strength from God [*vahegurū-khudah*]

It is the month of Jeth (May/June), the heat is unbearable. Today, the people of Lahore are sitting behind electric fans, and still they hardly can bear the heat. That time, when some faithful ladies sat in a crowded jail, it was in the same month of Jeth. On the one hand, fantastic stories were told to them to win their hearts. On the other hand, they were tortured to test their willpower. Each prisoner got one gulp of water and a handful of wheat (half of it salt) per day. Their prison work (*mushaqat*) consisted in grinding 10 kg of grain. Those who did not succeed were forced to bear a heavy stone of two man's weight on their chest and they were beaten up with bullwhips. The hungry babies cried in their laps. When the mother has not enough in her stomach, where should the nectar for the babies come from? But great is the honour of the mothers' loved ones. Watch the determination with which they bear the tortures.

Chand-ḍiunḍh (Chand in one and a half lines)[3]

The faithful women of the guru's house
    They were arrested by Mannu
The torture the poor ones had to endure
    What can I tell you about
Without committing a crime they were jailed
    It is the ruler's justice
Sitting in sorrow and grinding stones
    It is the destiny of god's children [*bhana ih ilāhī dā*]
One and a quarter of grain per person
    It is the order of the merciless
For their dharma they went through this agony
    It is the will of the Timeless One
Their meals consisting of a cup of water and barley
    The nights passed by like this
Having faith in the one Creator
    The favourites of the Guru

Hungry and thirsty they went through hardship [*taklīf*]
Not uttering a word of pain
Their root of faith could not be shaken
They tolerated all the trouble
God blessed the goddesses' wombs
So that they could all be successful[4]
What do you religious people know about this sorrow?
Seetal is telling you

These faithful women were tortured severely, but the brave hearted stuck to their faith. After a few days, they were summoned to the court of tyranny. The leader wanted to test their chastity. Thus they were sent to 'Nakhas Chauk' court.

Mirzā

Called by Mannu every single day, the Sikh ladies
Were requested to come to the crowded *darbār*
When the soldiers brought them in,
They vigorously shouted for God's victory [Sikh greeting]
They knew neither fear of death nor did they lose their faith
The leader of the *subā* burnt in rage
He promulgated vigorously
Stop being unbelievers and accept Islam
I have mercy with you
Become *begums* [concubines], and live in our houses
Why do you fill your life with sorrow?
If you do not agree, tomorrow the dagger of the Sharia
Will slash your head from the body
No one can escape my grasp, Seetal
Not even God can help you now

While entering the court, those faithful ones vigorously greeted the attendees with *fateh*. Hearing this, the ruler boiled with anger. His face went red and yellow, he threatened them. Showing the gleaming sword of tyranny, he said: Until today, no one could ever escape death. Don't you know what result it will have if you refuse to embrace Islam? This is the Sikh ladies reply he had to swallow:

Baiṃt

The female lions replied
Do not bore us day after day
We will not accept your Islam

Even if your life will be finished
The sword of tyranny you are holding in your hand
Will be used upon the innocent ones
Subjecting us to hard prison work, keeping us hungry
Cringing in pain children were pushed to death, Sube
Do whatever else you want to do
Do not show mercy on us and do us a favour, Sube
Once there will be justice, says Seetal
In the end you will be uprooted by the true god, Sube

Only a stern person could bear a 'No' from feebler ones than him. But where is this strength in Mannu? If he could bear this, where is the tyranny then? In rage he gave the order for another test.

Vār

Mannu burnt in rage
His eyes so red with blood
Quickly he called the executioner
In his anger he let him know the order
'Show me their faithfulness'
Bring the iron bars and heat them on hot pillars
Put them on the breasts and get them burned
From where they breastfed their babies
Take away the children from their laps
And let them hang on spears
Make little pieces of their loved ones
And put these pieces in their laps
Nobody can call me Mannu
If I do not make them confess my religion
Sitting on the same throne, says Seetal
He destroyed every single body

God (*khudā*) created tyrants. This is part of his nature; it is due to his grace that they are around. If there were no tyrants then how should one recognize the religious ones? And if there was no trial, then what would be the difference between the religious (*dharmī*) and unreligious (*adharmī*), immature (*kacce*) and mature (*pakke*) ones? All then would have to be called virtuous and faithful.

Move your attention away from the tyrants and see the ones who are suffering the burden. Babies are taken away from their mothers' laps. They are thrown into the air and gored by javelins. Dismembered pieces are then thrown in the laps of their mothers. The lap of the mother, where the baby used to sleep or drink the nectar of the breasts, is now filled with the sacred blood of the babies. Watch the heart-moving scene in the following lyrics:

Gaḍḍi

Hearing the order of the ruler
Grief-stricken, the executioner
Put the hot iron bars on the innocent
The merciless put them on their breasts
From where the milk would flow
From where now fountains of blood would spring
They snatched the crying babies
From the laps of their mothers
Like mushrooms they put them on long spears
Sorrow is unknown to the butcher
Putting them in front of the executioner
They made pieces out of the children
and put them in the laps of their mothers
The accepted destiny, Satiguru in their minds
They just hugged them with their heart
Great are those, says Seetal
Now let go, do not mourn
The fresh wound will not heal otherwise
It is not possible to tolerate what you hear
Eyes have dried up, no more tears
And yet, says Seetal
They cannot stop weeping

Only hearts can be filled with blood, a stone cannot. Instead of a heart, the despot had a stone planted in his chest. It was a very solid stone. Ground and sky shivered, but not the heart of the tyrant. Over there, the Sikh ladies had to bear all injustice while saying 'ਤੇਹਾ ਕੀਆ ਮੀਠਾ ਲਾਗੈ ।। ਹਹਿ ਨਾਮੁ ਪਦਾਹਥੁ ਆਸਾਂ ਪਹਥਤ ਨਾਨਕੁ ਮਾਂਗੈ ।।੨।।੪੨।।੯੩।। [Your actions seem so sweet to me. Nanak begs for the treasure of Lords Name. *Guru Granth Sahib*, p. 394, Asa, Guru Arjan]. In repeating these lines, they could bear the torture.

'What? They have still full trust in their faith?' The heart of the ruler began to burn even more. What happened next, no pen can write. The intestines of the babies were put in their mother's mouth. They got chains made out of the babies' and hung the pieces around the necks of their mothers.

Tarz: Es ishq vāle (Tune to those loving ones)

Kids were maltreated in front of the mothers, look at these mothers;
Taken away from their laps
The tyrants cut them into pieces
Chains of dismembered pieces were put on their necks, look at these mothers;

Kids were severely tortured, look at these mothers,
Seeing this transgression, even animals began to cry.
The trees, the jungle, the sky, all cried. Yes, even the sky burst into tears.
Alone the mothers of these martyred children did not utter a word of sorrow.

Sassī

Stop flowing, you tears of pain
Do not fill my eyes
The fire of the heart should stay there inside
Do not let it surge up
Do not leave it empty behind
Like the baby the mother's lap
Look upon my *Sikkhī*, says Seetal
It is not yet defamed.

Where once a flower of love used to giggle in the lap, there lays the dead body of the beloved. With the love she used to swing it to sleep, she now is handling the lifeless body.

Tarz: Shambū–Shambū (a lullaby)

Sleep my darling, I sing you a lullaby
Get close to my chest, I am dying for you
I embrace you, as I am full of worries
My feeling for you is as deep as the heart is wide
Sleep my darling, I sing you a lullaby
Open your lips my moon, my milk is shooting up
Suck it child, suck this milk, my life is getting uprooted
Sleep my darling, I sing you a lullaby
Open your lips child, my breasts are filled with milk
Speak my moon, just once speak to me
Sleep my darling, I sing you a lullaby
Why are you in such a hurry, so fast did you disappear
Like a wanderer who passes through this world,
Just one round you made
Sleep my darling, I sing you a lullaby
Get close to my chest, I am dying for you

The heart of mothers is a fountain of love. Mothers love healthy and handsome kids but also the ill and blemished ones. Yes, indeed! The love of mothers is infinite. They love their living child, and with the same affection they love their martyred ones.

Baiṃt

Patting the son's tormented body in her lap
The mother said: 'you are my all and everything'
My darling, my diamond, my beloved child, my moon
You are my life and the pride of Sikkhī
You let every joint be chopped for the sake of dharma
Faithful like Mani Singh you are
Winning over tyranny and self-centredness
Strong like Taru Singh you are
    Without fear in the storm of tyranny
    It seems you are a brave heart
    Seeing your faithfulness
    The tyrant's sword will shiver
Sleep my dearest son
Descendant of Boota Singh, you are
The soul of Shabeg and Shabaz Singh
The faithful warrior of Taru Singh you are
Who tolerated the tyranny of the sword
Gobind Singh's heroic son you are
The light of my blood you are
My lively picture you are
    The flower of my hopes!
    Tomorrow your flower will be buried
    Snatching away the body parts from the mothers
    Seetal asks: where will they be hidden?

How far can stretch the faith of the righteous ones? The virtuous (*dharmī*) mothers didn't lose their faith. But the tyrant was shaking (*kamb uṭhiā*). The ruler said: 'Lock them up in the basement, we will consider their fate later on. Right now, I do not feel well.'

When the Singhs came to know about these cruelties, they again started revolting in Punjab. When Mir Mannu came to know about this development, he prepared himself to catch them personally. He set his headquarters (*deṛā*) near Mulanpur. They captured the children of Singhs from the adjacent area. One group of Singhs was surrounded in a sugarcane field. While Mir Manu's soldiers unloaded their guns from outside, the Singhs started firing from within the field. Hearing this sudden noise, Mir Mannu's horse ran-off.

Kabbit

Then Mannu locked up the innocent ones in the cellar
Beat them and ordered guardians to the doors
Taking horses and an army of sinners

The honourable hunter is heading for Mulanpur
The army of the Khalsa hid in the sugarcane field
Firing on the ruler, God's name on their lips
Hearing this, the wild horse ran off
Death did not let you escape, think of it! [vichar ji]

'We are like mountains, we don't fear death' [Asa Parbat, original]. Mir Mannu could not realize his plan. His wish to extinguish the Sikhs did not come true. He could not bring his anxious horse under his control, so he fell from the saddle. But one foot got stuck in the strap. So he died while being pulled behind the horse. He had not paid his army for many months. So the army confiscated his dead body. They only gave back his dead body after Murad Begum paid their outstanding salary. Do you want to know how the body of the tyrant was deformed? Then listen:

Chand-ḍiunḍh (*Chand* in one-and-a-half lines)

Mannu started to give the horse full race
    Out of scare, he headed towards Lahore
With the stick in his hand he beat
    the flying animal
But they caught horse and rider,
    the mischievous sinner
They gave him the decisive blow
    It was his last moment
One foot was hanging in the strap,
    from the horse he fell
Banging his head on the ground,
    the irritated man began to cry
The horse got tired from the fast running,
    when they finally reached the camp
So many wounds he got,
    he had to die with grief
When they saw Mannu dead,
    women and men started to celebrate
Hiding the dead body before the army,
    was a difficult undertaking
Six months salary was left to pay
    Mannu did not pay his debt
So the dead body of the criminal lay scattered
    This is the work of God
For five days the body lay rotten
    Worms worked their way through it

See, you are a stranger to your own people
    All this shattered their hearts
Mannu's wife wept and cried
    'Oh my husband'
Throwing her hands up and down on her knees
    'Why have you turned away from me?
My boat has been uprooted because of my own deeds[5]
    Nobody is to be blamed
The pride and strength of the rule has been broken
    I am out of my senses
I request everybody to listen, my husband
    But no one is hearing my pleas
Your dead body is just decaying
    Ripping apart my heart
Homeless, lying there
    I feel depressed
Today nobody listens to my pleading
    My destiny is burning
Without any wish, there is nobody like me
    I am just holding on to you'
Nobody listens to the person without money
    Is the common saying
The begum thus began to think
    It is time for departure
Selling her jewellery, she paid the six months' salary
    Taking the dead body from Khan
Then she went to cremate Mannu
    And called Chandra the undertaker
The one who troubles the poor, says Seetal
    This is the way he is treated in the end

Here Mannu's dead body lay scattered, there the Singhs pulled down the wall of the prison. They set free the Sikh ladies and brought them to their homes.

Kalī

Here lay scattered Mannu's body
There the group of Singhs started to move
At the place of the massacre [*katal gaṛhi*] the lions started their attack
By pulling down the walls through the back entrance
The group of Sikh women, arrested in the basement,
Were set free by the arriving heroes
The liberated went on with their brothers

The ropes of tyranny were taken off
Inquiring after every single Sikh woman
They were all taken back to their homes with respect
Says 'Seetal', those who have done good deeds,
live as long as the world exists.

I remember a very sweet couplet of an Urdu poet:

'On the pyres of martyrs fairs will be held every year. These will be the lasting memories of martyrs (*vatan pahī miṇne vāle*)'

In the year 1935 the old building (*imārat*) of Shahidganj was being demolished for construction of the new surrounding wall; the devotional services that I saw at that time, will be glimmering in my soul forever (*sadā ātmā vic jhalkdā rohegā*). On one side, the outside foundation was being dug out, and on the other side, the (new) wall was coming up. On that day I saw Sikhs performing devotional services with dedication. If you want to see the verbal picture (*śabdī tasvīr*), then see it yourself (*āp vī tak lā'o*).

Gaḍḍi

Ascending the throne of sincerity-reliability [*gaḍḍī siddak-bharose*]
Arrived in Shahidganj
Reaching there [one] saw under the foundations
Digging out the rifts
Bones of innocent infants
Skulls, [of] heads
Chopped into pieces by the tyrant
In the laps of mothers
Lay the heads of many sincere [ones],
Whose heads were being sold
On the bazars of Muslim law.
They could feel the pain of saws [*kamchā*] and wheels
Those who had to bear it all
The bones of their bodies
The world bows and weeps passionately
Before their supreme sacrifice [*chand qurbānī*]
They could see the cellar
In which mothers were kept with their offspring
They saw the grinding mill with their own eyes
They could see the saw
Which was in the cellar
Blood still dripped from its dents
Countless scalpels and knives

And a huge stone of two men's weight
The head of the Subedar could be seen as well, listeners [*sangat*]
The sign of victory of the pure ones
No one should have to endure this martyrdom
No one is capable of doing such service
They carried baskets full of mud
Those, whose hands would feel dirty at the mere touch of their legs
Those, who would never leave their bed
Dragged the mud from within the gurdwara
Silk garments and mud on their head
It was like the flow of the nectar of love
One very old woman
Carried a heavy basket
Due to the heavy weight she could not walk
'I said, Mata Sahib Ji
Give it to me, let me carry the basket'
She said, 'No, child!
May I die under the basket
And may find a place in heaven, my son!'
Hearing this I said, 'Great are you,
Great are your Sikh gurus'
One's head is bowed by itself [*sir āpne āp jhuk jāve*]
At the sight of the Khalsa, Seetal!
Sevā! *Sevā*!
It will never end fruitless, you will be rewarded
Vāhe Guru jī dā Khālsā, Vāhe Guru jī kī Fateh!

Prasanga written 21 April 1935

Notes

1. I am grateful to Khushwant Singh, Harjot Singh, and Veena Nijhawan for their help with the translations. All remaining errors are entirely mine.
2. Throughout this text, Seetal uses old weight measures such as *ser* or man. One man amounts to approximately 40 kilogram.
3. The *chand* is a typical poetic form used in marriage ceremonies when the bridegroom is asked to recite poems for the female attendants and friends.
4. Obviously, this is an allusion to rape and unwanted children.
5. The boat is used as an idiom for life, a common metaphor in Punjab.

APPENDIX 2
Dhadi Performative Style

In cultural performance each event is unique as a social process. Therefore, we can find no master script for the event of a dhadi song recitation in contemporary Punjab. Performative contexts, narrative repertoires, and aesthetic forms, however, constitute a performative framework that is defined through its recognizable form and iterability. This appendix is intended to present a detailed description of these recurrent features, provided that the thematic discussion in my chapters does not allow such digressions in performative aesthetics.

Performative Context

To begin with, the traditional framework of a dhadi performance is the congregational gathering in the form of the mela or a religious ceremony. Both events give occasion to a large gathering of listeners. Historically this distinction becomes blurred, as the Punjabi mela was not only patronized by political leaders or landed gentry, but also by religious authorities like the Sufi Pirs and their successors. As a social institution, the mela creates a space in which musical performance, drama, and oratory function to vitalize the links between the participants. It gives rise to the staging of particular histories and songs that are associated with the locality or event. Following the religious calendar of such fairs, dhadi bards change their stories and melodies, adopting performative styles according to the local tastes and commemorative frameworks set by the localities and patrons such as in the case of the Mohan Singh mela that I have discussed in Chapter 7. Although currently melas are discarded by the modern middle class and urban elite as an occasion for 'low strata folk culture', reconstituted in utilitarian ways as a platform for election campaigns by politicians, and rejected by orthodox religious institutions as occasions of immoral conduct, it has not entirely lost its central role as a meeting point of local communities. The mela remains a cultural space characterized by particular forms of participation and aesthetic evaluations to which dhadi bards contribute with their performances.

FIGURE 20: Dhadi Jattha at a mela performance
Courtesy Michael Nijhawan

The spatial arrangement of a dhadi performance is rather informal and its duration depends on the kind of performed narrative and the capability of bards to keep listeners focused and involved. Modern melas, newly invented by folk institutions, societies, or well known public actors, are organized differently. As the set of expectations and time schedules of performance change, so does the performative meaning and nature of dhadi presentations. A singer is allotted a certain amount of time on the stage, while other groups are seated in the background waiting to be called by the stage-manager. There is a certain impact on the performer-audience relationship in such contexts to the extent that the distance between singer and audience increases. This distance has an impact on the multifaceted communicative system of bardic performance, as the immediacy of bodily gesture and movement that makes much of the patterned complexity of a performative event is to some extent lost.

In North India, bardic performance is known to create experiential spaces that can play a key role in the formation of religious experience. In Garhwal and Kumaon—regions in the Himalayan hills that border Punjab—dancers are possessed and chosen by deities to communicate to the participants of a ritual (Alter 2000; Leavitt 1997; Sax 1995). Bards are acknowledged here as entertainers and religious mediators. Significantly, some of the performative styles and forms of instrumentation are quite similar to that of the dhadi genre. Contrasting with their colleagues in the hills, however, dhadi bards are not known as diviners. What matters for participants in a dhadi darbar at the occasion of a religious festival, as for instance during the annual death celebration of a saint ('urs), are the musical skills, and the quality of the voice of the bards. During a Sufi ritual occasion, the dhadi singers would perform outside the immediate precinct of the shrine in what one might call minor congregational rituals. People gather in a half-circle around the group, listening; they sometimes join in the chorus and occasionally I also saw people beginning to dance ecstatically. This means that there are instances of ecstasy, even though in the eyes of the participant this does not necessarily constitute the central focus of 'urs celebrations, such as would certainly be the case with bardic performance in divination rituals.

As I have argued, in contexts of Sikh liturgy, there is a perceptible tendency toward narrative elaboration and oratory. Dhadi oratory consists of representations of Sikh history, preferrably narratives on Sikh martyrdom. In the Sikh gurdwara, the performers are placed to the right of the platform where the Adi Granth is kept and recited. They face the congregational gathering that is assembled on the ground. In such settings of Sikh dhadi performance too, there must be variations between narrative and song, and much of the audience's appreciation depends on the evaluation of the inspiring songs. Direct interaction between performers and audiences, however, is at a minimum. The most I heard were brief affirmative comments, voiced by individuals in the audience. A performance in a gurdwara usually lasts between 30 minutes to an hour, which is very short in terms of the usual epic length of Indian bardic performances. Exceptions are made in case the performers present are regarded as particularly gifted in oratory and musical performance.

Considering that, in bardic performances, the story is always already known, the interplay between storytelling and listening is essentially defined through its reflexivity. Performers are engaged in a process of listening, the focus is on a particular and nuanced understanding of selected plots and social relations. Dhadi performance can thus be conceptualized along a dialogic axis. It comprises the narrative strategy of the bards, the selective focus of the listeners, and the plot-structure of the reported narrative which, in turn, is not authorized or owned by either performer or audience. The bard's verbal performance challenges listeners to respond in their imagination. Persuasiveness rests as much on the capacity and reputation of a performer as it depends on the knowledge of the audience and the intensity of the act of listening. The interaction between bards and listeners has to be considered crucial to the extent that bardic agency is generated and shaped through such interaction. Listening, too, is not a passive state of mind; it is a central activity. As Malik has phrased it, listening 'provides the context for the speaker's utterance to unfold and make sense. Therefore, it is a non-verbal activity that engenders speech. Thus, the activity of singing and speaking is not solely about the singer's agency, but due to the audience's particular agency evoked through listening' (1999: 47). The expressive form of the dhadi genre, I suggest, is always based on this mediation between speaker and listener's agency at particular contexts of performance. The process of listening is not as limited by external guidelines and concepts as would be the case for the purely spiritual purposes of a religious ritual. Punjab's dhadi performances are oriented towards discursive contents as much as they are instantiations of aesthetic experience.

Performative Form

Dhadi bards usually perform in an upright position. In contrast to *qawwali* gatherings or kirtan congregational singing, dhadi performers never perform in a sitting posture. Typically, three musicians (two dhadd-players and one sarangi-player) form a group or dhadi jatthā. In the Sikh case they are led by the orator, who is not always a musician. Sikh dhadis mostly form a group of four performers.

The discursive framing of a dhadi performance begins with the invocation of spiritual authority, which is followed by the respectful greeting of the present audience for whom the story is performed. The allusion to divine voices is also common. Dhadi Idu Shareef, for instance, begins his recitation of the Hir Ranjha epos (Interlude IV) by evoking the name of the creator (*paidā karaṇ walā*), paying his special tribute to members of the spiritual lineage of a Sufi saint and only then addressing the audience: 'Friends! For one hour, we are going to present Hir Ranjha. All your yearlong ailments and sufferings will be healed.' This opening of the performance also indicates the modern measuring of narratives in time segments, which is due to the altered performative context during folk festival occasions on the stage. The fluidity and longevity of the oral epic narrative has certainly lost some of its essential characteristics in such circumstances. At the occasion of a dhadi performance on the Sikh stage, the opening greeting is: 'The Khalsa belongs to the Wonderful Guru! Victory belongs to the Wonderful Guru!' (*vāhegurū jī kā khālsā! vāhegurū jī kī fateh*). Depending on occasion, patrons or popular persons among the audience might be subsequently mentioned and welcomed. Otherwise, the orator would begin to introduce the topic of the performance.

I have pointed out in the introduction that dhadi performances fall into the group of song-recitation which, according to Blackburn and Flueckiger (1989: 9), is the primary form of bardic (oral epic) performance in India. Dhadi bards are vocalists in the first place, so that a characteristic element of their performance is the weaving together of oratory (or prosaic narrative) and song. In this respect, dhadi resembles the *ḍholā* performance of western Uttar Pradesh (Wadley 1989). Verbal aspects of performance and musical accompaniment are combined in each performance to complex poetical-musical patterns. Usually, the first part consists of verbal presentations without musical accompaniment. Concentration of performers and audiences firmly rests on the kind of telling and the development of the selected subplot. The case is somewhat special in the context of Sikh patronage. Although the heroic deeds and ailments of Sikh heroes are also widely known, Sikh performers perceive a strong didactic purpose in their presentation. The 'what' of the story is not just the background upon which their bardic performance unfolds; they evaluate the historical contents of dhadi narratives as constitutive element. The opening oratory of a Sikh dhadi performance can therefore be considerably detailed. A good speaker captures audiences by ornamenting historical discourse with poetic recitation, by altering his or her voice between exhilarating exclamations and calm deliberation. Performers and audiences alike assign transformative power to this poetic voice of the orator. The reputation of the dhadi orator is often cast in terms of his or her ability to essentially change the mood of the listeners. Sikh dhadi bards in particular have held a notion of the perfect orator as a 'master musician', quite similar to that of the European rhetorical tradition (Enders 1990).

In performative sequence, there is commonality too. The first musical item is performed by the sarangi, which is called the *alaṅkār* (ornamentation). The alaṅkār is a short item in which the sarangi plays the underlying melody. It can be repeated as an interlude and improvised at various instances. A chorus of two or three singers will then perform a vibrato that replicates the alaṅkār. This is called *hek lagauṇā*, the singing of a prolonged vibrating oral tune in a high pitch. In terms of a performance in a masterly fashion, the hek will evoke the emotive qualities of the song within a single dense musical metaphor. In the moment of singing the hek, the risk and potential of a good performance is located—it might draw everybody's attention to the stage, yet, as I witnessed several times, a bad apprentice might likewise cause listeners to withdraw their attention.

Finally, the entire dhadi chorus performs the song. The sarangi is played by one musician and resonates with the voice of the singers, the two dhadd players change their rhythmic patterns according to the genre that is played. The dhadds are considered hierarchically inferior to the sarangi. The string instrument clearly dominates the contemporary scene. Depending on the chant, the singing proceeds in formulaic or poetic couplets of two to four lines. It is up to the sarangi player to perform and sing the first hemistich. At the beginning of the second hemistich, a chorus of two or three singers (usually the dhadd players) comes in:

(Lead singer) *Hīr kahandī bhāī,* (chorus) *jā tak jīwān mahiyā,*
(Lead singer) *kaḍe nā harān Kaulām tū,* (chorus) *ithe uthe, dowī we jahānī*

(Hir says, as long as I shall live, my beloved
I shall not be defeated by the Kauls, whether in this or any other world)

Poetic lines and songs can be distinguished according to well established vernacular genres in which they are composed. Those which are specifically associated with the dhadi genre are called *jhoṛī*, baiṃt, *sākā*, *mirzā*, *kallī*, *talaṅg*, and particularly the var. They are associated with various narrative traditions in Punjab, as I have explored at various points in the text.

Following each song the verbal performance proceeds further in the compositions, thus introducing the next song element. In the case of the traditional performers, these prosaic parts are recited very rapidly. In the case of modern Sikh historical oratory, they are rhetorically structured, including pauses, variations in pitch intensity, and direct appeals to the audience. Oratory by Sikh dhadi performers often moves between historical and moral-religious discourse. We also find employed different speech genres, most popularly the recitation of short poems (which are also commented upon during oratory) but also proverbs, appellatives, citations, everyday talk, and others. The performance continues in this manner. Depending on the performative occasion, the pleasure it instills in the audience and the time allotted by the patron, the performance continues from half an hour to several hours. Participants in the congregation would step forward during the recitations and donate money to the group, which is usually shared among all members equally. The jattha then terminates the performance with a final song.

At the level of the actio of dhadi performance, there are notable differences between Sikh and Sufi bards. In his performance of the Hir Ranjha, Sufi dhadi Idu Shareef moves his body rhythmically, almost trance-like. The longer the performance, the more ecstatic and transformative it becomes. His movement is mediated by the playing of the sarangi that he holds at his left shoulder while using the bow with his right hand. The two drum players' movement is less ecstatic, but they clearly participate in the rhythm and movement set by the lead singer. This configuration of collective bodily movement is different from what Sikh dhadis perform. While Sikh bards share the 'taste' for grief and longing with their Sufi colleagues, the main emphasis of Sikh dhadi performances is placed on what I have called the heroic mood, or bir rasa. This is the second aesthetic concept explicitly framed in terms of the rasa theory. Sikh performers consider the musical-poetical metre of var and saka as particularly suited to create this state of bir rasa. They describe it in terms of bodily heat (the blood is brought to a boil—*khūn vic joś paidā hai*) and eruptive inner forces (*man andar ubāl āuṇā*). The body image of the Sikh dhadi bard is accordingly a different one: the performers hardly move their bodies, their pose is majestic and noble, and the eyes are fixed in one direction. The entire bodily dynamic consists of the raised oratory finger and the alteration of voice. When a var is performed, the voice is of very high pitch and intense (*tez*) on the vocal cords; whereas in a baiṃt, the voice is sweet (*mīṭhī*), prolonged and vibrating on the vowels, fashioned in a way to express a degree of mourning or lament.

Good performers are masters of these differently nuanced musical-poetical forms of voice production. The modes of voice production by singers are reflected in the play of the sarangi. As a metaphor the sarangi is also seen an extension of the human voice. A performer of reputation is able produce eager desire or pleasure (*shauk*, *amar*, *su'ād*), in the body of the listener, by fusing human and instrumental voice. Therefore, the singer-composer needs to be a master of voice and sarangi music. The quality of voice is evaluated in oratory too.

APPENDIX 3
Instrumentation

The following pages on musical instruments are based on a conversation with Pritam Singh of village Boparai Kalan some twenty miles west of Ludhiana (Figure 21). He is the only craftsman to provide dhadi groups with the two required instruments, the hourglass-shaped drum, dhadd, and the string instrument, sarangi. As for instrument makers in the Punjab, it is evident that this is a tradition on the verge of extinction. Good materials such as the *tuṇḍ*, *chamb*, and *ṭāli* (shisham wood) used for the sarangi are becoming rare or expensive. Moreover, the musical and practical skills (*riyāz*) of musicians have declined significantly. Pritam Singh is a carpenter and has only recently started to craft sarangi and dhadds. Presently he provides instruments for around 200

FIGURE 21: Lessons from sarangi craftsman Pritam Singh
Courtesy Michael Nijhawan

dhadi groups in the Panjab as well as in Europe, North America, and Singapore. Of the sarangis that are presently produced 90 per cent are of a new conventionalized style. Their body is smaller and less waisted as the classical or older folk sarangi.

Due to the sarangi's long history as a folk and classical instrument, it is found in different forms in India. As a bowed chordophone it is characterized by a waisted body and a wide neck normally carved out of a single piece of wood, three to four main strings that are played with a bow, while a set of sympathetic strings profoundly imitate the pitches of the human voice (Figure 22).[1]

Pritam Singh crafts instruments that are loud enough to be played without loudspeakers 'as it used to be earlier', he says. Loudness, however, has to be controlled and must not diminish the sweet voice which makes a good instrument. To produce this sound, the material basis is very important. It has to be carved from a single block, as the anchor strings and resonance string put strong pressure on the entire instrument. The anchor strings are fixed in the head of the instrument where they can be tuned by turning the pegs. There are large and small pegs to tune both the main strings and resonance strings. The resonance strings vibrate according to the notes played on the main strings. The sarangi player moves the fingers cn the finger-board on the left side of the neck where he or she touches the strings. The tones diverge according to the pressure put by fingerjoints on the side of the string. The usage of the bow results in the vibrant tune of the sarangi that resonates in the waisted belly.

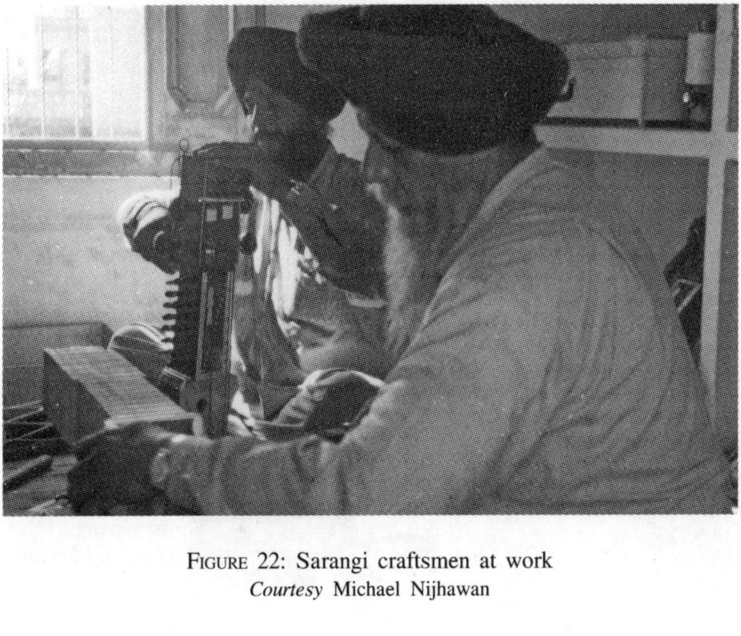

FIGURE 22: Sarangi craftsmen at work
Courtesy Michael Nijhawan

Depending on the wood and the size of the belly, the style and 'taste' (*su'ād*) of the sarangi changes significantly. The belly is covered with a thin parchment upon which a bridge is attached to stabilize the resonance strings. Despite its solid appearance, the sarangi is a fragile instrument. Crucial parts such as the bridge on the parchment or strings can break easily if they are not correctly handled. The instrument also needs the constant retuning of the main strings which, as I witnessed, has often to be done within a performance itself. Pritam Singh usually measures the quality of a sarangi by the wood and the number of resonance strings attached to it. Good musicians, using an instrument with a great number of resonance strings, would perform music of the dhadi *rāga* type as they would be able to produce a nuanced and varied sound system.

Two motifs of artistic and cultural refinement stand out markedly in traditional sarangis. Carved into the peg-boxes of the instrument are two outlets that are similar to elegant windows in the Mughal style architecture. This part of the classical sarangi is named as the mehrab (prayer niche) and minar (minaret). Another feature of the classical sarangi is a white fish (*macchlī*) inlay that symbolizes good fortune and is also an index to feudal Muslim culture. According to Qureshi (2000: 820) it can be 'found carved on Lucknow gates and buildings from palaces to the ruling dynasty's halls of worship, the Shi'a *imāmbaras*. It is also replicated in traditional jewelry and in the delicate containers for *surmā*, the kohl for lining the eyes'. Pritam Singh carves both ornamental designs onto his new sarangis. He regards them as mere artistic conventions and never made any reference to feudal or Muslim symbolism. The bridal metaphors that are used in the Muslim context to describe the body of the sarangi are also absent from Pritam Singh's description.

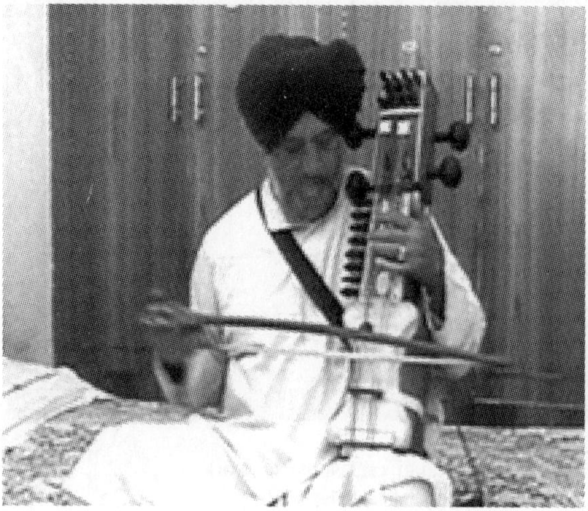

FIGURE 23: Dhadi Ajaib Singh Chandan playing the sarangi *Courtesy* Michael Nijhawan

Pritam Singh also produces the dhadd. The dhadd lies at the heart of contemporary and past dhadi performance, perhaps most significantly because it provides the genre with its name and the particular rhythmic style (Figure 24). The dhadd is a small hourglass shaped drum, six to eight inches long, and has the same form as the oldest of membraphones in South Asia, the *ḍamarū*. The main difference between the two is that the dhadd is played with the fingers of one hand while it is held in the other.[2] The dhadd is very similar to the *hurakī*, known in the Central Himalayas. As reported by Chandola (1977), the huraki is ten inches long and therefore of bigger size than the dhadd. Furthermore, pitch variation is created by means of a cotton string that is 'attached to the braces around the neck and can be moved towards either face of the drum, in order to raise the pitch' (ibid.: 34). The function of the dhadd in musical performance is the rhythmic patterning of the song by low and high pitches. Low pitches are produced by simply striking the face of the dhadd. High pitches are produced by pulling the cotton strings that are tied to the skin covering the faces of the drum. The high pitched sound of the drum is onomatopoeic in the word dhadd: it is a short stroke, abruptly brought to an end by tightening the strings, the tone thus fading out while momentarily rising in pitch. Its two faces as well as the strap (*tasmāh*) that is put around the lacing and which is used to alter the tone frequency are usually made of goatskin. A group usually has two dhadd players. Borrowing from classical Indian music, these are the instruments to produce the *tāl*, the essential rhythmical element.

FIGURE 24: Dhadi Shareef Idu and his sons playing sarangi and dhadd
Courtesy Michael Nijhawan

The sarangi and dhadd are not the only instruments used by dhadi performers. While the dhadd is always used, the sarangi is occasionally replaced by other percussion instruments, such as the *chimtyā* (iron tongs, sometimes with small cymbals attached) or the pair of cane duct flutes (*jhoṛī*). 'Dhādī Mohammad Shareef Ragi uses jhori that are played simultaneously based on a technique of circular breathing. The usage of the jhori instead of the sarangi reflects regional variations in musical style.[3] One of Mohammad Shareef's comments during our conversations is instructive. He felt uncomfortable that there have been some major changes in dhadi instrumentation. Earlier, he said, there used to be one *bānsurī* (flute) and no jhori (pair of flutes). Afterwards the *king* (a two string, plucked, spiked lute) was added. Both instruments are popular in the musical region of Faisalabad and thus it is likely that they might have been added to the dhadi genre after Ragi migrated to this region. Presently Ragi uses the harmonium, *tablā* and sometimes the mandolin in studio recordings in addition to the traditional instruments. This orchestration of dhadi sounds accommodates preferences of the studio producers.

Notes

1. For a description of the classical sarangi in musicological terms, see Bor (1987).
2. The *ḍamarū* (inscribed in old iconographies of Lord Shiva) is regarded as the most ancient of drum instruments in the subcontinent. The drummer turns the drum quickly back and forth, in a series of rapid 180-degree turns, so that the two stones tied to the strings strike against the drumheads.
3. I could not trace historically what regional form of dhadi was associated with what instruments. Faruqi et al. (1989) provide a musical survey and a compilation of instruments in west Punjab.

APPENDIX 4
Glossary of Punjabi Terms

Ādi Granth—'original book'; the holy book of Sikhism, that was compiled by the fifth Sikh Guru, Arjan Dev; first completed in 1604 and later authorized in its final version by Guru Gobind Singh.

Akālī—'follower of the timeless One'; the term was initially used for Khalsa Sikhs who followed Guru Gobind Singh's injunction to bear arms. In the early twentieth century it denoted Sikhs who fought during the gurdwārā liberation movement or Akali movement.

Akālī Dal, Shiromanī—an organization brought together to coordinate activities of the dispersed Akali groups in the early 1920s.

Akāl Takht—'the immortal throne'; refers to the sacred Sikh architecture that is erected opposite the Harmandir Sahib, in Amritsar. Initially constructed in the seventeenth century by the sixth Guru, Hargobind, as the place from where to issue political decisions and religious orders (*hukumname*), it had recently been destroyed (but later reconstructed) in the course of the Indian Army's military attack in 1984.

amrit—'elixir of life'; sugared water that is used for Sikh baptism.

amritdhārī—term for a baptized Sikh.

anjuman—assembly, meeting, or association.

ardās—daily Sikh (congregational) prayer in which Sikh gurus, heroes, and martyrs are commemorated.

Aryā Samāj—Hindu reform organization founded by Swami Dayananda at Lahore in 1875.

Babbar Akālī—name for a group of militant protesters in the 1920s; most members of the group were executed by the British at around 1923.

Bacittar Nāṭak—a hagiographical text included in the *Dasam Granth* on Guru Gobind Singh's life.

bai'āt—a vow of spiritual allegiance to a Sufi saint.

baiṃt—Punjabi poetic metre; used in the *qissā* genre; also a popular form in dhadi compositions.

barākat—'blessing power'; spiritual charisma that is also believed to heal various afflictions and maladies; associated with Sufi pirs.

bīr/vīr—denotes one who is courageous or brave; 'hero' or 'brother'; usually the term refers to a spirit of a well known figure killed in a battle.

birādarī—lineage, usually the maximal lineage within a *jātī*; often also used in a wider sense for 'brotherhood' or clan.

bhā'ī—'brother', title applied for acknowledged pious and learned Sikhs.

bhaktī—a form of Vaishnavite devotion; path of love; adoration of a personal god who is manifest in anthropomorphic form.

bhangrā—popular Panjabi dance form.

Damdami Taksāl—a seminary that was presumably established by the Sikh martyr Baba Deep Singh. Jarnail Singh Bhindrawale was the leader of this institution until his death in 1984.

durbār—'the royal court', public audience held by a person of royal status, a formal assembly.

dargāh—literally 'court'; a Sufi's tomb, at the same time a site of pilgrimage and 'urs' celebration.

Dasam Granth—'Tenth Book' a compilation of texts, that includes Puranic narratives of cosmic battle, hagiographic genres, and biographic texts that are associated with Guru Gobind Singh; the authenticity of most sections of this book is contested among Sikh scholars.

devī—'goddess'; generic term used for different goddesses that are mostly related to the Hindu goddess *Durgā* or *Kālī*; abundant references to be found in the mythological sections of the *Dasam Granth*.

dharam—righteousness, religion, proper moral conduct or duty.

dharamyudh—'holy war'; legitimized in Sikhism as the last possible means to uphold and defend righteousness and the integrity of the community.

dīwālī—the Hindu festival of lights, celebrated in the month of Kartik.

dīvān—Meeting at which *kirtan* is held and speeches and lectures made. Also keeper of treasuries, collection of poetry, ghazal.

dukh—'suffering', with both physical and spiritual implications.

ghar—house or household.

ghadr (*gadar*)—'revolution'; term used by Indian émigrés who started the revolutionary movement in California in the early twentieth century; also name of a publication issued by this group.

giānī—a traditional reputed scholar of Sikhism; well versed in all forms of Sikh literature and exegesis.

granthī—one who reads or recites the Sikh sacred scriptures and who is in charge of the gurdwara.

gurbāṇī—sacred utterances of the gurus, virtually the entire compilation of which is included in the Guru Granth Sahib.

gur-bilās—hagiographic literature about the lives of the Sikh gurus, usually traced back to the eighteenth and nineteenth century.

gurduārā (*gurdwārā,* pl. *gurdwāre*)—lit. 'the guru's door'; usually understood as: 'by means of the Guru's grace'; designates the Sikh architecture in which the 'Ādi Granth is kept and where Sikh worship takes place.

gurmat—the doctrines referred to as Sikhism.

gurmukhī—'from the mouth of the Guru'; the script in which hymns of the Adi Granth are written; also the modern Punjabi script.

gursikh—name for a pious Sikh.

gurū—lit. 'teacher', 'preceptor'; any of the ten Sikh gurus or the eternal Guru (*Ākāl Purakh*), that is believed to reside in *Adi Granth* and the Sikh panth. The historical Sikh Gurus are: Guru Nanak (1469–1539), guruship: 1469–1539; Guru Angad (1504–52), guruship: 1539–52; Guru Amar Das (1479–1574), guruship: 1552–74; Guru Ram Das (1534–81), guruship: 1574–81; Guru Arjan Dev (1563–1606), guruship 1581–1606; Guru Hargobind (1595–1644), guruship: 1606–44; Guru Har Rai (1630–61), guruship: 1644–61; Guru Har Krishan (1656–64), guruship: 1661–64; Guru Tegh Bahadar (1621–75), guruship: 1664–75; Guru Gobind Singh (1666–1708), guruship: 1675–1708.

Gurū Granth Sahib—revised version, and reverential term for the *Ādi Granth*; Guru Gobind Singh added compilations (of Guru Tegh Bahadur) to the original version of the *Ādi Granth*.

Harmandir Sāhib—also called the 'temple of god' or 'Golden Temple'. It designates the sacred place of Sikh worship in the city of Amritsar. The place was constructed in the sixteenth century during Guru Arjan's time.

hauṃaiṃ—'I-me', the principle of egoism or self-centeredness. This impulse was criticized by the Sikh gurus and is regarded as a hindrance to salvation.

hukam-nāmā—a 'decree' that is usually issued by the representative body of the Sikhs, from the *Akāl Takht*. The earlier decrees of the Sikh gurus are the model upon which this practice of authority rests.

Imām—a Muslim religious leader who leads the prayers in a mosque.

Jāp (*Jāpujī Sāhib*)—important prayer in Sikhism, that is recited daily. It was composed by Guru Nanak and can be found on the first pages of *Ādi Granth*.

Jaṭ—former tribal clan that was accommodated into an agrarian subcaste; *Jaṭs* form the numerically strongest kinship group within the Sikh panth.

jātī—lit. 'descent', 'origin'; term used to designate local castes; genereally jātī classifies biological species, kinship, ethnic groups, race, profession, musical forms.

jatthā (pl. *jatthe*)—a group, band.

jatthedār—a 'commander', term used for a leader of a jattha. The custodian of one of the five historic *takhts* is also called by this name.

kabit—praise song, Punjabi poetic genre.

kakār—the five bodily symbols that constitute the outer appearance (*bāṇā*) of a baptized Sikh. The different k's are: *kes*—wearing uncut hair, symbolizing adherence to the creator of mankind; *kaṅghā*—wooden comb that stands for purity; *kaṛā*—steel brass bangle, symbolizing the ubiquity of God; *kirpān*—sword, representing the worldly aspect of Sikhism; *kachairā*—tailored shorts, a symbol for a virtuous character.

kathā—the oral exegesis of some portion of the Guru Granth Sahib.

Kaur—'princess'; the traditional name given to a baptized Sikh woman.

kaviśar—designates a poet or bard, as well as the specific genre of speech-song. During the early nineteenth century, this name was sometimes used synonymously for dhadi.

Khālsā—the brotherhood of baptized Sikhs; founded in 1699 by the tenth Guru, Gobind Singh. The order is open to male and female initiates, regardless of their social standing or nationality.

khaṇḍe kī pāhul—baptismal ẹlixir, stirred by double-edged sword used during the Sikh initiation rite.

laṅgar—the Sikh community kitchen attached to every gurdwara. This institution is traced back to the times of the Sikh Gurus. Food is served here to all people without consideration of caste or social background.

mahfil-e sāmā—musical congregation, in Sufi devotional contexts.

Mājhā—region between the rivers Beas and Ravi defined by specific linguistic and cultural traits.

Mālwā—region extending south and southeast of the river Sutlej, and stretching from the districts of Patiala and Ludhiana to Ferozepur and Bhatinda at the Indo-Pak border.

marsiyā—an elegy; a short devotional poem on Imam Hussein's martyrdom.

maulvī—title held by an Islamic theologian, jurist, or religious leader.

melā (pl. *mele*)—'gathering', name for fairs and festivals (religious or secular).

mīrāsī—name for a traditional Punjabi musician; encompassing category for low strata Muslim musicians, bards, and genealogists.

mīrī-pīrī—principle that was institutionalized by the sixth Sikh Guru, Hargobind. It assumes the duality of temporal/worldly (*mīrī*) and spiritual power (*pīrī*).

misl—Sikh military band in the eighteenth century. The Sikh kingdom under Maharaja Ranjit Singh emerged from one of these organizations.

morchā—originally a Persian word for the embrasure in the wall of a fort; used by Sikh protesters in the twentieth century, as a term for the popular struggle against oppression and injustice.

mūl-mantar—the 'essential formula' or basic theological statement of Sikhism. This is the opening verse of *Ādi Granth.*

murīd—a disciple; in the Sufi context the position to which one is initiated in adherence to a Pir or his spiritual successor.

nām simraṇ—remembering the name; the Sikh discipline of meditating on the divine name.

nirguṇ—God in its formless qualities/without attributes.

Nirmalā—term for a person belonging to a group of traditional Sikh scholars, whose interpretation of the *Ādi Granth* draws on Vedic and Vedantic thought.

pañj piāre—'the five beloved ones'; the five Sikhs that were chosen by Guru Gobind Singh to represent the entire Sikh community.

panth—path or way, term designating the Sikh religious community.

pauṛī—a stanza, section of a var; this poetic form is frequently used in the *Ādi Granth.*

Pīr—a Sufi teacher; popular Sufi saint.

pīrkhānā—minor shrines of Sufi saints.

pracārak—a preacher, missionary, one who does the *pracār* (exegesis).

prasaṅga—episode, lecture, elaboration of a theme.

Punjabīyat—Punjabiness, expression of regional identity on the basis of cultural and linguistic referents.

Pūrāṇā—compilation of Hindu mythology, regarded as sacred texts by Hindus. Folk renderings of the epic battles depicted in these texts can be found in the *Dasam Granth.*

qaum—'community' or 'nation'; term used as a self-identification of a modern political religion.

rahitnāma—a manual in which the Sikh code of belief and conduct is formulated.

rāsdhārī—ancient drama form; the performance of Krishna and Radha songs.

śabad—'word'; the divine word that was mystically spoken by God, term used for a hymn in the *Ādi Granth.*

sabhā—union, organization.

saguṇa—visible form of a qualified God with attributes; devotional concept in Vaishnavite *bhaktī.*

śahīd—martyr, witness to truth.

śahīdī—the institution, act of martyrdom.

sajjādā nashīn—the 'one who sits on the carpet', successor of a Sufi saint.

sanātan—'ancient', 'eternal'. The name usually refers to Sant movement or in a broader sense to the pluralistic Sikh tradition, in the nineteenth century.

saṅgat—an assembly, a Sikh religious congregation.

sant—holy person, saint-poets of medieval India.

sant-sipāhī—a saint-soldier; one who combines the piety of the saint and the virtues of a soldier.

sāraṅgī—a bowed chordophone, one of the instruments used in dhadi performance.

sardār—leader; name for male Sikhs.

satyāgraha—request based on truth (and non-violence); the non-violent holding to the truth; applied to the non-cooperation and the civil disobedience movements initiated by Mahatma Gandhi.

Shī'ā—'party'; the party of 'Ali. Name for all those Muslims who regard the son-in-law of the prophet Muhammad, 'Ali and his descendants as the only legitimate leaders (*imām*s) of the Muslim community. Distinct from the *Sunni.*

Shiromani Gurdwara Prabhandak Committee (SGPC)—Sikh institution founded in 1925; administrates and controls the Sikh gurdwaras.

sikkhī—the Sikh faith.

Sikh Rahit Maryādā—a proscriptive text and code of conduct issued in 1950.

silsilā—a Sufi order; chain of mystics.

Singh—'lion', surname used by baptized male Sikhs.

Sufi—an Islamic mystic.

swarāj—self-rule; the rallying idiom of Indian nationalist movement.

takht—'throne'; In the Punjab five such thrones are recognized as the institutions of Sikh worldly authority.

tehsil—'district', territorial administrative unit.

udāsī—Order of ascetics, often celibate, tracing their origin to Siri Chand, the son of Guru Nanak.

'urs—(lit. 'marriage'); the ritual to celebrate and commemorate the death anniversary of Sufi saint.

Vāhegurū jī kā khālsā, Vāhegurū jī kī Fateh—'The Khalsa belongs to the Wonderful Guru! Victory belongs to the Wonderful Guru!' Sikh greeting; traditional opening of a public speech or address also used by orthodox Sikhs as personal greeting.

vār—a Punjabi poetic metre; designates epic poetry; frequently used in martial-sacrificial dhadi compositions.

Bibliography

Primary Sources: Books and Dhadi Booklets in Gurmukhi

Gohalvaria, Gurcharan Singh. 1998. *Jīvan te Racnā*. Amritsar: Wigyan Bharati, Guru Nanak Dev University.

Gukewalia, Sohan Singh. 1964 (n.d.). *Dhāḍī Kiranā*. Amritsar: Bhai Chatar Singh, Jiwan Singh.

——— 1964 (n.d.). *Dhāḍī Hañjhūṃ*. Amritsar: Bhai Chatar Singh, Jiwan Singh.

——— 1964 (n.d.). *Dhāḍī Taraṅgāṃ*. Amritsar: Bhai Chatar Singh, Jiwan Singh.

Kasel, Kirpal S., Parminder Singh, and Gobind Singh Lamba. 1998. *Panjābī Sāhit dī Utapatī te Vīkās*. Ludhiana: Lahore Book Shop.

Rae, Gurdev Singh. 1998. *Azādī Parvāne*. Jalandhar: Rae Sahit Prakashan.

Sandhu, Wariam Singh. 1994. *Samāj-Śastrī Triśtī toṃ Sohan Singh Sītal dī Nāval-Racnā dā Adhi'ain*. Doctoral Dissertation. Panjab University, Chandigarh.

——— 1997. Sohan Singh Seetal (Interview) in Raghbir Singh (ed.), *Mulākātāṃ* (*Das Prasidh Nāvalkārām Nāl*). Amritsar: Ravii Saahit Prakashan.

Seetal, Sohan Singh. 1944. *Sikh Rāj Kīveṃ Gayā*. Ludhiana: Sītal Pustak Bhaṇdār.

——— 1948. *Panjāb dā Ujaṛā*. Amritsar: Mastar Sher Singh, Khazan Singh.

——— 1962a. *Tuṭāṃ Wālā Ku'ā*. Ludhiana: Sītal Pustak Bhaṇdār.

——— 1962b. *Vahinde Hañjūṃ*. Ludhiana: Sītal Pustak Bhaṇdār.

——— 1966. *Icogil Nahir Tak*. Ludhiana: Sītal PustakBhaṇdār.

——— 1972. *Jug Badal Gayā*. Ludhiana: Sītal Pustak Bhaṇdār.

——— 1980. *Merī Itihāsak Laikcār*. Ludhiana: Lahore Book Shop.

——— 1981a. *The Sikh Misals and the Punjab States*. Ludhiana: Lahore Book Shop.

——— 1981b. *Sikh Itihās de Some*. Ludhiana: Lahore Book Shop.

——— 1983. *Vekhī Māni Duniā*. Ludhiana: Sītal Pustak Bhaṇḍār.
——— 1989. Meñāṃ abhul Yadaṃ. Ludhiana: Sītal Pustak Bhaṇḍār.
——— 1993 (1945). *Sītal Taraṅgāṃ*. Ludhiana: Sītal Pustak Bhaṇḍār.
——— 1994 (1942). *Sītal Kiranā*. Ludhiana: Sītal Pustak Bhaṇḍār.
——— 1998 (1955). *Sītal Umaṅgāṃ*. Ludhiana: Lahore Book Shop.
——— 1998 (n.d.). *Sītal Sugātā*. Ludhiana: Lahore Book Shop.
Singh, Ganda. 1990. *Panjāb diāṃ Vārāṃ*. Patiala: Punjabi University Publication House.

Secondary Sources: Books and Articles

Abu-Lughod, Lila. 1986. *Veiled Sentiments: Honor and Poetry in a Bedouin Society*. Berkeley: University of California Press.
Allué Marta. 1999. La Douleur en Directe: Anthropologie et Societés, 23(2): pp. 117–37.
Appadurai, Arjun, Frank J. Korom, and Margaret A. Mills (eds). 1991. *Gender, Genre and Power in South Asian Expressive Traditions*. Philadelphia: University of Pennsylvania Press.
Arendt, Hannah. 1970. *On Violence*. Orlando, Florida: Hartcort and Brace.
Asad, Talal. 1993. *Genealogies of Religion: Discipline and Reasons of Power in Christianity and Islam*. Baltimore: John Hopkins University Press.
——— 1999. 'Religion, Nation-State, Secularism', in Peter van der Veer and Hartmut Lehmann (eds), *Nation and Religion: Perspectives on Europe and Asia*. Princeton, New Jersey: Princeton University Press.
——— 2003. *Formations of the Secular*. Stanford, California: Stanford University Press.
Axel, Brian Keith. 2001. *The Nation's Tortured Body: Violence, Representation, and the Formation of a Sikh 'Diaspora'*. Durham and London: Duke University Press.
Bakhtin, Mikhail. 1981. *The Dialogic Imagination* (Michail Holmquist ed.). Austin: University of Texas Press.
——— 1986. 'The Problem of Speech Genres', in G. Emerson and M. Holmquist (eds), *Speech Genres and Other Late Essays: M.M. Bakhtin*. Austin: University of Texas Press, pp. 60–102.
Barthes, Roland. 1977. *Image, Music, Text*. New York: Hill and Wang.
Basgöz, Ilhan. 1978 (1972). 'Folklore Studies and Nationalism in Turkey', in Felix J. Oinas (ed.), *Folklore, Nationalism, and Politics*. Columbus, Ohio: Slavica Publishers, pp. 123–38.
Bauman, Richard and Charles L. Briggs. 1992. 'Genre, Intertextuality, and Social Power', *Journal of Linguistic Anthropology*, 2: pp. 131–72.
Bauman, Richard and Americo Paredes (eds). 1970. *Towards New Perspectives in Folklore*. Austin and London: University of Texas Press.

Bedi, Sohinder Singh. 1971. *Folklore of the Punjab*. Delhi: National Book Trust.

Bell, Catherine. 1992. *Ritual Theory, Ritual Practice*. Berkeley: University of California Press.

Ben-Amos, Dan. 1972. 'Toward a Definition of Folklore in Context', in Americo Paredes and Richard Bauman (eds), *Toward New Perspectives in Folklore*. Austin and London: University of Texas Press, pp. 3–15.

——— 1984. 'The Seven Strands of Tradition: Varieties in its Meaning in American Folklore Studies', *Journal of Folklore Research*, 21: pp. 97–131.

Bhalla, Alok. 1999. 'Memory, History and Fictional Representations of the Partition', *Economic and Political Weekly*.

Bhatti, H.S. 2000. *Folk Religion: Change and Continuity*. Jaipur, New Delhi: Rawat Publications.

Bhogal, Balbinder. 2001. 'On the Hermeneutics of Sikh Thought and Praxis', in Christopher Shackle, Gurharpal Singh, and Arvind Pal Singh Mandair (eds), *Sikh Religion, Culture and Ethnicity*. London: Curzon Press, pp. 72–96.

Blackburn, Stuart. 1996. *Inside the Drama House: Rama Stories and Shadow Puppets in South India*. Berkeley: University of California Press.

Blackburn, Stuart and Joyce Burkhalter-Flueckiger (eds). 1989. *Oral Epics in India*. Berkeley: University of California Press.

Blackburn, Stuart and A.K. Ramanujan (eds). 1986. *Another Harmony. New Essays on the Folklore of India*. Berkeley: University of California Press.

Bor, Joep. 1987. 'The Voice of The Sarangi', *Quarterly Journal of the National Centre for the Performing Arts*, 15: pp. 6–178.

Bourdieu, Pierre. 1977. *Outline of a Theory of Practice*. Cambridge: Cambridge University Press.

Brass, Paul. 1979. 'Elite Groups, Symbol Manipulation and Ethnic Identity among the Muslims of South Asia', in David Taylor and Malcom Yapp (eds), *Political Identity in South Asia*. London: Curzon Press, pp. 35–77.

Briggs, Charles. 1988. *Competence in Performance: The Creativity of Tradition in Mexicano Verbal Art*. Philadelphia: University of Pennsylvania Press.

——— 1993. 'Metadiscursive Practices and Scholarly Authority in Folkloristics', *Journal of American Folklore*, 106: pp. 387–434.

Briggs, Charles and Amy Shuman. 1993. 'Theorizing Folklore: Toward New Perspectives on the Politics of Culture', *Western Folklore*, p. 52.

Bruner, Edward M. 1986. 'Experience and Its Expression', in Edward M. Bruner and Victor W. Turner (eds), *The Anthropology of Experience*. Urbana and Chicago: University of Chicago Press, pp. 3–30.

Butalia, Urvashi. 1998. *The Other Side of Silence: Voices from the Partition of India*: Delhi: Viking.

Butler, Judith. 1997a. *Excitable Speech: A Politics of the Performative*. London: Routledge.

——— 1997b. *The Psychic Life of Power: Theories in Subjection*. Stanford: Stanford University Press.

Campbell, Shirley. 2001. 'The Captivating Agency of Art. Many Ways of Seeing', in Christopher Pinney and Thomas Nicholas (eds), *Beyond Aesthetics: Art and the Technologies of Enchantment*. Oxford: Oxford University Press, pp. 117–36.

Caton, Steven C. 1990. *Peaks of Yemen I summon*. Poetry as Cultural Practice in a North Yemeni Tribe. Berkeley: University of California Press.

Chakrabarty, Dipesh. 2000. *Provincializing Europe*. Princeton: Princeton University Press.

Champion, Catherine. 1996. 'Tradition Orales dans le Monde Indien: Introduction', *Purusharta*, 18: pp. 1–22.

Chandra, Bipan. 1989. *India's Struggle for Independence 1857–1947*. Delhi: Penguin Books.

Chandola, Anoop. 1977. *Folk Drumming in the Himalayas*. New York: AMS Press.

Chatterjee, Partha. 1993. *The Nation and Its Fragments*. Princeton: Princeton University Press.

Chatterjee, Partha and Anjan Ghosh (eds). 2002. *History and the Present*. Delhi: Permanent Black.

Chatterji, Roma. 1998. 'Gender, Genre and Voice: Poetic Expression of Personal Voice', *Loyola Journal of Social Sciences*, 12: pp. 12–22.

——— 2000. Why does Shyamola Sing? The Poetic Expression of Personal Voice in one Musical Genre in Purulia. Unpublished Manuscript.

——— 2003. 'The Category of Folk', in Veena Das (ed.), *The Oxford India Companion to Sociology and Social Anthropology*. Delhi: Oxford University Press, pp. 567–97.

Chaturvedi, Vinayak (ed.). 2000. *Mapping Subaltern Studies and the Postcolonial*. London and New York: Verso.

Chhabra, G.S. 1960. *Advanced History of the Punjab. Volume I: Guru and Post-Guru Period upto Ranjit Singh*. Jalandhar: Sharanjit.

Coccari, Diane M. 1989. 'Protection and Identity: Banaras's Bir Babas as Neighbourhood Guardian Deities', in Sandria Freitag (ed.), *Culture and Power in Banaras*. Berkeley: University of California Press, pp. 130–46.

Cocciara, Giuseppe. 1981. *The History of Folklore in Europe*. Philadelphia: Institute for the Study of Human Issues.

Cole, Juan Richardo Irfan. 1988. *Roots of North Indian Shi'ism in Iran and Iraq*. Berkeley: University of California Press.

Corrucini, Robert S. and Samvit S. Kaul. 1990. *Halla: Demographic Consequences of the Partition of the Punjab 1947*. Lanham: University Press of America.

Crapanzano, Vincent. 2000. 'Fragmentarische Überlegungen zu Körper, Schmerz und Gedächtnis', in Klaus-Peter Köpping und Ursula Rao (eds), *Im Rausch des Rituals. Gestaltung und Transformation der Wirklichkeit in körperlicher Performanz*. Münster: LIT Verlag, pp. 218–39.

Dalmia, Vasudha. 1997. *The Nationalization of Hindu Traditions*. Delhi: Oxford University Press.

——— 2001a. 'Women, Duty and Sanctified Space in a Vaisnava Hagiography of the Seventeenth Century', in Francoise Mallison (ed.), *Constructions Hagiographique dans le Monde Indien*. Paris: Librarie Honoré Champion, pp. 205–19.

——— 2001b. 'Vernacular Histories in Late Nineteenth Century Banaras: Folklore, Puranas and the New Antiquarianism', *The Indian Economic and Social History Review*, 38: pp. 59–79.

Daniel, Valentine. 1996. *Charred Lullabies: Chapters in an Anthropography of Violence*. New York: Princeton University Press.

Das, Veena. 1987. 'The Anthropology of Violence and the Speech of Victims', *Anthropology Today*, 3(4): pp. 11–13.

——— (ed.). 1990. *Mirrors of Violence. Community, Riots and Survivors in South Asia*. Delhi: Oxford University Press.

——— 1995a. 'Counter-concepts and the Creation of Cultural Identity: Hindus in the Militant Sikh Discourse', in Vasudha Dalmia and Heinrich von Stietencron (eds), *Representing Hinduism*. Delhi: Sage, pp. 358–68.

——— 1995b. *Critical Events. An anthropological perspective on contemporary India*. Delhi: Oxford University Press.

——— 1997. 'Language and Body: Transactions in the Construction of Pain', in Arthur Kleinman, Veena Das and Margaret Lock (eds), *Social Suffering*. Berkeley: University of California Press, pp. 67–92.

——— 2000. 'The Act of Witnessing: Violence, Poisonous Knowledge, and Subjectivity', in Veena Das, Arthur Kleinman, and Pamela Reynolds (eds), *Violence and Subjectivity*. Berkeley: University of California Press, pp. 205–25.

Das, Veena Arthur Kleinman, Mamphela Ramphele, and Pamela Reynolds (eds). 2000. *Violence and Subjectivity*. Berkeley: University of California Press.

Das, Veena and Rajiv Singh Bajwa. 1994. 'Community and Violence in Contemporary Punjab', *Purusharta*, 16: pp. 245–60.

Datta, Nonika. 1999. *Forming an Identity: A Social History of the Jats*. Delhi: Oxford University Press.

Datta, Pradip K. 1999. *Carving Blocs: Communal Ideology in Early Twentieth-Century Bengal*. Delhi: Oxford University Press.

Devji, Faizal Fatehali. 1993. *Muslim Nationalism: Founding Identity in Colonial India*. Doctoral Dissertation. Chicago University, Chicago.

Douwes, Dick and Linda Herrera. 2004. Editorial. *ISIM Newsletter*, 14: p. 4.

Dow, James and H. Jost Lixfeld. 1991. 'National Socialist Folklore and Overcoming the Past in the Federal Republic of Germany', *Asian Folklore Studies*, 50: pp. 117–53.

Dundes, Alan 1977. 'Who are the Folk?', in W.R. Bascom, *Frontiers of Folklore*. Colorado: Westview Press, pp. 17–35.

——— (ed.). 1999. *International Folkloristics: Classical Contributions by the Founders of Folklore*. Lanham: Rowman and Littlefield.

Eaton, Richard M. 1978. *The Sufis of Bijapur 1300–1700: Social Roles of Sufis in Medieval India*. Princeton, New Jersey: Princeton University Press.

——— 1984. 'The Political and Religious Authority of the Shrine of Baba Farid', in Barbara D. Metcalf, *Moral Conduct and Authority: The Place of Adab in South Asian Islam*. Berkeley: University of California Press, pp. 333–57.

——— 1996. *The Rise of Islam and the Bengal Frontier, 1204–1760*. Berkeley: University of California Press.

Enders, Jody. 1990. 'Visions with Voices: The Rhetoric of Memory and Music in Liturgical Drama', *Comparative Drama*, 24: pp. 34–54.

——— 1999. *The Medieval Theatre of Cruelty: Rhetoric, Memory, Violence*. Ithaca and London: Cornell University Press.

Faruqi, Farhana et al. 1989. *Musical Survey of Pakistan: Three Pilot Studies*. Islamabad: Lok Virsa Research Centre.

Feld, Steven. 1982. *Sound and Sentiment*. Philadelphia: University of Pennsylvania Press.

Feldman, Allen. 1991. *Formations of Violence: The Narrative of the Body and Political Terror in Northern Ireland*. Chicago: Chicago University Press.

——— 2000. 'Violence and Vision: The Prosthetics and Aesthetics of Terror', in Veena Das, Arthur Kleinman, Mamphela Ramphele, and Pamela Reynolds (eds), *Violence and Subjectivity*. Berkeley: University of California Press, pp. 46–78.

Fenech, Louis E. 2000. *Martyrdom and the Sikh Tradition*. Oxford: Oxford University Press.

Fernandez, James W. 1986. *Persuasions and Performances: The Play of Tropes in Culture*. Bloomington: Indiana University Press.

Finnegan, Ruth. 1977. *Oral Poetry: Its Nature, Significance, and Social Context*. Cambridge: Cambridge University Press.

Flueckiger, Joyce Burkhalter. 1996. *Gender and Genre in the Folklore of Middle India*. New York: Cornell University Press.

Flueckiger, Joyce Burkhalter and Laurie J. Sears (eds). 1991. *Boundaries of the Text: Epic Performances in South and Southeast Asia*. Michigan: Center for South and Southeast Asian Studies.

Freitag, Sandria. 1989. *Culture and Power in Banaras: Community, Performance, and Environment, 1800–1980*. Berkeley: University of California Press.

Fuchs, Martin. 1996. 'Metaphor of Difference: Culture and the Struggle for Recognition', *Anthropological Journal on European Cultures*, 5(1): pp. 63–94.

——— 1999. *Kampf um Differenz. Repräsentation, Subjektivität und soziale Bewegungen: Das Beispiel Indien*. Frankfurt am Main: Suhrkamp.

——— 2000. 'Articulating the World: Social Movements, The Self Transcendence of Society and the Question of Culture', *Thesis Eleven*, 61: pp. 65–85.

Gade, Anna M. 2002. 'Taste, Talent, and the Problem of Internalization: A Qur'anic Study in Religious Musicality from Southeast Asia', *History of Religions*, 41(4): pp. 328–68.

Gandhi, Surjit Singh. *Sikhs in the Eighteenth Century: Their Struggle for Survival and Supremacy.*

Geertz, Clifford. 1973. *The Interpretation of Cultures*. New York: Basic Books.

Gell, Alfred. 1998. *Art and Agency: An Anthropological Theory*. Oxford: Oxford University Press.

Gerstin, Julian. 1998. 'Reputation in a Musical Scene: The Everyday Context of Connections between Music, Identity and Politics', *Ethnomusicology*, 42: pp. 385–414.

Giddens, Anthony. 1979. *Central Problems in Social Theory: Action, Structure and Contradiction in Social Analysis*. Berkeley: University of California Press.

Gill, Harjeet Singh. 1985. 'The Human condition in Puran Bhagat: An Essay in Existential Anthropology of a Punjabi Legend', *Contributions to Indian Sociology*, 19: pp. 133–52.

Gilmartin, David. 1984. 'Shrines, Succession, and Sources of Moral Authority', in Barbara D. Metcalf (ed.), *Moral Conduct and Authority: The Place of Adab in South Asian Islam*. Berkeley: University of California Press, pp. 221–40.

——— 1988a. 'The Shahidganj Mosque Incident: A Prelude to Pakistan', in Edmund Burke and Ira M. Lapidus (eds), *Islam, Politics, and Social Movements*. Berkeley and Los Angeles: University of California Press, pp. 146–68.

——— 1988b. *Empire and Islam. Punjab and the Making of Pakistan*. Berkeley: University of California Press.

——— 1991. 'Democracy, Nationalism and the Public: A Speculation on Colonial Muslim Politics', *South Asia*, 14(1): pp. 123–40.

——— 1998. 'A Magnificent Gift: Muslim Nationalism and the Election Process in Colonial Punjab', *Comparative Studies in Society and History*, 40: pp. 415–36.

Girard, René. 1977. *Violence and the Sacred*. Baltimore: John Hopkins Press.

Gnoli, Raneirio. 1956. *The Aesthetic Experience According to Abhinavagupta*. Rome: Instituto Italiano Per il Medio ed Estremo Oriente.

Good, Edwin M. 1990. *In Turns of Tempest: A Reading of Job with a Translation*. Stanford, California: Stanford University Press.

Gold, Ann Grodzins., 1992. *A Carnival of Parting*. Delhi: Munshiram Manoharlal.

Grewal, J.S. 1976. *Guru Tegh Bahadur and the Persian Chroniclers*. Amritsar: Guru Nanak Dev University.

——— 1984. 'The World of Waris', in Sudhir Chandra (ed.), *Social Transformation and the Creative Imagination*. Delhi: Allied Publishers, pp. 107–26.

——— 1986. *The Emergence of Punjabi Drama: A Cultural Response to Colonial Rule*. Amristar: Guru Nanak Dev University.

——— 1998a. *Contesting Interpretations of the Sikh Tradition*. Delhi: Manohar.

——— 1998b. 'Sikh Identity, the Akalis and Khalistan', in J.S. Grewal and Indu Banga (eds), *Punjab in Prosperity and Violence: Administration, Politics and Social Change 1947–1997*. Chandigarh: Institute of Punjab Studies, pp. 65–103.

——— 1990. *The Sikhs of the Punjab*. New York: Cambridge University Press.

——— 2004. 'Historical Geography of the Punjab'. *Journal of Punjab Studies*, 11(1): pp. 1–18.

Guha, Ranajit. 1988. 'The Prose of Counter-Insurgency', in: Ranajit Guha and Gayatri C. Spivak (eds), *Selected Subaltern Studies*. Oxford: Oxford University Press, pp. 45–88.

Hans, Surjit Singh. 1984. 'Ramavtar in Dasamgranth', *Journal of Sikh Studies*, 11: pp. 59–65.

——— 1986. 'Anthropology of Violence and Warfare and Sikh religion in the eighteenth century', *Journal of Sikh Studies*, 13(2): pp. 55–74.

——— 1987. 'The Partition Novels of Nanak Singh', in A.K. Gupta (ed.), *Myth and Reality: The Struggle for Freedom in India, 1945–47*. Delhi: Manohar, pp. 365–77.

Hasan, Mushirul. 1993. *India's Partition: Process, Strategy and Mobilization*. Delhi: Oxford University Press.

——— (ed.). 1997. *Legacy of a Divided Nation. India's Muslims since Independence*. Boulder, Colorado: Westview Press.

Hawley, John Stratton. 1984. *Sur Das: Poet, Singer, Saint*. Delhi: Oxford University Press.

——— 1987. 'The Sant in Sur Das', in Karin Schomer and W.H. McLeod (eds.), *The Sants: Studies in a Devotional Tradition of India*. Delhi: Motilal Banarsidas, pp. 191–211.

Herscher, Andrew and Andras Riedlmayer. 2000. 'Monument and Crime'. *Grey Room 01*, Fall 2000: pp. 109–22.

Herzfeld, Michael. 1986 (1982). *Ours Once More*. Austin: University of Texas Press.

Hirschkind, Charles. 2001. 'Civic Virtue and Religious Reason: An Islamic Counterpublic', *Cultural Anthropology*, 16(1).

Hobsbawm, Eric and Terence Ranger (eds) 1984. *The Invention of Tradition*. Cambridge: Cambridge University Press.

Hodson, H.V. *The Great Divide: Britain-India-Pakistan*. Karachi, Oxford University Press, 2001 (1969).

Højbjerg, Christian Kordt (2002), 'Religious Reflexivity. Essays on Attitudes to Religious Ideas and Practice', in: *Social Anthropology*, 10(1): pp. 1–10.

Houseman, Michael and R. Severi. (1998). *Naven or the other self. A relational approach to ritual action*. Leiden: Brill.

Human Rights Watch. 1991. *Punjab in Crisis: Human Rights in India*. New York: Human Rights Watch Asia.

——— 1994. *Dead Silence: The Legacy of Abuses in Punjab*. New York: Human Rights Watch.

Ibbetson, Sir Denzil. 1994 (1883). *Panjab Castes*. Lahore: Sang-e-Meel Publications.

Jackson, Jean. (1994). 'Chronic pain and the tension between the body as subject and object', in Thomas Csordas (ed.), *Embodiment and Experience: The Existential Ground of Culture and Self*. Cambridge: Cambridge University Press, pp. 201–28.

Jalal, Ayesha. 2000. *Self and Sovereignty: Individual and Community in South Asian Islam since 1850*. London and New York: Routledge.

Jantzen, Grace M. 1989. 'Mysticism and Experience', *Religious Studies*, 25: pp. 296–315.

——— 1990. 'Could there be a Mystical Core of Religion?', *Religious Studies*, 26: pp. 59–71.

Jeffrey, Robert. 1986. *What's Happening to India?: Punjab, Ethnic Conflict and the Test for Federalism*. Basingstoke: Macmillan.

——— 1987. 'Grappling with History: Sikh Politicians and the Past', *Pacific Affairs*, 60: pp. 60–73.

Jodhka, Surinder Singh. 2001. 'Looking back at the Khalistan Movement. Some Recent Researches on its Rise and Decline', *Economic and Political Weekly* (http://www.epw.org.in/previous/rev.htm).

Jones, Kenneth W. 1989. *Arya Dharm: Hindu Consciousness in the 19th Century Punjab*. Delhi: Manohar.

——— 1994. *Socio-Religious Reform Movements in British India*. Cambridge: Cambridge University Press.

Joshi, Varsha. 1995. 'Drums and Drummers', in: N.K. Joshi and Rajendra Joshi (eds), *Folk, Faith and Feudalism*. Jaipur and New Delhi: Rawat Publications, pp. 112–26.

Juergensmeyer, Mark. 1982. *Religion as Social Vision*. Berkeley: University of California Press.

——— (ed.). 1991. *Violence and the Sacred in the Modern World*. London: Frank Class and Co.

——— 2000. *Terror in the Mind of God*. Berkeley: University of California Press.

Kalra, Virinder. 2005. 'Cultural, Linguistic, and Political Translations', Paper on Dhadi Urban Music at Conference: Translating Culture, Sikh and Punjab Studies in Global Perspective, University of California at Berkeley, 11–12 November 2005.

Kapferer, Bruce. 1988. *Legends of People, Myths of State*. Washington and London: Smithsonian Institution Press.

Karlekar, Malavika. 1995. 'Case Studies of Women's Empowerment in India', *AJWS*, 1: pp. 127–51.

Kaur, Madanjit. 1984. 'Folklore as a Source of History with Special Reference to the Study of Medieval Punjab', *The Panjab Past and Present* 18: pp. 58–70.

Keane, Webb. 1997a. *Signs of Recognition. Power and Hazards of Representation in an Indonesian Society*. Berkeley and Los Angeles: University of California Press.

——— 1997b. 'From Fetishism to Sincerity: On Agency, the Speaking Subject, and their Historicity in the Context of Religious Conversion', *Comparative Studies in Society and History*, 39: pp. 674–93.

——— 1997c. 'Religious Language', *Annual Review of Anthropology*, 26: pp. 47–71.

——— 2001. Voice. In: A. Duranti (eds), *Key Terms in Language and Culture*. Oxford: Blackwell Publishers, pp. 268–72.

Kermani, Navid. 1996. 'Revelation in its Aesthetic Dimension', in Stefan Wild (eds), *The Qur'an as Text*. Leiden: Brill, pp. 213–24.

——— 2000. *Gott ist schön: Das aesthetische Erleben des Koran*. München: Beck.

Khalsa, Sant Singh. 1995. *Guru Granth Sahib* (with revised translation). San Mateo, Anaheim: Sikh Center of Orange County (CD-ROM).

Khosla, Gopal Das. 1989 (1948). *Stern Reckoning: A Survey of the Events Leading up to and Following the Partition of India*. Delhi: Oxford University Press.

Köpping, Klaus-Peter und Ursula Rao (Hrsg.) 2000. *Im Rausch des Rituals: Gestaltung und Transformation der Wirklichkeit in körperlicher Performanz*. Münster: LIT Verlag.

Krämer, Sybille. 2002. 'Sprache—Stimme—Schrift: Sieben Gedanken über Performativität als Medialität', in: Uwe Wirth (ed.), *Performanz. Zwischen Sprachphilosophie und Kulturwissenschaften*. Frankfurt a.M: Suhrkamp, pp. 323–46.

Kumar, Nita. 1988. *The Artisans of Banaras: Popular Culture and Identity, 1880–1986*. Princeton, New Jersey: Princeton University Press.

Lamb, Jonathan. 1995. *The Rhetoric of Suffering*. Oxford: Clarendon Press.

Layton, Robert. 2003. 'Art and Agency: A Reassessment', *Journal of the Royal Anthropological Institute* (N.S.), 9: pp. 447–64.

Le Breton, David. 1995. *Anthropologie de la douleur*. Paris: Métailié.

Leavitt, John. 1997. 'The Language of the Gods: Craft and Inspiration in Central Himalayan Ritual Discourse', in John Leavitt (ed.), *Poetry and Prophecy. The Anthropology of Inspiration*. Ann Arbor: The University of Michigan Press, pp. 129–68.

Longinovic, Tomislav. 1996. The Perpetual Resurrection of the Past: The

Kosovo Legacy and Serbian Nationalist Discourse. Bogradski Krug/ Belgrade Circle No 3–4/96 and 1–2/97: pp. 370–91.

——— 1997. 'The Perpetual Resurrection of the Past: The Kosovo Legacy and Serbian Nationalist Discourse', *Belgrade Circle*, 3–4/96 and 1–2/97: pp. 370–91.

——— 2000. 'Music Wars: Blood and Song at the End of Yugoslavia', in Ronaldo Radano and Philip V. Bohlman (eds), *Music and the Racial Imagination*. Chicago and London: The University of Chicago Press, pp. 622–43.

Madan, T.N. 1997. 'Modern Myths, Locked Minds', *Secularism and Fundamentalism in India*. Delhi: Oxford University Press.

Magrini, Tullia. 2000. 'Manhood and Music in Western Crete: Contemplating Death', *Ethnomusicology*, 44: pp. 429–59.

Mahmood, Cynthia Keppler. 1996. *Fighting for Faith and the Nation: Dialogues with Sikh Militants*. Philadelphia: University of Pennsylvania Press.

Malik, Aditya. 1999. *Divine Testimony: The Rajasthani Oral Narrative of Devnarayan*. Habilitationsschrift, Universität Heidelberg.

Malik, Iftikar. 1998. 'Pluralism, Partition and Punjabisation: Politics of Muslim Identity in the British Punjba', *International Journal of Punjab Studies*, 5: pp. 1–27.

Mandair, Arvind Pal Singh. 2001. 'Thinking Differently about Religion and History: Issues for Sikh Studies', in Christopher Shackle, Gurharpal Singh, and Arvind Pal Singh Mandair (eds), *Sikh Religion, Culture and Ethnicity*. London: Curzon Press, pp. 47–72.

Mann, Gurinder Singh. 2001. *The Making of Sikh Scriptures*. Oxford: Oxford University Press.

Mansukhani, Gobind Singh. 1984. 'A Survey of the Poetry and Music of Sri Guru Ram Das', *Journal of Sikh Studies*, 11(2): pp. 66–86.

Marcus, Scott L. 1989. 'The Rise of a Folk Music Genre: Biraha', in Sandria B. Freitag (ed.), *Culture and Power in Banaras*. Berkeley: University of California Press, pp. 93–113.

Matringe, Denis. 1996. '"Listen to what Bullhe Shah Says!" The Oral Tradition of Sufi Poetry in Punjabi in Pakistan Today', *Purusharta*, 18: pp. 39–50.

——— 1988. *Hir Varis Shah*. Pondicherry: Institut Francais de Pondichery.

Mauss, Marcel. 1950. 'Les Techniques du Corps', *Anthroplogie and Sociology*. Paris: Presses Universitaires de France.

Mayaram, Shail. 1997. *Resisting Regimes: Myth, Memory and the Shaping of a Muslim Identity*. Delhi: Oxford University Press.

McLeod, Hew. 1989. *Who is a Sikh? The Problem of Sikh Identity*. Oxford: Clarendon Press.

——— 1992. *Popular Sikh Art*. Delhi: Oxford University Press.

——— 1994. 'Cries of Outrage: History Versus Tradition in the Study of the Sikh Community', *South Asia Research*, 14: pp. 121–34.

——— 1997. *Sikhism*. New York: Penguin.

McMahon, Suzanne C. (ed.). 2001. *Catalogue of the Exhibition 'Echoes of Freedom: South Asian Pioneers in California, 1899–1965'*. Berkeley: Center for South Asia Studies, University of California.

Menon, Ritu and Kamla Bhasin. 1993. 'Recovery, Rupture and Resistance: The Abduction of Women During Partition', *Economic and Political Weekly*, 28: WS2–WS11.

——— 1998. *Borders and Boundaries: Women in India's Partition*. New Brunswick, New Jersey: Rutgers University Press.

Metcalf, Barbara D. 1982. *Islamic Revival in British India: Deoband 1860–1900*. Princeton: Princeton University Press.

——— 1999. 'Nationalism, Modernity, and Muslim Identity in India before 1947', in Peter van der Veer and Hartmut Lehmann (eds), *Nation and Religion*. Princeton, New Jersey: Princeton University Press, pp. 129–43.

Meier, Sabine. 1992. 'A Generation Led Astray, Communal Singing as a Means for Nationalist Socialist Indoctrination of Youth'. Dissertation, University of London, Goldsmiths' College.

Mitchell, Timothy. 1988. *Violence and piety in Spanish folklore*. Philadelphia: University of Pennylvania Press.

Miyazaki, Hirokazu. 2000. 'Faith and its Fulfilment: Agency, Exchange, and the Fijian Aesthetics of Completion', *American Ethnologist*, 27: pp. 31–51.

Nayyar, Adam. 2000. 'Musical Regions: Punjab', in Alison Arnold (ed.), *The Garland Encyclopedia of World Music*. New York and London: Garland Publishing, INC, pp. 762–72.

Nazir, Pervaiz. 2001. 'Modernity, Re-Islamization, and Waris Shah's Heer', *ISIM Newsletter* 08/01, p. 13.

Neuman, Daniel M. 1980. *The Life of Music in North India*. Detroit, Michigan: Wayne State University Press.

Nijhawan, Michael. 2003. 'From Divine Bliss to Ardent Passion: Exploring Sikh Religious Aesthetics through the Dhadi Genre', *History of Religions*, 42(4): pp. 59–85.

——— 2004. 'Shared Melodies, Partitioned Narratives. An Ethnography of Sikh and Sufi Dhadi Performance in Contemporary Punjab', *International Journal of Punjab Studies*, 10(1–2): pp. 57–77.

——— 2005. 'Ritual, Identity, Reflexivity', in B. Leistle, P. Köpping and M. Rudolph (eds), *Ritual and Identity: Performative Practices as Effective Transformations of Social Reality?* Hamburg/Münster/London: LIT.

Noorani, A.G. 2001. 'Ayodhya in Reverse. The Story of the Shahidganj Mosque in Lahore', *Frontline*, 18(3), February 3–16, *http://www.flonnet.com/fll803/18030890.htm*

Oberoi, Harjot S. 1997. *The Construction of Religious Boundaries: Culture, Identity and Diversity in the Sikh Tradition*. Delhi: Oxford University Press.

O'Hanlon, Rosalind. 1988. 'Recovering the Subject: Subaltern Studies and Histories of Resistance in colonial South Asia', *Modern Asia Studies*, 22: pp. 189–224.

Oinas, Felix J. 1978 (1972). 'The Political Uses and Themes of Folklore in the Soviet Union', in Felix J. Oinas (ed.), *Folklore, Nationalism, and Politics*. Columbus, Ohio: Slavica Publishers, pp. 77–96.

Orsini, Francesca. 2004. 'Qutubshatak, Delhi and early Hindavi', Unpublished Paper presented at the 18th European Conference on Modern South Asian Studies, Lund, 8 July 2004.

Ortner, Sherry B. 1984. 'Theory in Anthropology since the Sixties', *Comparative Studies in Society and History*, 26: pp. 126–66.

——— 1990. 'Patterns of History: Cultural Schemas in the Founding of Sherpa Religious Institutions', in E. Ohnuki-Thierney (ed.), *Culture Through Time. Anthropological Approaches*. Stanford: Standford University Press, pp. 57–93.

——— 1999. 'Thick Resistance: Death and the Cultural Construction of Agency in Himalayan Mountaineering', in S.B. Ortner (ed.), *The Fate of 'Culture': Geertz and Beyond*. Berkeley: University of California Press, pp. 136–63.

Pande, Trilochan. 1963. 'The Concept of Folklore in India and Pakistan', *Schweizerisches Archiv für Volkskunde*, 59: pp. 25–30.

Pandey, Gyanendra. 1991. 'In Defence of the Fragment: Writing about Hindu-Muslim Riots in India Today', *Economic and Political Weekly*, March 91 issue.

——— 1995. 'The Appeal of Hindu History', in Vasudha Dalmia and Heinrich V. Stietencron (eds), *Representing Hinduism*. Delhi: Sage Publications, pp. 369–88.

——— 1997. 'Community and Violence: Recalling Partition', *Economic and Political Weekly*, 32: pp. 2037–45.

——— 2001. *Remembering Partition: Violence, Nationalism and History in India*, Cambridge.

Pannke, Peter. 2002. 'Sufis, Pilger, Troubadoure. Heinrich von Morungen, ein Minnesänger auf Orientfahrt', *Lettre International*, 57: pp. 70–6.

Paredes, Americo. 1993 (1978). 'The Problem of Identity in a Changing Culture: Popular Expressions of Culture Conflict along the Lower Rio Grande Border', in Richard Bauman (ed.), *Folklore and Culture on the Texas-Mexican Border*. Austin: CMAS Books, pp. 19–48.

Pettigrew, Joyce. 1978. *Robber Noblemen: A Study of the Political System of the Sikh Jats*. Delhi: Ambika Publications.

——— 1987. 'In Search of a New Kingdom of Lahore', *Pacific Affairs*, 60: pp. 1–25.

——— 1992. 'Songs of the Sikh Resistance Movement', *Asian Music* (Fall 1991–92), pp. 85–118.

——— 1995. *The Sikhs of the Punjab: Unheard Voices of State and Guerilla Violence*. London: Zed Books.

Pinney, Christopher. 1997. *Camera Indica: The Social Life of Indian Photographs*. Chicago: University of Chicago Press.

Prakash, Gyan. 1991. 'Becoming a Bhuinya: Oral Traditions of and Contested Domination in Eastern India', in Douglas Haynes and Gyan Prakash (eds), *Contesting Power: Resistance and Everyday Social Relations in South Asia*. Berkeley: University of California Press, pp. 145–74.

Puri, Harish K. 1983. *The Ghadar Movement: Ideology, Organisation, and Strategy*. Amritsar: Guru Nanak Dev University Press.

Puri, Harish et al. (eds). 1999. *Terrorism in Punjab: Understanding Grassroots Reality*. New Delhi: Har Anand Publishers.

Qureshi, Regula. 1995 (1986). *Sufi Music of India and Pakistan: Sound, Context and meaning in Qawwali*. Cambridge: Cambridge University Press.

——— 2000. 'How Does music Mean? Embodied Memories and the Politics of Affect in the Indian *Sarangi*', *American Ethnologist*, 27: pp. 805–38.

Qureshi, Regula Burkhard. 1997. 'The Indian Sarangi. Sound of Affect, Site of Contest', *Yearbook of Traditional Music*, XXIX: pp. 1–38.

Raheja, Gloria G. and Gold Ann Gordzins. 1994. *Listen to the Heron's Words: Reimagining Gender and Kinship in North India*. Berkeley: University of California Press.

Ramanujan, A.K. 1993. 'On Folk Mythologies and Folk Puranas', in Wendy Doniger (ed.), *Purana Perennis: Reciprocity and Transformation in Hindu and Jaina Texts*. Albany: State University of New York Press, pp. 101–20.

——— 1999a (1988). 'Where Mirrors are Windows: Towards an Anthology of Reflections', in Vijay Dharwadker (ed.), *The Collected Essays of A.K. Ramanujan*. Oxford and New York: Oxford University Press, pp. 6–33.

——— 1999b (1988). 'Who Needs Folklore?', in Vijay Dharwadker (ed.), *The Collected Essays of A.K. Ramanujan*. Oxford and New York: Oxford University Press, pp. 532–52.

——— 1999c. 'Is There an Indian Way of Thinking?', in Vijay Dharwadker (ed.), *The Collected Essays of A.K. Ramanujan*. Oxford and New York: Oxford University Press, pp. 34–51.

Ramaswamy, Sumathi. *Passions of the Tongue: Language Devotion in Tamil India, 1819–1970*. Berkeley: University of California Press.

Ray, Niharranjan. 1970. *The Sikh Gurus and the Sikh Society: A Study in Social Analysis*. Patiala: Punjabi University Press.

Rizvi, Saiyid Athar Abbas. 1986. *A Socio-Intellectual History of the Isna 'Ashari Shi'is in India (AD 16th to 19th century)*. Volume II. Canberra: Ma'rifat Publishing House.

Robinson, Francis. 1979. 'Islam and Muslim Separatism', in David Taylor and Malcolm Yapp (eds), *Political Identity in South Asia*. London: Curzon Press, pp. 78–112.

——— 1991. 'Perso-Islamic Culture in India from the Seventeenth to the Early Twentieth Century', in R.L. Canfield (ed.), *Turko-Persia in Historical Perspective*. Cambridge: Cambridge University Press, pp. 104–31.

Rose, H.A. 1970 [1892]. *A Glossary of the Tribes and Castes of the Punjab and North-Western Frontier Province*. Patiala: Languages Department Punjab.

Sarkar, Sumit. 1982. *Modern India 1885–1947*. Madras: Macmillan.

——— 2000. 'The Decline of the Subaltern in *Subaltern Studies*', in Vinayak Chaturvedi, *Mapping Subaltern Studies and the Postcolonial*. London, New York: Verso, pp. 300–24.

Sax, William (ed.). 1995. *The God at Play: Lila in South Asia*. New York: Oxford University Press.

Scarry, Elaine. 1985. *The Body in Pain*. Oxford: Oxford University Press.

Schechtman, Joseph B. 1949. *Population Transfers in Asia*. New York: Hallsby Press.

Schimmel, Annemarie. 1975. *Mystical Dimensions of Islam*. Chapel Hill: The University of Carolina Press.

——— 1986. 'Karbala and the Imam Husayn in Persian and Indo-Muslim literature', *Al-Serat*, 12.

Schmid, Anna. 1997. *Die Dom zwischen sozialer Ohnmacht und kultureller Macht: Interethnische Beziehungen in Nordpakistan*. Stuttgart: Franz Steiner Verlag.

Schomer, Karin and W.H. McLeod (eds). 1987. *The Sants: Studies in a Devotional Tradition of India*. Delhi: Motilal Banarsidas.

Serres, Michel. 2000 (1991). *The Troubadour of Knowledge*. Ann Arbor: University of Michigan Press.

Shackle, Christopher. 1993. 'Early Vernacular Poetry in the Indus Valley: Its Contexts and its Character', in Anna Liberia Dallapiccola and Stephanie Zingel-Ave Lallement (eds), *Islam and Indian Religions*. Stuttgart: Franz Steiner, pp. 259–90.

Sharma, Suresh and Javeed Alam. 1998. 'Remembering Partition', *Seminar*, 461: pp. 98–103.

Shastri, B.N. 1989. 'Folksongs of Punjab', *Folklore*, 30: pp. 120–36.

Sher, Sher Singh. 1996. 'Contribution of Sikh Gurus to Indian Musicology', in Kharak Singh (ed.), *Current Thoughts on Sikhism*. Chandigarh: Institute of Sikh Studies, pp. 319–27.

Shiach, Morag. 1989. *Discourse on Popular Culture: Class, Gender and History in Cultural Analysis, 1730 to the Present*. Oxford: Basil Blackwell.

Shils, Edward. 1981. *Tradition*. Chicago: University of Chicago Press.

Singh, Arvind Pal. 1996. 'Interrogating Identity: Cultural Translation, Writing, and Subaltern Politics', in Gurharpal Singh and Ian Talbot (eds), *Punjabi Identity: Continuity and Change*. Delhi: Manohar, pp. 187–228.

Singh, Bhai Baldeep. 2001. 'The tradition of kirtan and its discipline', in Prithipal Singh Kapur and Dharam Singh (eds), *Perspectives on Sikhism*. Patiala: Punjabi University Publication Bureau.

Singh, Chetan. 1988. 'Centre and Periphery in the Mughal State: The Case of Seventeenth-Century Panjab', *Modern Asia Studies*, 22: pp. 299–318.

Singh, Daljeet and Kharak Singh (eds). 1997. *Sikhism: Its Philosophy and History*. Chandigarh: Institute of Sikh Studies.

Singh, Daljinder. 1980. 'Qadir Yar's Poetry in Relation to His Age', in J.S. Grewal and Indu Banga (eds), *Maharaja Ranjit Singh and His Times*. Amritsar: Guru Nanak Dev University, pp. 227–43.

Singh, Fauja. 1998. 'A Brief Account of the Freedom Movement in the Punjab', in Parm Bakshish Singh and Devinder Kumar Verma (eds), *Punjab and the Freedom Struggle*. Patiala: Punjabi University Patiala, pp. 9–50.

Singh, Gurharpal. 2000. *Ethnic Conflict in India: A Case Study of Punjab*. London: MacMillan Press.

Singh, Gurtej. 2000. *Chaktavyuh*. Chandigarh: Institute of Sikh Studies.

Singh, Giani Bachittar. 1996. 'Akal Takht—Concept of Miri-Piri', in Kharak Singh (ed.), *Current Thoughts on Sikhism*. Chandigarh: Institute of Sikh Studies, pp. 216–47.

Singh, Harbans (ed.). 1992. *The Encyclopedia of Sikhism, Volume 1*. Patiala: Punjabi University.

——— 1994. *The Heritage of the Sikhs*. Delhi: Manohar.

——— (ed.). 1996. *The Encyclopaedia of Sikhism, Volume II*. Patiala: Punjabi University.

——— (ed.). 1998. *The Encyclopaedia of Sikhism, Volume IV*. Patiala: Punjabi University.

Singh, Jane. 1990. *Echoes of Revolution: The Role of Literature in the Gadar Movement*. Doctoral Dissertation. University of California, Berkeley.

Singh, Kavita. 1996. 'Changing the Tune. Bengali Pata Painting's Encounter with the Modern', *India International Centre Quarterly*, 23: pp. 61–78.

Singh, Mohinder. 1978. *The Akali Movement*. Delhi: Macmillan.

Singh, Narinder. 1974. 'Shiromani Gurdwara Prabandhak Committee, Amritsar', in J.C.B. Webster (ed.), *Popular Religion in the Punjab Today*. Delhi, Batala: Christian Insitute of Sikh Studies.

Singh, Nikki-Guninder Kaur. 1993, *The Feminine principle in the Sikh Vision of the Transcendent*. Cambridge: Cambridge University Press.

Starrett, Gregory. 2003. 'Violence and the Rhetoric of Images', *Cultural Anthropology*, 18(3): pp. 398–428.

——— 2004. *Religious Violence as Religious Experience*. Unpublished Manuscript.

Stokes, Martin. 1992. *The Arabesk Debate: Music and Musicians in Modern Turkey*. Oxford: Clarendon Press.

——— 1994. 'Local Arabesk, the Hatay and the Turkish-Syrian border', in Hastings Donnan and Thomas M. Wilson (eds), *Border Approaches*. Lanham: University of America Press, pp. 31–51.

——— 1998. 'Imagining "the South": Hybridity, Heterotopias and Arabesk on the Turkish-Syrian Border', in Hastings Donnan and Thomas M. Wilson (eds), *Border Identities*. Cambridge: Cambridge University Press, pp. 263–88.

Talbot, Ian. 1996. 'State, Society and Identity: The British Punjab, 1875–1937', in Gurharpal Singh and Ian Talbot (eds), *Punjabi Identity: Continuity and Change*. Delhi: Manohar, pp. 7–34.

——— 1998. 'From Pakistan to Punjabistan? Region, State and Nation Building', *International Journal of Punjab Studies*, 5: pp. 179–91.

Talib, Gurbachan Singh (ed.). 1976. *Guru Tegh Bahadur: Background and the Supreme Sacrifice*. Patiala: Punjabi University.

——— (ed.). 1984. *Sri Guru Granth Sahib*. English Translation. Patiala: Patiala University Press.

Tambiah, Stanley J. 1981 (1979). 'A Performative Approach to Ritual', *Proceedings of the British Academy*, 105: pp. 113–69.

Tatla, Darshan Singh. 1999. *The Sikh Diaspora: The Search for Statehood*. Seattle: University of Washington Press.

Temple, Richard C. 1962 [1899]. *The Legends of the Punjab* (Volumes 1–3). Patiala: Language Department, Punjab.

Thandi, Shinder Singh. 1996. 'Counterinsurgency and Political Violence in Punjab, 1980–94', in Gurharpal Singh and Ian Talbot (eds), *Punjabi Identity: Continuity and Change*. Delhi: Manohar, pp. 159–86.

Thompson, E.P. 1977. 'Folklore, Anthropology, and Social History', *The Indian Historical Review*, 3(2): pp. 247–66.

Trawick, Margaret Egnor. 1986. 'Internal Iconicity in Paraiyar "Crying Songs"', in Stuart Blackburn and A.K. Ramanujan (eds), *Another Harmony: New Essays on the Folklore of India*. Berkeley: University of California Press, pp. 294–343.

Turner, Victor. 1969. *The Ritual Process: Structure and Anti-Structure*. Chicago: Aldine Publishing.

Uberoi, J.P.S. 1999 (1996). *Religion, Civil Society and the State: A Study of Sikhism*. Delhi: Oxford University Press.

Van der Veer, Peter. 1996. *Religious Nationalism: Hindus and Muslims in India*. Delhi: Oxford University Press.

Van der Veer, Peter and Hartmut Lehmann (eds). 1999. *Nation and Religion*. Princeton, New Jersey: Princeton University Press.

Vaudeville, Charlotte. 1962. *Les Duhā de 'Ḍholā-Māru: Une ancienne ballade du Rajasthan*. Pondichéry: Institut Français d'Indologie.

——— 1964. 'Kabir and Interior Religion', *History of Religions*, 3: pp. 191–201.

——— 1999. 'Leaves from the Desert: The Dhola-Maru-ra Dhuha—An ancient Ballad of Rajasthan', in Charlotte Vaudeville, *Myths, Saints and Legends in Medieval India* (edited by Vasudha Dalmia). Delhi: Oxford University Press, pp. 273–334.

Wade, Bonny C. 1998. *Imaging Sound: An Ethnomusicological Study of Music, Art and Culture in Mughal India*. Chicago and London: The University of Chicago Press.

Wadley, Susan S. 1989. 'Choosing a Path: Performative Strategies in a North Indian Epic', in Stuart Blackburn and Joyce Burkhalter-Flueckiger (eds), *Oral Epics in India*. Berkeley: University of California Press, pp. 75–101.

Wagner, Roy. 1985. *Symbols That Stand for Themselves*. Chicago and London: The University of Chicago Press.

Wulff, Donna M. 1986. 'Religion in a New Mode. The Convergence of the Aesthetic and the Religious in Medieval India', *Journal of the American Academy of Religions*, 54: pp. 673–88.

Yong, Tan Tai. 1994. 'Prelude to Partition: Sikh Responses to the Demand for Pakistan, 1940–47', *International Journal of Punjab Studies*, 1: pp. 167–95.

Index